POWER IN THE LAND

THE RAMSDENS AND THEIR HUDDERSFIELD ESTATE, 1542–1920

Essays to commemorate the centenary of the purchase of the estate by Huddersfield Corporation in 1920

edited by
Edward Royle

UNIVERSITY OF HUDDERSFIELD PRESS
IN ASSOCIATION WITH HUDDERSFIELD LOCAL HISTORY SOCIETY
2020

Published by University of Huddersfield Press

University of Huddersfield Press
The University of Huddersfield
Queensgate
Huddersfield HD1 3DH

Email enquiries university.press@hud.ac.uk

Text © The Authors 2020

This work is licensed under a Creative Commons Attribution 4.0 International License

Images © as attributed

Every effort has been made to locate copyright holders of materials included and to obtain permission for their publication.

The publisher is not responsible for the continued existence and accuracy of websites referenced in the text.

A CIP catalogue record for this book is available from the British Library.

ISBN: 978-1-86218-176-2

Designed by Dawn Cockcroft

Front cover illustration © Kirklees Image Archives

Back cover illustration © Huddersfield Examiner/Reach plc

Sir John William Ramsden (1831–1914), c.1890s.
Kirklees Image Archive

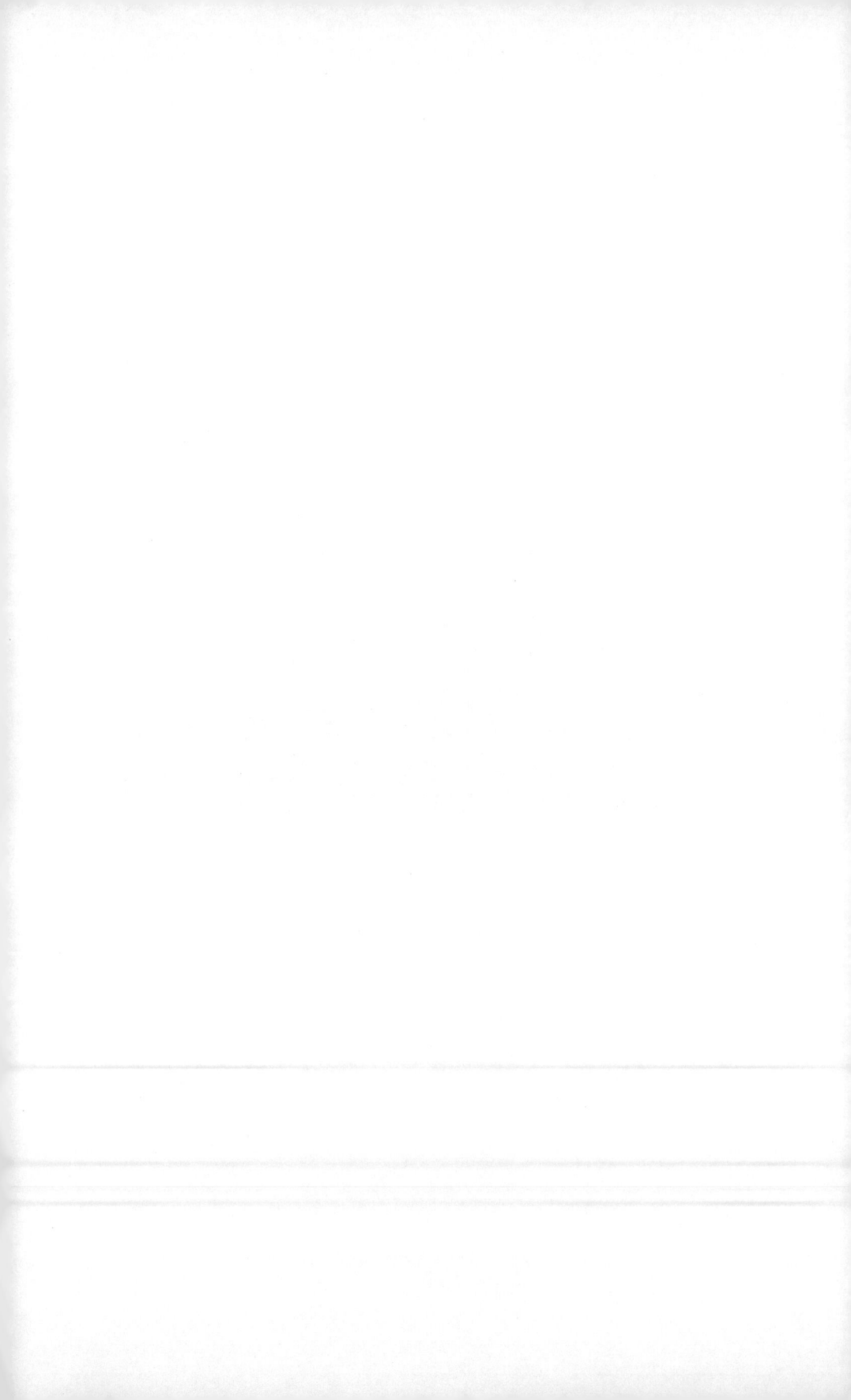

Acknowledgements

THE PUBLISHERS, EDITOR and authors are grateful to the following for kind permission to reproduced images in their collections: AHR Building Consultancy Ltd; *Huddersfield Examiner*/Reach plc; Huddersfield Local Studies Library, Kirklees Libraries; Jarrolds Publishing; Kirklees Museums and Galleries; Lafayette Photography Ltd; Leeds University Library Special Collections; Matthew Beckett, Lost Heritage; The National Portrait Gallery; The Pennington family of Muncaster Castle; The Ramsden family; and West Yorkshire Joint Services, Kirklees Archive. Individual acknowledgement of permissions granted to the University of Huddersfield to reproduce images is given in the list of illustrations on page IX-XIII, and the source of the image is given with each caption.

We also wish to thank all the librarians and archivists who have helped and advised in the research for this book, especially the staff at the Heritage Quay, University of Huddersfield, and at Huddersfield Central Library in Local Studies and in the Kirklees Archive office, for whom nothing has been too much trouble. The editor is also grateful to Megan Taylor, Zoë Johnson, Dawn Cockcroft and the staff of the University of Huddersfield Press, and to David Griffiths and Brian Haigh of Huddersfield Local History Society, for their assistance, and to all his fellow authors for their willing co-operation with their second editor following Hilary Haigh's untimely death.

Contents

FRONTISPIECE	III
ACKNOWLEDGEMENTS	V
ILLUSTRATIONS AND PERMISSIONS	IX
ABBREVIATIONS	XV
A NOTE ON CONTRIBUTORS	XVII
PREFACE	XIX
THE RAMSDENS OF LONGLEY, 1542–1920: A FAMILY TREE	XXII

CHAPTER ONE

Longley Hall: the Huddersfield Seat of the Ramsdens   1
Brian Haigh

CHAPTER TWO

The Ramsdens and the Public Realm in Huddersfield, 1671-1920   43
David Griffiths

CHAPTER THREE

The Ramsden Estate Dispute of 1850-1867   87
John Halstead

CHAPTER FOUR

Religion and Philanthropy   115
Edward Royle

CHAPTER FIVE

Architectural patronage in early-Victorian Huddersfield: 145
the Ramsdens, William Wallen and J. P. Pritchett
Christopher Webster

CHAPTER SIX

Buying Huddersfield for the People   173
   Stephen Caunce and Edward Royle

CHAPTER SEVEN

A Ramsden Family Perspective   195
   Meriel Buxton

BIBLIOGRAPHY   221

INDEX   233

Illustrations and Permissions

COVER
: Ramsden Estate Buildings, Westgate (1870), by W.H. Crossland
by kind permission of Kirklees Museums and Galleries

FRONTISPIECE
: Sir John William Ramsden (1831–1914), c.1890s   III
by kind permission of Kirklees Museums and Galleries

1. Longley Old Hall before restoration   2
   by kind permission of Huddersfield Local Studies Library, Kirklees Libraries

2. Longley Old Hall after restoration, 1885   3
   by kind permission of Huddersfield Local Studies Library, Kirklees Libraries

3. Longley Hall, rebuilt eighteenth-century south side   6
   by kind permission of Huddersfield Local Studies Library, Kirklees Libraries

4. Longley Hall, eighteenth-century west front   7
   by kind permission of Huddersfield Local Studies Library, Kirklees Libraries

5. The Hon. Mrs Isabella Ramsden (1790–1887)   9
   by kind permission of the Pennington family of Muncaster Castle

6. George Loch (1811–1877)   9
   by kind permission of the National Portrait Gallery

7. Alexander Hathorn (1816–1892)   11
   by kind permission of Huddersfield Local Studies Library, Kirklees Libraries

8.	Isaac Hordern (1829–1912) *by kind permission of Kirklees Museums and Galleries*	11
9.	Longley Hall, north front, 1874 *by kind permission of Huddersfield Local Studies Library,* *Kirklees Libraries*	15
10.	Longley Hall, Ground Plan, 1866 *by kind permission of West Yorkshire Archive Service, Kirklees*	18
11.	Longley Hall Stables, North Elevation, 1855. *by kind permission of West Yorkshire Archive Service, Kirklees*	22
12.	Longley Hall, Ground Plan of W. H. Crossland's hall of 1871–3 *by kind permission of West Yorkshire Archive Service, Kirklees*	30
13.	Longley Hall, Elevations, 2008 *by kind permission of AHR Building Consultancy Ltd*	30–31
14.	Longley Hall after 1873, view of the south and west fronts *by kind permission of Huddersfield Local Studies Library,* *Kirklees Libraries*	32
15.	Tudor chimney piece, removed from Longley Hall to Muncaster Castle, 1920 *by kind permission of the Pennington family of* *Muncaster Castle and Jarrolds Publishing*	35
16.	Longley Old Hall, interior *by kind permission of Kirklees Museums and Galleries*	37
17.	Cloth Hall, erected 1766 and enlarged in 1780 and 1863 *by kind permission of Kirklees Museums and Galleries*	48
18.	Sir John Ramsden, 4th Bt (1755–1839) *by kind permission of the Pennington family of Muncaster Castle*	49
19.	Market Place, the old George Inn (centre) and the Brick Buildings, erected in the 1770s *by kind permission of Kirklees Museums and Galleries*	50
20.	Ramsden estate map of central Huddersfield, 1778 *by kind permission of West Yorkshire Archive Service, Kirklees*	50

ILLUSTRATIONS AND PERMISSIONS   XI

21. Thomas Dinsley map of central Huddersfield, 1828   51
     by kind permission of West Yorkshire Archive Service, Kirklees

22. Railway Station (1846–51)   59
     by kind permission of Kirklees Museums and Galleries

23. George Hotel (1848–1851)   59
     by kind permission of Kirklees Museums and Galleries

24. Ordnance Survey street map, 1907 (1:25,000),   75
     showing central Huddersfield
     by kind permission of Huddersfield Local Studies Library, Kirklees Libraries

25. Joshua Hobson (1810–76)   88
     by kind permission of Kirklees Museums and Galleries

26. Wright Mellor (1817–93)   104
     by kind permission of Kirklees Museums and Galleries

27. Huddersfield old parish church   133
     by kind permission of Kirklees Museums and Galleries

28. Huddersfield new parish church (1834–6)   133
     by kind permission of Kirklees Museums and Galleries

29. St John, Birkby (1851-3)   136
     by kind permission of Kirklees Museums and Galleries

30. Almondbury parish church before restoration   137
     by kind permission of Kirklees Museums and Galleries

31. Almondbury parish church after restoration in 1876   137
     by kind permission of Kirklees Museums and Galleries

32. St Michael, Somerset Road (1913–15)   139
     by kind permission of Kirklees Museums and Galleries

33. Ramsden Street Congregational Chapel (1824)   149
     by kind permission of Kirklees Museums and Galleries

34. Huddersfield Collegiate School (1839–40)   154
     by kind permission of Kirklees Museums and Galleries

35.	Huddersfield College (1839–40) *by kind permission of Kirklees Museums and Galleries*	154
36.	St Paul, Shepley (1845-8) *by kind permission of Special Collections, Leeds University Library*	157
37.	Riding School (1846) and Zetland Hotel (1846–7) *by kind permission of Kirklees Museums and Galleries*	160
38.	Castle Hill hotel (1851) *by kind permission of Huddersfield Local Studies Library, Kirklees Libraries*	164
39.	Wilfrid Dawson (1871–1936 *by kind permission of the Huddersfield Examiner/Reach plc.*	176
40.	Samuel William Copley (1859–1937) *by kind permission of Lafayette Photography Ltd*	176
41.	Sir John William Ramsden, 5th Bt (1831–1914) age 30 *by kind permission of the Ramsden family*	198
42.	Sir John William Ramsden, 5th Bt (1831–1914) *by kind permission of Kirklees Museums and Galleries*	200
43.	The Hon. Lady Helen Guendolen Ramsden (1846–1910) *by kind permission of the Pennington family of Muncaster Castle*	200
44.	Opening of Somerset Bridge by Lady Guendolen Ramsden, 1874 *by kind permission of Kirklees Museums and Galleries*	203
45.	Portrait group at the Yorkshire Agricultural Show, Longley Hall, 1888 *by kind permission of Huddersfield Local Studies Library, Kirklees Libraries*	204
46.	Laying of the corner stone of the Victoria Tower, Castle Hill by John Frecheville Ramsden, 1898 *by kind permission of the Ramsden family*	204

ILLUSTRATIONS AND PERMISSIONS XIII

47. Byram Hall 206
    by kind permission of Matthew Beckett, Lost Heritage

48. Sir John Frecheville Ramsden (1877–1958) 214
    by kind permission of the Ramsden family

COVER (BACK)
    Crests of the Ramsden Family, the Huddersfield Improvement Commissioners and Huddersfield Corporation

    by kind permission of the Huddersfield Examiner/Reach plc

Abbreviations

CLWC	Commissioners of Lighting, Watching & Cleansing
DF	Dawson File
HBC	Huddersfield Borough Corporation
H(D)C	*Huddersfield (Daily) Chronicle*
H(D)E	*Huddersfield (Daily) Examiner*
HHE	*Huddersfield and Holmfirth Examiner.*
HWC	Huddersfield Waterworks Commissioners
HIC	Huddersfield Improvement Commissioners
ICBS	Incorporated Church Building Society
JFR	Sir John Frecheville Ramsden
JWR	Sir John William Ramsden
KIA	Kirklees Image Archive
L & Y	Lancashire & Yorkshire Railway
LI	*Leeds Intelligencer*
LM	*Leeds Mercury*
ODNB	*Oxford Dictionary of National Biography*
PCO	Privy Council Office
TNA	The National Archives, Kew
TRDA	Tenant-Right Defence Association
WYAS	West Yorkshire Archive Service
YAS	Yorkshire Architectural Society
YEP	*Yorkshire Evening Post*

A Note on Contributors

MERIEL BUXTON studied jurisprudence at St Hugh's College, Oxford, and is now a free-lance writer who lives in Leicestershire, married to a great-nephew of Joan Ramsden, née Buxton, wife of Sir John Frecheville Ramsden. She has written several books including biographies of the missionary/explorer, David Livingstone, and of Mary, the 'High-Flying' Duchess of Bedford. Her *Poverty is Relative,* published by Woodperry Books in 2017, tells the story of the Ramsden family during the lifetimes of the 5th and 6th baronets, Sir John William Ramsden (1831-1914) and his son Sir John Frecheville Ramsden (1877-1958). Now retired from the magistracy, Meriel has more time to spend with her husband, children, grandchildren, dogs, horses and Dexter cattle.

STEPHEN CAUNCE is a native of south Lancashire, and has a BA from University College, London. His PhD, from Leeds University, investigated the lives of farm horsemen in Yorkshire by taping oral testimony and was published as *Amongst Farm Horses*. He also taught at Leeds, after twelve years working in museums. He recently retired as a Senior Lecturer in History at the University of Central Lancashire, where he also conducted collaborative work with the heritage sector and developed an innovative BA in History, Museums and Heritage. He still researches and publishes, mainly on various aspects of northern England's transformation between 1600 and 1939. He gives lectures in many different settings and is writing a book about the origins of the Industrial Revolution.

DAVID GRIFFITHS has lived in Huddersfield for over 30 years and worked for Kirklees Council in corporate management roles. Much of his retirement has been spent in researching the development and governance of 19th-century Huddersfield. His most recent publications are *The Villas of Edgerton: Home to Huddersfield's Victorian Elite* (2017)*;* and, as editor*, Making up for Lost Time: The Pioneering Years of Huddersfield Corporation* (2018). He is active in several local history and heritage groups and is a frequent speaker, walk leader and contributor to local and national journals.

BRIAN HAIGH is a retired museum professional who specialised in social history, education and interpretation. He cared for wide-ranging collections from natural history specimens to works of art which was reflected in the diversity of the exhibition programmes he organised. He was responsible for galleries exploring the Amazon rainforest and Ancient Egypt. He managed the restoration of the Cloth Hall shelter in Ravensknowle Park and the conservation of the stonework and re-pointing of the Victoria Tower on Castle Hill. He is the author and editor of a number of books for schools, and has written on local history topics.

JOHN HALSTEAD studied at Highburton Church of England elementary school, Penistone Grammar and the London School of Economics. He was a civil servant for ten years, leaving the administrative class at the Home Office in 1965 for a career teaching coal miners, steel and other workers at the University of Sheffield. He became active in the Society for the Study of Labour History in the 1960s and was a long-time editor of its *Bulletin* and its continuation as *Labour History Review*. He currently serves as one of the Society's Vice-Presidents. He stood down in September 2016 after a twenty-one year period on the board of housing associations, but not believing in retirement he continues to write and be concerned about modern economic and social issues.

EDWARD ROYLE was born in the Colne Valley, educated in Almondbury and then after Cambridge returned to teach at the University of York where he is now Professor (Emeritus) in History. He has published widely on nineteenth-century British topics as diverse as popular atheism, radical politics and Methodism. Since retirement he has published editions of Yorkshire *Visitation Returns of the Clergy* (1858 and 1865), and edited a study of the *Great Yorkshire Election of 1807*. He has frequently been drawn through his research back to his Huddersfield roots and wrote a history of the *Queen Street Chapel and Mission* for the Huddersfield Local History Society of which he is a founder-member.

CHRISTOPHER WEBSTER is an architectural historian who has specialised in the buildings of late-Georgian England, and published extensively on the subject. Currently, he is nearing completion of a monograph on church-building and churchgoing at that time. He is also interested in the development of the architectural profession in the provinces in the early-nineteenth century, with several publications on West Yorkshire architects, their training and their patrons. He is retired, after a long career in higher education, and is currently a Research Associate in the Centre for Eighteenth Century Studies at the University of York.

Preface

ON MICHAELMAS DAY 1920 Huddersfield Corporation bought from Sir John Frecheville Ramsden the land and rights held by his family in and around the town of Huddersfield, thus bringing to an end a relationship that had begun in 1531 when William Ramsden married Joanna Wood of Longley Hall. Over the decades the Ramsdens extended their property, acquiring the manors of Huddersfield in 1599 and Almondbury in 1627. By the end of the nineteenth century they owned a considerable part of the land on which central Huddersfield was built. They invested in and benefited from the urban and industrial expansion of Huddersfield in the later-eighteenth and nineteenth centuries, but were never primarily industrial or commercial entrepreneurs: they were ground landlords who, from the later-17th century, lived 30 miles away at Byram. They retained their local seat at Longley New Hall but, as absentees, acted through local agents. They seldom visited the town in person until the coming of convenient rail travel in the second half of the nineteenth century.

This collection of essays has been brought together to celebrate the centenary of the 1920 purchase. It does not attempt a comprehensive history but is focused on aspects of the relationship between the Ramsdens and Huddersfield, especially in the nineteenth century during the lifetime of Sir John William Ramsden (1831-1914) for which the archives are particularly rich and when the greatest expansion of the town and Ramsden influence occurred.

Some outline of events is offered in chapter 1 by Brian Haigh, who looks at Longley Hall, its inhabitants and the uses to which the buildings were put. David Griffiths then follows in chapter 2 with an analysis of the evolving and sometimes fractious relationship between the town and the family, especially in the nineteenth century. One of the most controversial – as well as economically important – issues in the nineteenth century concerned the terms governing the relationships between the Ramsden estate and its tenants, the intricacies of which are pursued in chapter 3 by John Halstead. Religion and philanthropy, while no doubt sincerely meant, were also a useful means by which the Ramsdens managed not only their tenants but the whole community, and this is the theme of chapter 4 by Edward Royle. One expression of such activity was the construction of churches and other public buildings: in chapter 5 Christopher Webster provides studies of William Wallen and James Pigott Pritchett, two architects who did important work for the Ramsden estate in the 1840s and 1850s, giving the town two of its most impressive buildings – the George Hotel and the Railway Station. The final two chapters are concerned with the sale itself. In chapter 6 Stephen Caunce and the editor re-examine critically the 'Dawson File', first used by Clifford Stephenson in 1972 to celebrate rather uncritically the story of 'The Town that Bought Itself'; and in chapter 7 Meriel Buxton gives new insights into the reasons why Sir John Frecheville Ramsden wished to sell the town and how the sale was brought about. Her chapter also provides a personal perspective on some of the key members of the Ramsden family in the nineteenth century, drawing on private family archives.

Archival references are given in the end notes to each chapter. Where no location is given, the documents referred to will be found in the West Yorkshire Archive Service Kirklees office in Huddersfield. References to secondary works in the end notes are to the composite bibliography at the end of the book.

The idea for this book was conceived and commissioned by the late Hilary Haigh, formerly Huddersfield Archivist and Local History Librarian, then until her retirement archivist at the Polytechnic/University, and a founder-member and long-serving secretary of the Huddersfield Local History Society. The completed project is dedicated to her memory.

EDWARD ROYLE
SEPTEMBER 2020.

The Ramsdens of Longley, 1542–1920

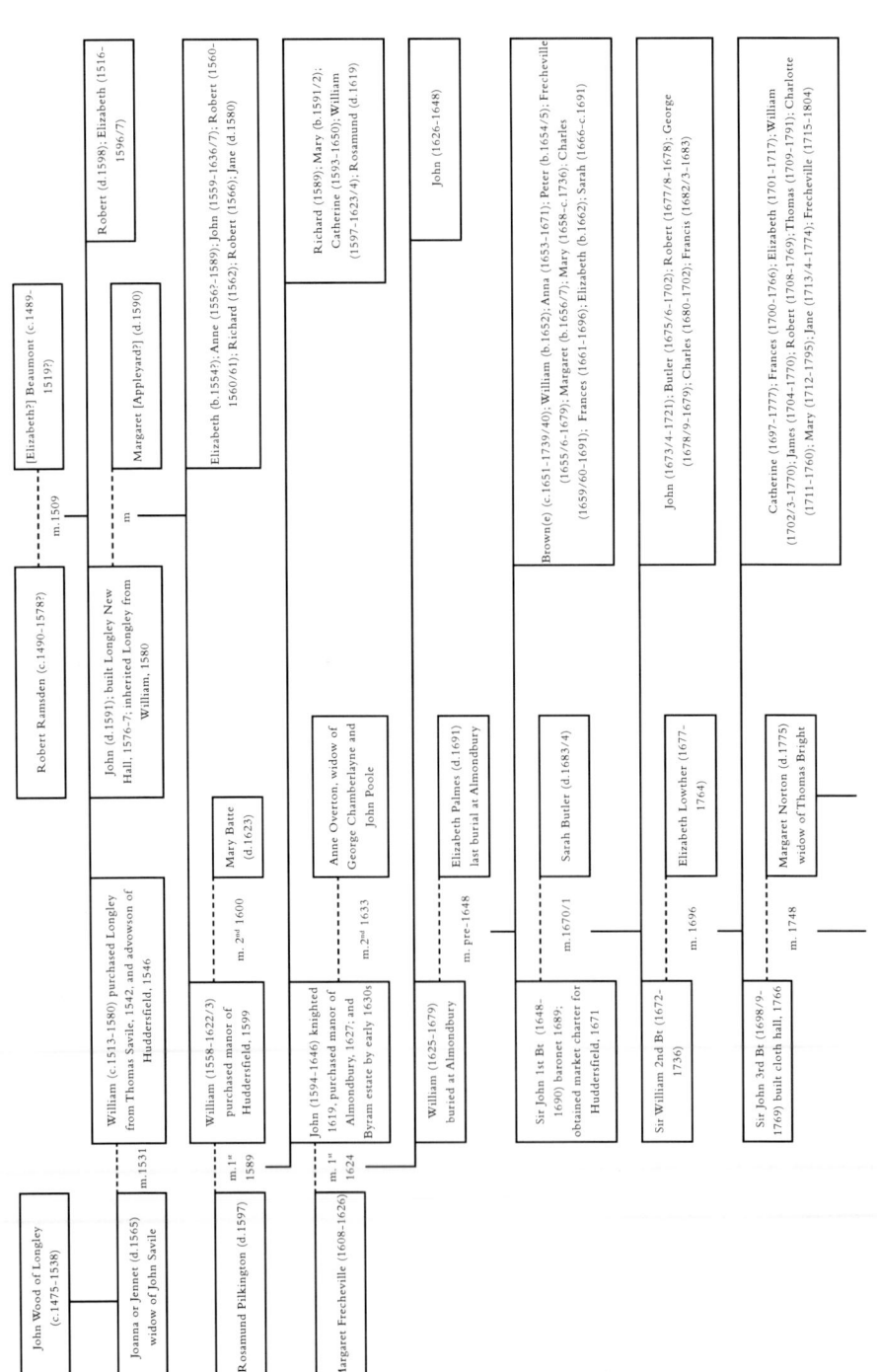

XXIII

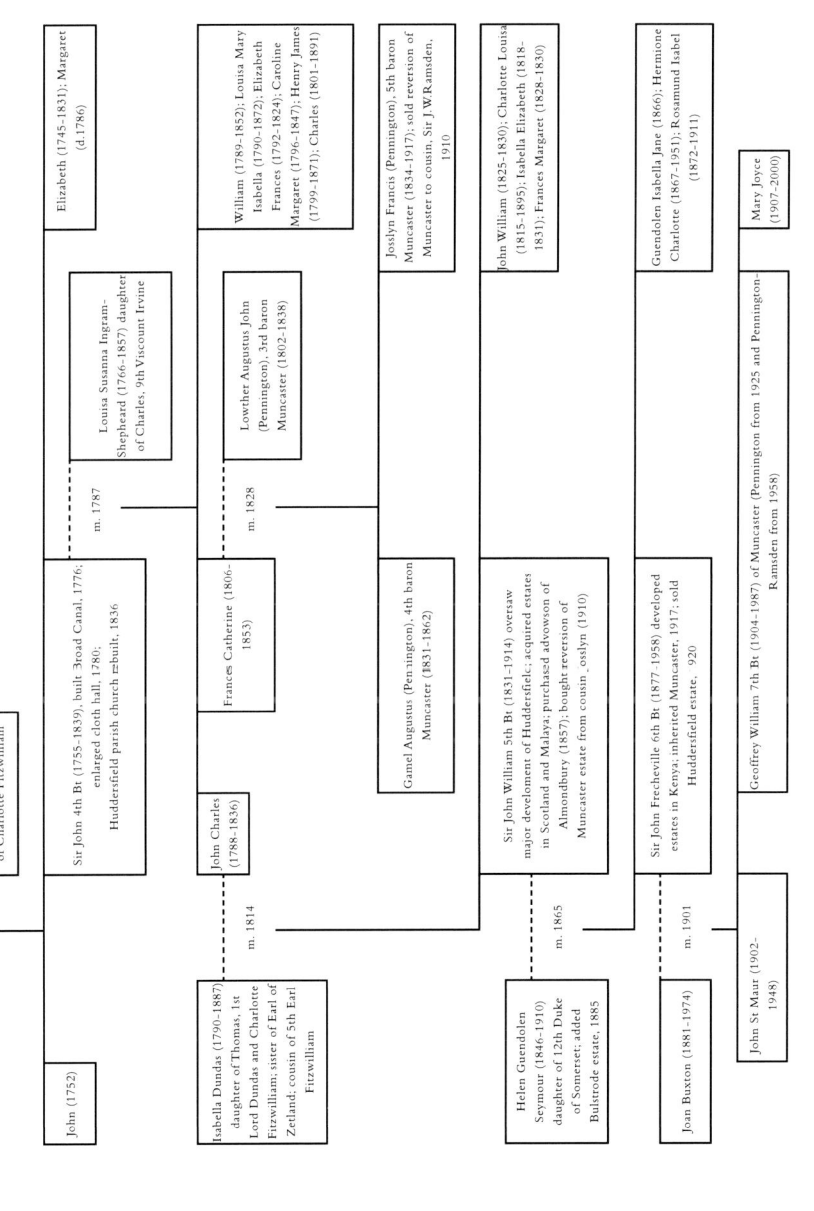

Before 1538 there were no parish registers; dates after that still remain imperfect; uncertain and estimated information is indicated by a question mark and/or brackets. Baptismal years are taken as surrogates for births.
Until 1752 the legal year began on 25 March, not 1 January, so dates for the first quarter before 1752 are given with both legal and calendar years to avoid ambiguity.

CHAPTER ONE

Longley Hall: the Huddersfield Seat of the Ramsdens

BRIAN HAIGH

IN 1531 WILLIAM RAMSDEN (c.1513–1580) married Joanna Wood, one of three daughters of John Wood who was among the wealthiest men in the community. Within a short time, he had acquired all John Wood's properties to add to his own growing portfolio. The acquisition of Longley, the Wood family home for over two centuries, bought from his wife's brother-in-law, Thomas Savile, in 1542, was his great prize.

Longley was typical of the homes of the lesser gentry of the district. Timber framed, it consisted of a central hall open to the roof, and two cross wings forming an 'H' plan house. Elements of the original structure have survived the numerous changes which have been undertaken over the centuries. Dendro-chronological analysis of some of the timbers suggests a date of around 1380 and there is documentary evidence for a house on the site from earlier in the 14th century. This house was probably enlarged during the following century and there were further changes after 1542 when the Ramsdens gained possession.[1]

Having consolidated his Huddersfield landholdings, William began to speculate in monastic property which had recently come on the market. He spent much of his time away from home and it has been concluded that he and Joanna had separated. She died childless in 1565, whilst William settled his dynastic ambitions on his brothers John and Robert.[2] From 1559, John (151? - 1591) rented Longley as a home for his growing family. Proceeds from rearing cattle and sheep, wool sales, money-lending and the profits of the fulling and corn mill, leased from the Crown, made John a man of substance. This enabled him to encase the old house in stone, enlarge the hall range to align with the cross wings to create a new unbroken elevation, and to insert mullion windows. Re-building probably also included the insertion of a ceiling in the open hall to allow for the creation of a living room and parlour on the ground floor with chambers or bedrooms above.[3]

1. Longley Old Hall before restoration.
Huddersfield Local Studies Library

It also established John Ramsden's status as a member of the county gentry – a position which was confirmed in 1575 by his being granted the right to bear arms. Despite having recently re-modelled Longley, in the following year he started to build a new hall a mile or so further down the hill to the north. The Ramsden Commonplace book records that work began on the Thursday in Easter week, 26 April 1576, and was completed on 3 August 1577. The total cost of labour was £17-0-5.[4]

The New Hall

To maintain continuity with the Wood and Ramsden inheritance, he took with him the name 'Longley'. Described in the 1584 Survey of Almondbury as the New Hall, it has also been known as Longley Hall, Nether or Lower Longley (as opposed to Longley Old Hall, Over or Upper Longley). The 'capital messuage' which had 'been built within the memory of man' was replete with 'two gardens, two orchards, one springe of wodde' and a number of closes.[5]

Other than a chimney piece, now at Muncaster Castle [see Illustration 15, p. 35], nothing of this New Hall now survives above ground. Canon Hulbert

2. Longley Old Hall after restoration (1885).
Huddersfield Local Studies Library

(1804-1888), long-serving vicar of Almondbury and author of a history of the parish, described the hall as having been built in the Tudor style on three sides of a courtyard with the main entrance on the east side.[6] It is not clear what evidence he had for this statement and it seems more likely that he was merely describing a typical gentry house of the area in this period. On Timothy Oldfield's survey map of 1716, the hall is shown as a long, narrow building aligned north west – south east.[7] The main entrance would have been on the eastern elevation. With the ranks of the gentry growing at this time, the Ramsdens were not alone in establishing their new-found place in society through building. New gentry homes sprang up across the Pennine region. They were typically built to an 'H' or 'E' plan. Varying in size, these stone-built houses were firmly rooted in the vernacular tradition, with only superficial reference to the classical influences which inspired the prodigy houses of the Elizabethan and Stuart age.[8]

Other houses, such as nearby Woodsome, the family home of the Kayes, were being re-built, enlarged or, like Old Longley, encased in stone; and another neighbour, Richard Beaumont, was replacing an earlier timber framed house at Whitley with one in stone to an 'E' plan.[9] Longley was one of the larger houses, being assessed on 25 hearths in the 1672 Hearth Tax; Woodsome was taxed on 22 hearths and Whitley Beaumont on 17. Of the 132 houses in the West Riding listed as having 10 or more hearths, only six had 25 or more; one of these was Byram, which had been acquired in about 1630 by John Ramsden's grandson, another John (1594-1646) – distinguished from his grandfather by having been knighted in 1619 – who had inherited the Ramsden estates on his father's death in January in 1622/3.[10]

Byram was probably a grander house than Longley and it had the further advantage of being nearer to York, the centre of county government, to which the Ramsdens like other members of their class were drawn. With gentry status came responsibility. Local government was county-based and depended on the active participation of the gentry. Sir John undertook a number of administrative and judicial roles. A JP from 1627, he was elected MP for Pontefract in 1628 and 1640. A visit to the town 'to know what service the townsmen would command' may have introduced him to Byram only four miles away.[11]

Set within a deer park, Byram was ideal for entertaining, which was essential to the development of political and commercial alliances. This was made much easier for the widowed Sir John after 1633 when he married twice-widowed Anne Poole, a substantial heiress. Longley had become very much a secondary home, despite the purchase of the Manor of Almondbury in 1627, but it was to become a place of safety for the family in the troubled times that lay ahead.

As High Sheriff of the county in 1636-7, Sir John bore the responsibility for collecting Ship Money, a levy instituted by the Crown without parliamentary sanction. Despite its unpopularity, he was successful in collecting £11,800 of the £12,000 charged on the county. When Parliament finally sat in April 1640, Ship Money was one of the many grievances which occupied members. Matters were unresolved when Charles dissolved the sitting after only three weeks. The lines for future conflict were drawn. In 1642, Sir John sold land near Saddleworth to raise funds for a regiment, settled his estates and made a will. The family retreated to Longley which was at a distance from the main centres of military activity in the civil wars which followed. Whilst Sir John's regiment fought at Marston Moor in July 1644, he had himself been captured at the Battle of Selby in April and sent to the Tower. Upon release he joined the forces besieging Pontefract Castle before moving on to defend Newark, where he died in 1646.

Now in Royalist hands, Pontefract Castle came under siege for a third time in October 1648 with Cromwell briefly taking charge of proceedings. On 6 November, news reached Parliament that 'Lieut. General *Cromwel* is at *Biron House* near *Pontefract*, and there continues 'till he hath so settled the several

Posts, as that the Enemy may not, as they have done, break forth, plunder and undo the County; which done, he goes to the Head-Quarters, as expected.'[12] Cromwell probably spent no more than a week at Byram before crossing the River Aire and taking up residence at Knottingley. The well-provisioned and strongly-fortified garrison was still holding out when Cromwell left for London in December; it was the last Royalist stronghold to surrender in March 1649, two months after Charles I's execution.

Thanks to the arrangements made by his father, William Ramsden (1625-1679) was able to avoid sequestration and succeeded to the family estates. Newly married, he continued to live at Longley where the first of his four sons was born in 1648. It was to remain their principal home for the rest of their lives, William dying there in 1679 and his wife, Elizabeth, in 1691. Byram, which was probably in no fit state for immediate occupation after the billeting of parliamentary forces, did not become a family home again until John Ramsden (1648-1690) brought his new wife Sarah Butler there in 1670/1. Their eldest son, William was born at Byram and baptised at Brotherton on 22 October 1672. Involvement in county affairs and national politics meant that John spent little time at Longley, though he was successful in obtaining a licence to hold a weekly market in Huddersfield in 1671. After he came into his inheritance, he relied on a steward to manage the Huddersfield and Almondbury estates.

John's support of William III was rewarded with a baronetcy in 1689. Within a year the title had passed to his 17-year old son. In 1696, Sir William (1672-1736) married Elizabeth, daughter of the first Viscount Lonsdale, a prominent figure at Court, thus marking a further rise up the social ladder for the Ramsdens and necessitating alterations and improvements at Byram. Meanwhile, Longley became a backwater with rooms retained for no more than occasional use. To maintain the lifestyle now expected of him, Sir William took a keen interest in the management of his estates and kept a close eye on his revenues. His successor's interests were in national politics, serving as an MP for 27 years, and required him to maintain a household in the capital. Sir John, 3rd baronet (1698/9-1769) was 49 years of age when he married Margaret Norton on 8 August 1748; a longed-for son and heir was born in 1755.

'A Modern House'

A year earlier, on 24 September, according to local attorney John Turner, 'Longley Hall pulled down'.[13] No other record for this action has been found, but in his account of the hall, Canon Hulbert notes 'a modern house had been added in the last century, in the plain style of the day, looking towards the West and North'.[14] J. S. Fletcher remarks that this new house replaced the

3. Longley Hall, rebuilt eighteenth-century south side, enclosing part of the original Tudor building.
Huddersfield Local Studies Library

existing buildings. Recalling the Huddersfield of his youth, Mr. D. Schofield noted that '... Longley Hall, [was] at that time a brick building, plastered over and lime washed, standing on the site of the present hall'.[15]

Taken at its face value, John Turner's journal entry would lead to the conclusion that John Ramsden's New Hall had been demolished in its entirety, a view supported by the statements of Fletcher and Schofield. Canon Hulbert stands alone in observing that the 'modern house' was an addition, from which it must be concluded that only part of the earlier house was pulled down in 1754. Two photographs in the collections of Huddersfield Local Studies Library confirm this.[16] They show respectively, the west elevation and the south-west corner of the hall in or about 1871 before this 'modern house' itself was demolished and replaced. It is clearly a somewhat utilitarian addition to an earlier gabled building. The three by one bay extension in plain Georgian style has sash windows which have also been introduced beneath the hood mouldings of the older part of the building where they presumably replaced stone mullions. The newer part of the building has been lime rendered and was in need of attention at the time that this photograph was taken.

4. Longley Hall, rebuilt eighteenth-century west front.
Huddersfield Local Studies Library

This new addition must have been part of a re-organisation and refurbishment of the hall, which included moving the main entrance from the east to the west elevation. The front door beneath a semi-circular light is recessed behind a pair of Tuscan columns forming a portico. Together with the treatment of the windows – tri-partite openings with simple pediments on the ground floor and arched on the first floor – suggest a date later in the 18th century. Local historian, Philp Ahier, was of the opinion that it dated from after the building of the extension to the Cloth Hall in 1780.[17] He does not give his reasons for this, though stylistically he is on good grounds. It may have been the use of brick in a predominantly stone-built area which encouraged this speculation. Brick was used for the building of the Cloth Hall and its extension, and surplus bricks from this project had been used in the construction of the New Row near the Market Place.

More difficult to explain is why there was such a long gap between the demolition of part of the hall and the building of a new wing, and why this project was begun at a time when the 4th baronet was preoccupied with the improvements he was making to Byram under the direction of John Carr,

Robert Adam and Lancelot 'Capability' Brown.[18] It seems unlikely that Sir John (1755-1839) ordered the work because he intended to spend more time in Huddersfield. He had succeeded his father in 1769, and spent most of his time in London and Byram, relying on his trustees and agents to manage his estates. So far as is known, he never stayed at Longley and, despite his long tenure, he famously visited the town from which he derived a considerable part of his income and which allowed him to live a life of pleasure, only once, in 1822.[19]

Whilst the 'modern house' had been incorporated into the older property, it could, quite easily stand alone. With the appearance of a modest gentleman's property or a somewhat grander farmhouse, was this, perhaps, occupied by a tenant who acted as agent and custodian of the hall? William Hirst, Corn factor, Dealer and Chapman, was living at Longley Hall when his creditors were invited to a meeting at the 'House of Samuel Mortimer, known by the sign of the George' on 22 September 1769, to make a dividend of the bankrupt's estate and effects.[20]

In a valuation of 1843, Margaret Holt is listed as the occupier of Longley Hall and the tenant of 24 acres of land, which she held on preferential terms.[21] She shared her home with her two sisters, Sarah and Mary, who were said to be in poor health and deaf.[22] Together they made a living through needlework and keeping a cow or two.[23] They were the daughters of John Holt, who is listed as tenant of the King's Mill in 1797. He was obviously a man of some substance, paying an annual rent of £266 for the mill and 19 acres. In Baines' 1822 *Yorkshire Directory* he is shown as residing at Longley Hall and acting as an agent, architect and land surveyor. In this capacity he was employed by Sir John Ramsden and was said to be 'the general measurer of buildings in Huddersfield' with 'long and considerable experience in that line'.[24]

As heir presumptive to the estate and baronetcy, John Charles Ramsden (1788-1836) accompanied by his wife, the Hon. Isabella, visited Huddersfield in 1829. Arriving in the town on the evening of Saturday 27 June, they took up residence at Longley Hall, attending morning and afternoon services at Almondbury Church on the Sunday. On Monday morning Isabella was 'visited by several of the principal ladies'. Members of the family having visited the town only once in the previous half century, the couple aroused a great deal of interest and crowds gathered to witness the laying of the foundation stone of the new infirmary, the purpose of their visit. 'Mrs. Ramsden appears much younger than her husband, and is a very elegant and lady-like woman. Mr. Ramsden is a tall slender man, and his general appearance produces an impression of aristocracy. His matter is tolerable, but he has an impediment in his speech, which disqualifies him from figuring as a public speaker'.[25]

5. The Hon. Mrs Isabella Ramsden (1790–1887),
wife of John Charles Ramsden and mother of Sir John William Ramsden.
Muncaster Castle

6. George Loch (1811–1877), Ramsden agent 1847–1853,
by unknown artist, stipple engraving, late 19th century.
National Portrait Gallery

John Charles was in fact only two years older than his wife, but she was to outlive him by over 50 years. He predeceased his father leaving Isabella Ramsden guardian of his son and heir, John William, who became the fifth baronet at the age of only seven years. Meanwhile, under the terms of the fourth baronet's will, oversight of the estate passed to trustees, the most influential of whom was his mother's cousin and brother-in-law, Earl Fitzwilliam (1786-1857) who first visited the town on Tuesday 5 November 1844 'for the purpose of inspecting and interviewing on the proposed improvements, the sites of new churches &c'. After looking around the Cloth Hall, where he bought a piece of fancy cloth, he visited the Parish Church and the Ramsden Street and Queen Street chapels. On Wednesday and Thursday of the same week, the 13 year-old John William, who was making his first visit to the town, joined the agent, George Loch, at the George Hotel to receive the half-yearly rents, estimated to amount to £30,000.[26]

Estate Office and Resident Agent

Rooms at Longley must have been kept ready for these occasional visits. At other times, the windows would have been shuttered and the furniture covered by dust sheets. Isabella was happy to receive some of the principal ladies of the town during her stay in 1829 but there is no record of any major work having been undertaken in preparation for that visit. She encouraged George Loch to make use of Longley after he took over the management of the estate: 'I am afraid you will have very uncomfortable quarters at the George Inn, pray go and look at Longley Hall and consider if you would not be fitter lodged there'.[27] Earlier in the year, Loch had made a fact-finding visit to the town uncovering three decades of mismanagement and neglect. Some of this was the responsibility of Sir John's steward, John Bower, who visited the town twice a year when rents were due, staying for about two weeks on each occasion to conduct business. Like his predecessor, John Crowder, he would have stayed at Longley. The trustees accepted Loch's recommendations, which included the appointment of a resident agent.[28] Mrs Ramsden was impatient for the resident to take up the post and wished 'he was installed in his office and a site chosen for an Estate office &c. and the building planned'. A town centre location was envisaged as she pondered whether it might be better to wait until the site of the railway station had been determined 'and have the Estate Office &c. at a convenient distance from it'.[29]

In the meantime, Edward Blore (1787-1879) had been consulted about plans for an extension to Longley. At that time, the architect was employed in building New Worsley Hall for Loch's major employer, the Duke of Bridgewater. George Loch maintained an office at Worsley Old Hall to which

7. Alexander Hathorn (1816–1892), resident agent for Huddersfield, 1844–1861.
Huddersfield Local Studies Library

8. Isaac Hordern (1829–1912), estate clerk and cashier, 1846–1909.
Kirklees Image Archive

much of the Ramsden estate correspondence in this period was directed. Blore along with Sir William Tite advised George Loch and the trustees on building proposals, designing some new farm buildings for the estate. He wrote from Dover *en route* to Belgium in September 1844, suggesting that he had been set a difficult task. He could not match the plans he had been given to the internal arrangement of the proposed extension, but he felt he could not improve on the design without adding to the costs. He assumed that the extension would be in an 'old English' style rather than 'Roman'[30]. Despite Mrs Ramsden's wishes, plans for new estate offices appear to have been put on hold for the time being at least.

Alexander Hathorn (1816-1892) took up the post of resident agent in October 1844. He had been a secretary in James Loch's offices in Albemarle Street before moving to the Bridgewater Offices in Manchester. James Loch (1780-1855) made his reputation as agent to the vast Sutherland and Bridgewater estates; George followed in his father's steps. Hathorn became a lodger at Longley Hall where an estate office was set up in the existing building. Seventeen year old Isaac Hordern joined the office in March 1846 about the same time as three fireproof safes arrived for the storage of account books and deeds.[31] Longley was no longer a temporary site for the resident agent's offices and, in May 1847, Hathorn was ready to set out his ideas for proposed additions and alterations to the hall and for the creation of new estate offices:

> I do not see that any portion of these proposed additions can be made at either end of the Hall – I mean in the shape of wings – I would propose that the new buildings should be placed so as to run from near the kitchen door up the side of the plantation, leaving sufficient space at either end for entrance into the garden, larder and the croft beyond.[32]

It was envisaged that the extension would be of two storeys, the ground floor of which would comprise a waiting room, clerks' office and agent's room, whilst the upper floor would connect with the main house and provide additional accommodation. Part of the latter might be required for the agent's office if a stone fireproof safe were to be constructed at the end of the clerks' office, which Hathorn recommended. He also favoured an "Elizabethan' style and rough sandstone work. For this, Thomas Brook, who worked in the office, provided an estimate of about £300, but Hathorn remarked that, 'as the season is now considerably advanced, & masons & all other kind of works so very expensive' he would recommend postponing any work to the end of the year or the beginning of the next.[33]

While Hathorn was awaiting instruction about the proposed extension and the go-ahead to paint and decorate both the interior and exterior of the existing buildings, which was said to be much in need, Mrs Ramsden intervened. She had at last received the letter relating to the plans whilst staying at Easthorp Southern, the Warwickshire home of the Vyners: 'If Longley Hall is found on trial as suitable situation for the abode of the Resident Agent, I sh[oul]d say, hasten to build the wing you propose'. She reminded Loch that at the time of his appointment he had considered that some buildings, including an estate office and residence for an agent, might be required. Summing up, she insisted that there was no economy in postponing the required additions: 'pray proceed with the consideration of the plans for making it commodious for the intended purpose'. She regretted that the work had not been started. 'Had the work been set about in May, what progress there might have been made this fine summer!' She was equally positive about the painting and decorating. It is 'much wanted' and 'must certainly be done' though May would have been a better time for interior painting than July or August'.[34]

Spurred on, Hathorn was able to report to Loch on 24 August 1847 that 'the kitchen has been painted and whitewashed & otherwise repaired … Miss Holt's parlour, Servants Hall & all the Bedrooms occupied by them [the Holt sisters] & by the servants have been painted, papered and whitewashed'. This was the first work to have been undertaken in the house for over 14 years and the rooms occupied by the Misses Holt were in quite a state. After attending a lecture on public health earlier in the year, Hathorn was convinced that 'the cleanliness of the habitation the more necessary and important for the preservation of health'.[35]

A late start had been made on the alterations and additions to the hall and good progress made by the end of August 1847. The front door and portico were painted at the same time as the kitchen, but the work was halted before the expected arrival of George Loch so that he 'should not be annoyed with the smell of the paint'. Four rooms were ready for decorating. Hathorn sought advice on the papers to be chosen. A man had been set on to find a supply of water in the field above the hall. Hathorn was confident that a suitable source would be found and that the pressure would be good enough to carry the water up to the bedrooms. Here, Hathorn probably means the bedroom floor rather than the individual bedrooms. Housemaids would have been expected to fill pitchers 'with water and other matters' in a closet on the landing between the old and new parts of the house. Once the water supply was proved, the pipes could be installed and the painting commence. This would be a considerable improvement; Hathorn had had no running water for three months and had to rely on a well he had dug two years earlier.[36]

As Hathorn had suspected, there was little likelihood of all the building work being completed before the end of the season, leaving the new estate offices to be erected the following year. Work resumed in March 1848 but was halted when a dispute arose about the cost of the outstanding work. In January 1848, William Wallen had estimated the mason's work on the new offices at £300 with other costs at £315.³⁷ This is the first mention of Wallen's involvement in the project; his plans for the buildings do not appear to have survived. Estimates in March 1848 put the total cost of the work at £712, the discrepancy being accounted for by a higher estimate from Catton, the mason. Wallen explained that since January, 'the workmen have "struck" and there is now a general demand for an increase of 6d a day for labour'. Furthermore, Wallen noted, the quarry that had been chosen to supply the stone, which was the only source of suitable stone for the job, charged higher rates for its product and, if that were not enough, problems had been found when excavating the foundations, the ground being 'made' rather than 'natural'. Hathorn recommended that the estimates be accepted and the work proceeded.³⁸

The new offices survived the later rebuilding at Longley Hall in the form of the two gabled bays and a single storey castellated extension on the eastern side of the building [see Illustration 9, p. 15]. W. H. Crossland was to place his new main entrance in this wing, which he converted from agent's offices to domestic offices. Wallen employed the local vernacular, with hood mouldings to the mullioned windows which would have fitted in with the remaining parts of the original building. On the easternmost gable the Ramsden arms are carved in stone, whilst a roundel on the other gable included a clock. There are close similarities between the agent's offices and the former Castle Hill Hotel for which Wallen was probably responsible two years later [see Illustration 38, p. 164]. The Georgian wing, which included the principal reception rooms and bedrooms and which were re-decorated at this time, has not survived.

With the new buildings in place, Hathorn felt that the old buildings looked dirty and dingy. He recommended that Thomas Clayton, 'who coloured the Cloth Hall so successfully and has discovered some preparation which prevents the weather from having the usual effect upon whitewashed or coloured Buildings', be employed to colour the hall to match the stone of the new offices. Approval for this must have been forthcoming as Clayton was given two additional days' work to repair and replace the ridge tiles and slates which had been found in need of attention.³⁹

Fitting out the new building started in earnest in 1849. Wallen sought advice concerning the chimney pieces to be installed in the rooms to be occupied by Hathorn and members of the Ramsden family. The specification had provided for stone fireplaces, which would be in a Gothic style, though plain and well executed. Alternatives in marble were offered, but this would add at least £10 to the final cost. And cost was an issue. Loch had already

9. Longley Hall, north front. Engraving by Rock & Co. of London, 15 May 1873.

The two gables on the left formed part of the Estate Offices, designed in 1848-9 by William Wallen, enclosing the old Tudor building. The porch by W. H. Crossland was added in 1873 when the whole western side of the Hall was replaced: the ground floor rooms under the two gables to the right were the ante room and the library.

Huddersfield Local Studies Library

complained that the ceilings were 'too expensive and rich'. Wallen disagreed. All the plasterers' work had been included in the contract and any additional work had been approved. Wallen considered their prices to be fair as there was 'great competition in the plasterers' work'.[40]

Loch carefully scrutinised all estimates and accounts with the aim of keeping down the costs of the alterations and additions to the hall. Due economy was observed by the re-use and refurbishment of fixtures and fittings, but even the workmen questioned some of the decisions. Mr Wilson, who attended in October 1849 in order to measure the four rooms in the new offices for carpets, was asked to include the entrance, hall, staircase and landings in his measurements. Somewhat dismayed, he opined that 'anything new put on the floor of the Hall & staircase will not correspond well, or at all with the present condition of the walls and ceiling'. Hathorn confirmed that the ceiling was so black that before it could be whitewashed again, it would have to be papered first. Indeed, the four large front square rooms were in want of being papered and painted throughout as they 'are hardly fit to receive either Lord Fitzwilliam, Sir John Ramsden or yourself'.[41]

Local tradesmen were encouraged by the Ramsdens' revived interest in the town and the new developments that were taking place in the wake of the arrival of the railways in Huddersfield. Wallen, Hathorn observed in January 1849, was 'already set to work in preparing the necessary papers and measurements by which the several builders may be enabled to deliver tenders'.[42] Messrs Roebuck did not wait to be invited to compete for work, sending a letter and circular detailing their joinery work. Hathorn was keen to employ them and Loch had expressed a wish that 'a greater portion of the recent furnishings had been done by Huddersfield tradesmen'.[43] With this in mind, Hathorn had sought estimates for painting and papering at Longley from Burman & Calvert of whom 'Mr Wallen has the highest opinion'. Moreover, they were tenants on the estate and, like others in their position, 'they always appear glad to be employed'.[44] On this occasion, it was not to be. Mrs Ramsden wrote announcing that she had been to the Duppa & Collins showrooms in Oxford Street and selected the papers for Longley Hall and 'they wish to put them up & say it will not encrease [sic] the expense as they have workmen now employed near Leeds'.[45]

If employing London tradesmen incurred no additional monetary costs, it did cost a great deal of the goodwill which Hathorn had fostered, providing Joshua Hobson and the recently-established *Huddersfield Chronicle* with ammunition to aim against the estate and its absentee owners who were already under fire over the issue of Tenant Right [see chapter 3]:[46]

> … the majority of the inhabitants of Huddersfield are tenants under the estate of Sir J.W. Ramsden at the hands of whose Trustees they have had many concessions of a wise and comprehensive character conceded to them, and we believe that the Right Honourable Baronet in return draws a rent-roll of £60,000 a-year from the people of Huddersfield and the neighbourhood. So far there has, we think been a quid pro quo. Now there is standing within a short distance of Huddersfield, a mansion pretty generally known as Longley Hall in connection with which a suit [sic] of offices has been erected by the Ramsden Trustees… where the matters of detail pertaining to the management of the estate are transacted. The shell of these buildings having been carried up, and the exterior erections completed [local tradesmen expected to be called upon to tender for painting and papering]. …those hopes and expectations of being patronised by their landlord have, within the last

week been completely dispelled; for within the last few days a number of painters, paper-hangers, decorators &c. have arrived from London ... accommodation having in the meantime been provided for them at a neighbouring inn....Were we not convinced to the contrary we should be led to infer that the tradesmen of Huddersfield are not competent to undertake the decoration of these baronial offices.[47]

Sir John William read these criticisms at his home in Upper Brook Street but did not realise the extent of the opposition to the estate's leasing policy nor did he anticipate that it would lead to battle in the courts. He felt that the *Chronicle* was indulging in hyperbole. And, as for ordering paper and curtains in London, this was a 'very far fetched grievance indeed'.[48]

Alexander Hathorn's progress reports, together with the Duppa & Collins account for work at Longley, give a fuller picture than is usual of what was involved in decorating a country seat, and compensate for the absence of plans or illustrations of the finished rooms.[49] During May 1850, the suitability of the chimney pieces in each room was considered. A marble chimney piece in the surveyors' office was moved to the drawing room; others were relegated to the bedrooms and new grates and mantels ordered. These had all been installed before painting and papering was commenced in June. The woodwork in all the rooms was prepared, rubbed down, filled, and any rotten wood replaced. All the windows were given two coats of paint whilst the doors, the woodwork in the dining room, passage and stairs were given three coats in readiness for the grainer's arrival. Outside, after preparation, the wooden window frames were given two coats of paint, which was also applied to the stone jambs and sills.

There were four principal rooms on the ground floor, including a drawing room and dining room. Hathorn had a bedroom on the upper floor, where there were three more new bedrooms, two of them larger than the others, presumably set aside for Sir John William's use although nothing had been finalised and Miss Holt was anxious to know how the rooms were being allocated. These rooms received three coats of paint before papering. Observing the progress made, Hathorn felt that the work would be well-done, but he was less happy with the workmanship in the offices and bedrooms above, recommending that these rooms be re-varnished. Additionally, he requested that the Servants' Hall be whitewashed and the walls papered in oak together with the passage leading to the Entrance Hall.

Duppa & Collins provided a detailed account for the work they had undertaken in one of the four original reception rooms. After washing off the old colour from the ceiling, any cracks exposed were cut out and stopped in readiness for the application of a cream tint which was also applied to 111 feet

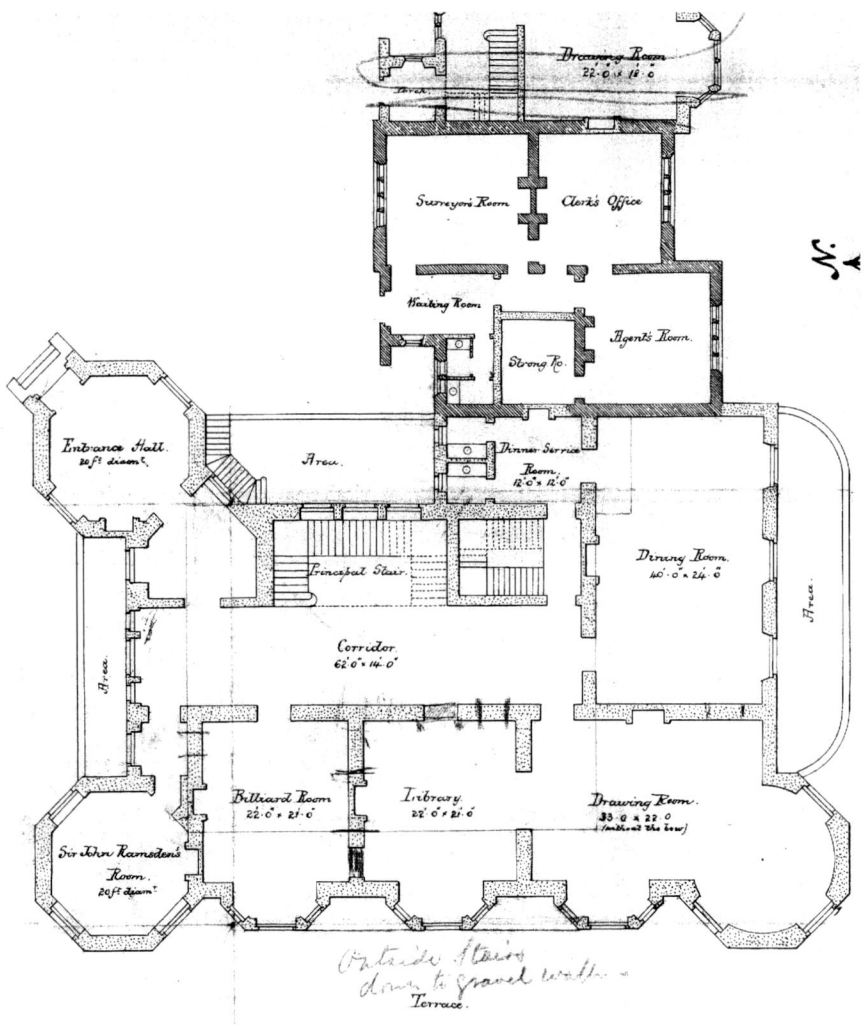

10. Longley Hall, Ground Plan (1866), showing William Wallen's Estate Offices of 1848 and the proposed 'mansion' by William Burn.

The walls of the 1848 building are picked out in solid shading; the walls of Burn's proposed mansion at the bottom (west) of the plan are stippled. The buildings to the east of the estate offices (top) represent one of the proposals for the agent's residence.

WYAS Kirklees, DD/RA/C/33/6

of cornice. The walls had been covered with a flock paper mounted on canvas stretched over battens and tacked. The fixings were concealed beneath a gilt moulding or fillet. This was carefully dismantled, the old canvas restored and replaced where necessary before sheets of green and gold paper were applied and the gilt mouldings re-fixed. Paid in September 1850, the account totalled £31-5-7, including £1-17-9. to cover the paperhanger's railway fares, time travelling and lodgings. The fashionable decorators' services extended to supplying, making and fitting curtains, and repairing and re-upholstering seat furniture as well as supplying items of furniture, all of which were required at Longley. Where possible, the existing furniture was retained. A set of 12 dining room chairs was re-furbished and the seats covered in leather. The claw feet of a matching pair of armchairs needed to be re-carved before the seats were stuffed and covered with leather. Some of the furniture was found to be beyond repair including the bed in Hathorn's room, the North Bedroom. It was replaced with an iron bed which both Sir John and his mother thought ' would be more easily kept clean and [would be] more durable'. Six old bedroom chairs were covered in chintz and one placed in each of the bedrooms. On the recommendation of Hanson, the upholsterer, velvet and damask were chosen for the new covers of the large armchairs in the dining and drawing rooms. And there was new furniture too – a consignment of mahogany furniture arrived from Lambs of Manchester on 16 October 1849.

Sir John had not visited Huddersfield since 1844. He had not, as expected, joined Earl Fitzwilliam at the laying of the foundation stone of the railway station in 1846; and a planned stay at Longley in autumn 1849 had been postponed at the last minute. In view of the mounting criticism of the estate's policies, Loch wanted the young baronet to be seen by his tenants. With the new bedrooms partially furnished, he wrote to Mrs Ramsden saying that they were '… very nice … very comfortable…I shall hope to see you and your son in them next year.[50] A date was finally fixed. Sir John would join his mother at the laying of the foundation stone of the new church at Bay Hall in which they had taken a keen interest, on 16 October 1851 [see pp. 134-6]. This allowed plenty of time to complete outstanding work and to furnish the rooms at Longley as well as to improve the approach to the house by widening and fencing the carriage road and erecting a new gate and gate piers at the entrance.[51]

The visit proved a great success. Isabella was overjoyed: '…no mother and son could be greeted and supported with more warmly expressed kindly feeling than we were'.[52] But their stay was short. They stayed overnight at Longley, entertained Earl Fitzwilliam to lunch, and returned to Byram after the ceremony 'as our time is not at our own disposal', wrote Isabella. She hoped that this would not be misconstrued by our friends and she was sorry to think that any ladies and gentlemen might be encouraged to 'come up the hill to Longley Hall' and find them not at home.[53]

Whilst congratulating Loch on their reception in the town, the Ramsdens appear not to have recorded what they thought of the improvements at Longley nor their appreciation of all the work that Hathorn had undertaken on the house and grounds. Given approval to have the garden 'made to look a little tidy' not long after his arrival at Longley, Hathorn set about this task with enthusiasm.[54] The plantations were thinned out and older fruit trees in the orchard taken away. Despite the exceptionally cold weather, Armitage the gardener was creating a new walk leading towards the house. He proposed to plant lilacs and roses on the bank which ran alongside.[55] Writing in 1847, George Searle Phillips described the garden and the improvements which had been made in the intervening years:

> [The garden] is situate on top of a pleasant hill surrounded by trees; and below it lies a deep dell, the banks of which slope in rather sudden declivities to the bottom. A short time ago, this dell was wild and uncultivated; but the present occupier of the hall having an eye both to use and beauty, has broken it up into a garden, and planted the hillsides with potatoes and other vegetables. He has likewise built a green house there, and cut a deep trough to carry off the water which comes down the hill; and on either side the trough he has planted shrubs and flowers, which I remember had a very beautiful appearance in the early part of the summer. Then there is a fine shadowy walk, running to the end of the dell, amongst tall and graceful trees.[56]

Phillips was of the opinion that these improvements reflected the character of the man who had wrought them: 'he is a man who will war with disorder, and put up with no wild nonsense either from men or nature'. He went further, considering that a man 'who can turn a savage stony dingle into a garden is just the man to stop all nuisances of what sort soever, and look well after the sanatory matters within his authority'.

Whilst he might have enjoyed free rein in the garden, Hathorn was answerable to Loch and the family. He carried out their instructions and sought their approval on estate matters which not infrequently extended to matters of detail. Phillips described Longley as being 'once the seat of the Ramsden family and now occupied by a gentleman acting in the capacity of an agent.' As far as Hathorn was concerned it remained a seat of the family where he merely had rooms and where his offices were located. In the 1851 Census, he was described as a 'lodger', the eldest of the Holt sisters, Mary, being described as head of the household. Her youngest sister, Sarah, who acted as housekeeper, asked the family through Loch how the new rooms were to be allocated, and Hathorn had had no say in the decoration and furnishing of the rooms. The family even chose the door furniture, expressing a preference for white china door knobs and finger plates over ones in brass.[57]

So much for the house Hathorn believed he had been promised as an incentive to make the move over the Pennines. But that was not his only grievance. Not unsurprisingly, he felt that he was being taken for granted. He complained to Loch that he was not adequately remunerated for the work he did as resident agent. He had been in post for over six years and in that time had devoted himself to the service of the estate, so much so, he argued, that 'I may without any exaggeration, call it 9 years'. During that time, the business of the estate had grown with the acquisition of neighbouring estates and the 'healthy increase of the Town' and with that had come 'new duties, anxieties and responsibilities'. Yet, despite previous approaches, his salary had not been increased in line with this additional burden. And, if that were not enough, he had had to meet the cost of keeping a horse without which he could not do his job. He reminded Loch of his loyalty to him and his father James over almost 14 years. 'My great object now is to get everything into as perfect order as possible by the time of Sir John Wm Ramsden's attaining his majority.'[58]

In achieving this objective, Hathorn became increasingly reliant on Isaac Hordern, the clerk who had arrived at Longley from the Bridgewater offices not long after he had taken up the post of resident agent. When an opportunity for advancement arose following the suspension of Dyke, one of the clerks, on account of his 'reckless conduct and extraordinary actions', Hathorn happily supported Hordern's application. Not only was he familiar with every department of the business, but 'he has very good taste in Architecture, and has at various times by his suggestions and otherwise assisted me very materially in the arrangement & laying out of Land for Building purposes'.[59]

New Longley

Hordern was able to leave his mark on Longley when called upon to draw up plans for new stables, barn and coach house. The chosen site was to the north east of the hall and the buildings, on two sides of a rectangular plot, forming an 'L' shape, survive, though the interiors have been stripped of their original features. The walls and gate on the other two sides of the rectangle, which formed the stable yard, have also disappeared. Built of coursed dressed local sandstsone in a plain gothic style, buttresses separate one bay from the next. A string course forms a dado around the whole building. Windows are emphasised by hood mouldings and decorative stonework whilst the doors are Early English arches. Narrow slit openings on the north and west elevations

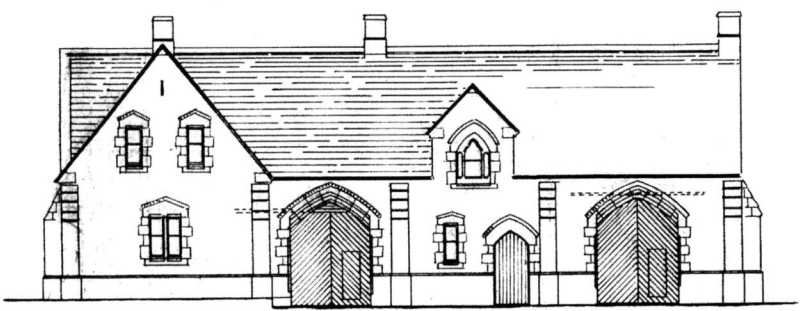

11. Longley Hall Stables, North Elevation by Isaac Hordern (1855), from a plan by
Huddersfield Corporation Architects
WYAS Kirklees, CBH/A/321.

are given a similar treatment. The double doors of the barn and coach house necessitate Tudor arched openings. Most of the building was single storey, but there was a floor above the harness room at the southern end of the building to provide accommodation for groomsmen and above the coach house at the eastern end for coachmen and visiting servants. Windows and a dormer indicate the second floors.[60]

In his notebook, Hordern recorded the completion of the stables in 1855, with which he appears to have been very pleased, noting that, 'Mr Matthews, Sir W Tite's repr[esentative] spoke very well of them when he visited Huddersfield'. Later historians have attributed the building to Edward Blore and the overall appearance of the barn and stables does owe much to him. There are similarities between Hordern's plans and those provided by Blore for George Green's farm approximately 10 years earlier.[61]

Loch stayed at Longley to oversee the celebrations to mark Sir John William Ramsden's coming of age. These took place on Wednesday 15 September 1852, the day after the birthday to avoid competition with the business of the Tuesday market, and were deemed to be a success despite the rain. Neither

Sir John nor any member of the family attended, but it was anticipated that Sir John would become more actively involved in Huddersfield affairs.[62] With the health of his father deteriorating, Loch was spending more time on the Sutherland estate, the running of which he took over following James Loch's death in 1855.[63] Sir John attended the soiree at the Mechanics' Institute on 18 May 1853 and, on the following day toured the town with Earl Fitzwilliam and Thomas Nelson, a London-based solicitor.[64] The latter took on Loch's role at a time when many local people were concerned about the costs of leases, the security of their property and their position as tenant-right holders of property. Nelson's actions exacerbated the situation.[65] Looking back, Hordern confided: 'I said the Estate would not recover from his Management for 30 years. It never has'.[66]

Sir John was all too well aware of shortcomings in the management of his affairs. Following a rent dinner, which Nelson had failed to attend, Sir John reviewed his own situation:

> During my recent stay at Huddersfield I became painfully conscious of the manner in which I had hitherto neglected my duties there – and of the injurious extent to which it had reacted [reflected?] on my own character and interests. As an absentee I was very ignorant of my own property & a very indolent & very careless Proprietor, I had delegated to you a vast amount of business which ought properly to have been discharged by myself. ... Many circumstances brought this forcibly to my mind at Huddersfield & showed that I had relied too exclusively on my Agents instead of acting for myself. ... I determined therefore to adopt an entirely new course - to take the management of my own affairs, as in duty bound, into my own hands – & in all local matters to carry on the ordinary business by direct instructions to Mr. Hathorn as my resident & local Agent & referring to you for advice assistance on more special and important matters properly falling under your functions.[67]

Nelson did not last long and after his departure, Alexander Hathorn was appointed general manager of the estate in June 1860, reporting directly to Sir John. Nelson had spent little time in the town, leaving Hathorn as resident to face the critics of the estate's leasing practices, and deal with the consequences of ongoing legal challenges. Not even a substantial pay rise assuaged Hathorn's grievances. He reminded Sir John that he had given the best years of his life to the estate, pointing out that the business of the estate was 'of a very varied nature' and differed 'widely from the ordinary run of Estates'. For much of that time, he complained, he had not been adequately remunerated. Had he been given a separate residence, as promised, his salary would not have been sufficient to enable him to keep it in a manner commensurate with his position. This had undoubtedly impacted on his career and on his prospects of marriage and family life. Nevertheless, he had 'become much attached' to Longley Hall.[68]

But he was not too attached and when offered a partnership with a Mr. Chadwick in a public accountancy practice and agency in Manchester, Hathorn accepted, leaving Longley in December 1861. He was succeeded in March 1862 by John Noble who made no mark on the estate or Longley. He retired on 31 October 1864, leaving Hordern to complain that he was away from business for 96 days between 1 January 1864 and 6 August 1864: 'I had a busy time of it'.[69]

Agent's House and Mansion

Captain Richard Hewley Graham (1834-1885) took up the post in December 1864. The son and grandson of leading Yorkshire Evangelical clergymen, the 30 year old bachelor had been in the army until the previous year, having recently served as aide-de-camp to the Governor of Malta.[70] For the next 20 years, he brought to the role of agent and advisor 'firmness of character, gentlemanly courtesy and common sense'. He proved to be the right man to heal the wounds which the tenant right case had exposed, spending time looking after the social, educational and spiritual needs of the tenantry. He also took seriously responsibility for members of his own family: two unmarried sisters were living with him at Longley in 1871.[71]

It seems that Sir John had agreed to provide a residence at Longley where Graham could live independently. To this end, and to avoid the situation which had arisen because of the estate's failure to provide Hathorn with a suitable residence, he had shown William Burn (1789-1870) over the site sometime in the summer of 1865.[72] A pioneer of the Scottish baronial, Burn worked in a variety of styles but became known for the layout and planning of country houses. Sir John would have become aware of Burn's houses on his visits to Scotland, the beginning of a love affair with the country that would lead to his building Ardverikie on the shore of Loch Laggan, Inverness. From 1844, Burn lived at and practised from Stratton Street, a short walk from the Ramsdens' London home. In the months following his visit, the prolific architect produced a number of plans for the agent's house and the 'mansion'.

In his initial exchanges with Burn, Sir John had also discussed the possibility of providing a suitable residence for himself. Reviewing the various options and 'considering the separate requirements of the Mansion House and the Agent's residence', Burn wrote, 'it appeared to me indispensable to look at the whole subject, as from their close connexion, it became necessary to see how far advantages could be taken of any part or portions of either for the general benefit, and mutual convenience be best promoted'.[73] With this in mind, in August 1865, Burn produced a ground plan showing both elements of the proposals.[74]

At the centre of the ground plan, which formed an irregular 'E' shape, was Wallen's 1848 estate office [see Illustration 10, p. 18]. To the east, the agent's house with dining and drawing room, kitchen and domestic offices; to the west, the mansion with its principal reception rooms. Burn had tried to take into account all Sir John's wishes regarding the number, size and position of the public apartments in his proposals for the mansion, but he did not feel he could achieve this within the existing walls which he proposed to replace. The re-built walls would occupy a larger rectangular footprint approximately 60 by 95 feet with octagonal towers on three of the building's four corners. That on the north east formed the entrance hall; the one to the north-west, Sir John's room, whilst that to the south-west formed a light and airy extension to the drawing room. 'The Drawing Room, Library, or ante drawing room, Billiard room will all open on to the Terrace, and beneath the latter will be all the offices [the domestic office rather than the agent's], the public entry to which will be from the area at the back of the principal staircase'. The latter was located on a corridor running from north to south which afforded entry to the main reception rooms.

Having given a good deal of thought to fulfilling Sir John' requirements, Burn deferred providing plans for the basement and bedroom floors until these proposals were accepted.[75] Sir John lost little time responding to Burn's plans from the Glenfeshie estate where he was spending the summer. He liked the arrangement of the dining room, drawing room and library and thought the new main entrance well-placed. However, he wanted a waiting room adjacent to the entrance hall and a doorway from there into his room in order that visitors did not have to go through the private rooms. He wondered if there might be a door from the entrance hall to the service quarters to make it easier for the staff to respond to callers. He had seen such an arrangement at Oxenfoord Castle, to which Burn had made significant alterations for Lord Stair in 1841. He felt the billiard room unnecessary but wanted his room to be larger though not as large as the dining room. Although he liked the large octagon angle towers, which he considered a fine feature, he felt that 'a room consisting of nothing else, would be too much like a lantern to be comfortable and would have no comfortable corners by the fireside'. As an adjunct to the drawing room, an octagon would make 'a charming variety to an ordinary shape of rooms'.[76]

Graham does not appear to have raised any objections to the accommodation provided in the agent's house. His main concerns centred on the adjoining offices. In particular, he insisted that more space be set aside for the strong room and the waiting room which was 'sometimes full & under pressure of business Callers'. He did not approve of the proposed siting of the water closets, and was anxious that the surveyors' office should be located on the south side where it would benefit from the maximum amount of daylight. An alternative might be to move it upstairs into one of the bedrooms, but this was not thought to be as convenient as having all the offices on one floor. Graham did express an interest in the bedrooms above the offices being part of the agent's house.[77]

Burn did his best to take on board the comments of Sir John and his agent, responding at length on 1 September 1865. He did not foresee any obstacles to accommodating these and other requirements, but there was now no real urgency as it appears that Sir John had intimated to Burn that he was not ready to proceed with the mansion at that time. The reasons for this are unclear. Sir John had consulted Burn in order to fulfil promises made to Captain Graham on his appointment and perhaps he now felt that he had been manoeuvered into taking on a grander scheme. On the other hand, it may have been simply to do with cash flow.[78]

Whatever the reason, no final decisions had been made by November 1865 when Burn wrote to his patron requesting an interview when he was next 'in Town … there being many matters connected with the proposed buildings at Longley Hall that could be so much better considered and explained at a meeting than by sheets of correspondence'. Possibly to prepare himself for a meeting with the architect, Sir John asked Graham to send copies of the latest plans to Byram. It seems likely that they did meet, but not until March 1866 when Burn forwarded tracings of the proposed attic and bedroom floors. Not previously discussed, the attic was to provide accommodation for single ladies and gentlemen as well as servants' quarters. A secondary staircase would allow access to the former and the private stairs to the latter.[79]

At that meeting in March 1866, the architect told his client that there would be time to build the agent's house and make alterations to the offices if the go-ahead were given as soon after Easter as possible. Sir John wrote four weeks after Easter, asking if there would still be time to complete the work that season and requesting that he proceed with the working drawings immediately. He was anxious to have the agent's house and estate offices completed during that year so that 'Mr. Graham could move into his new House at the very beginning of next year – and leave the old House in time to be pulled down … to clear the ground & make the most of the building season of 1867, for getting on with the "Mansion"'. Sir John did not want Burn to do any work on the drawings for the mansion as he was likely to require further changes, but he did not want any more changes to the plans for the agent's house as he did not want the money he had allotted for the works to be exceeded.

It was Burn's assistant William Bunn Colling (1813-1886) who replied. The 77 year-old architect was 'too unwell to write for himself or give any attention to business'. The working drawings, 'which have been thoroughly arranged by Mr. Burn,' would be ready in a week when they would be sent to Longley together with specifications in order that estimates could be obtained from local contractors.[80] A month later, Burn himself wrote apologising that influenza, bronchitis and lumbago had prevented his working on the drawings and specifications which he had now completed and which he would send to Graham.[81] The set of five drawings for the agent's house, dated May 1866 and now in the archive of Historic England, are either Burn's office copies or the originals which were never sent.[82] They illustrate a roughly 'L' shaped two storey addition to the north and east of the extended estate office which had been built in 1848. The accommodation included a south facing drawing room (18 x 22 feet) with a large bay window, a dining room (18.5 x 22 feet), domestic offices, with cellarage, and upwards of eight bedrooms. Externally plain, the elevations were to be enlivened by tall chimney stacks, gables with kneelers, dormers and the use of dressed stone quoins, window and door frames. Despite Sir John's haste earlier in the year, these proposals for the agent's residence were then shelved; there had been another change of plan.

A New Plan

The long-running tenant right case had caused a review of the management of the estate and its leasing practices, necessitating a private Act of Parliament to effect these changes and modify the settlement established by the fourth baronet's will and subsequent estate acts. John Beasley (1801-1874), the influential agent of the Spencer estate, was commissioned to write a report on the Huddersfield and Almondbury estate, which he presented in 1866. He was adamant that the new estate offices should be built in a central situation in the town and recommended the site of the Cherry Tree Inn.

> The agent is necessarily obliged to be in the town if not every day, nearly every day in the week, and sometimes twice a day; he has to see not only the solicitor to the estate, but solicitors to the lessees and other parties, and much time is lost on both sides in passing between Longley Hall and the town … the cashier has instantly to go to the bank, and probably the assistants in the office reside in the town.[83]

At the same time, he did not consider it necessary for the agent's house to be attached to the offices and, taking his own experience into account, he was of the opinion that it was better if this was not so.

The Ramsden Estate Act of 1867 took on board Beasley's recommendations. If a new Estate Office were erected in a convenient and central situation, 'it would be a great convenience to the tenants and occupiers of the [estate], and would materially facilitate the economical and efficient management of the said Estates'. Another clause set out the desirability of erecting a residence for the agent on part of the estate and for the provision of a suitable residence for Sir John William and his successors: 'the only house upon the said Estate available for that purpose is an old mansion house called Longley Hall, altogether inadequate and unsuitable for the accommodation of the said Sir John William Ramsden and his establishment.' Provision was made for the demolition and replacement of Longley or for its re-building commensurate with Sir John's standing and the value of the Huddersfield estates, in the £75,000 which the act allowed to be raised for developing the estate. This included £8,000 for the new estate offices and agent's residence and £10,000 for the mansion at Longley, 'with such out-offices, stables, coach houses, outbuildings, gardens and pleasure grounds' as thought necessary.[84]

Work began on the site of the proposed estate buildings, which included shops, offices, warehouses and rooms for the Huddersfield Club in addition to the Ramsden estate offices, in the summer of the following year. By November, the *Chronicle* could report that 'the quaint old Cherry Tree is no more'.[85] Construction began in 1869 and was completed in August 1870. On 14 September 1870 the business of the estate was transferred to the new offices from Longley [see front cover].[86] According to Hordern, Sir John now agreed to the old offices being connected with the hall. 'Mr. Graham started to do this, but found it difficult & asked me to make suggestion.' Although Sir John approved of the scheme, he thought it better to consult W. H. Crossland, the architect of the Estate Buildings. 'My plan was sent to him and he enlarged upon it'. In the absence of these plans, tracings of which Hordern had placed in an envelope in his drawer, it is not possible to determine to what extent they influenced Crossland's scheme. It seems unlikely that the accomplished architect whose reputation was riding high had need of advice from the estate cashier; maybe the architect merely wanted to humour his pretensions. It is surprising that in his notes on the estate, Hordern makes no mention of the earlier abandoned proposals by William Burn.[87] Nothing that went on in the estate offices escaped his attention and he would have seen the plans, copies of which were made by the surveyors.

Huddersfield-born William Henry Crossland (1835-1908) was the son of a stone merchant who rented a quarry from the Ramsdens.[88] He trained in the offices of George Gilbert Scott before setting up in practice in Halifax in 1858 and later in Leeds. It may have been his work on local churches which drew him to the attention of Sir John William Ramsden but it seems more than likely that it was his prize-winning designs for Rochdale Town Hall (1864-1871), which enhanced the architect's reputation nationally, that led to his being commissioned to work on estate projects. By 1869, Crossland had moved to the capital and opened an office in Regent Street in premises once occupied by Scott.

In Crossland's plan for the mansion, which was to provide accommodation for both the agent and Sir John on his occasional visits, Wallen's estate offices were retained, but with new internal arrangements and changed functions.[89] These domestic offices occupy the area to the east of the main entrance marked externally by twin gables, one bearing the Ramsden arms. Beyond is a castellated single storey extension housing the kitchen court and offices.[90] To the right (west) of the entrance porch occupying two storeys with an attic are the principal reception rooms which lead off an entrance hall with a grand staircase which follows the curve of the outer wall, leading up to a gallery which provides access to the bedrooms. The arrangement of the ground floor rooms closely follows that of William Burn's abandoned scheme. To the right of the entrance an ante room, which could be used by the private secretary or visitors waiting to see Sir John or his agent, leads into the library on the western corner. The remainder of the north front was occupied by two interconnected drawing rooms, one with a canted bay. These could be opened up to form a large reception room. A dining room with a semi-circular bay window occupying the full width of the room and facing west adjoins the drawing room.

There do not appear to have been many changes to Crossland's proposals. Sir John was generally happy with the arrangements. His response to the attic plans was that more would be an improvement. Graham recommended dormers in place of skylights in the attics 'though this would increase the cost' – something which Sir John was unwilling to do.[91] He had no wish to exceed his budget. But he was insistent that the new house should be thoroughly warm, something he had earlier impressed on William Burn, who was called upon to take extra precautions, 'especially on the north side to keep out the cold' from this 'cold and exposed situation'.[92] With this in mind, Crossland replaced the 30 inch thick walls of the old buildings with 21 inch walls with an additional inner brick wall, and felted the roof.[93]

If the plans drawn up by Burn and Hordern influenced Crossland's layout of the rooms of the house, the elevations are very much his own work. Building on Wallen's vernacular, Crossland introduced elements of French Renaissance and 'Tudorbethan' style to give the impression of a house which had evolved

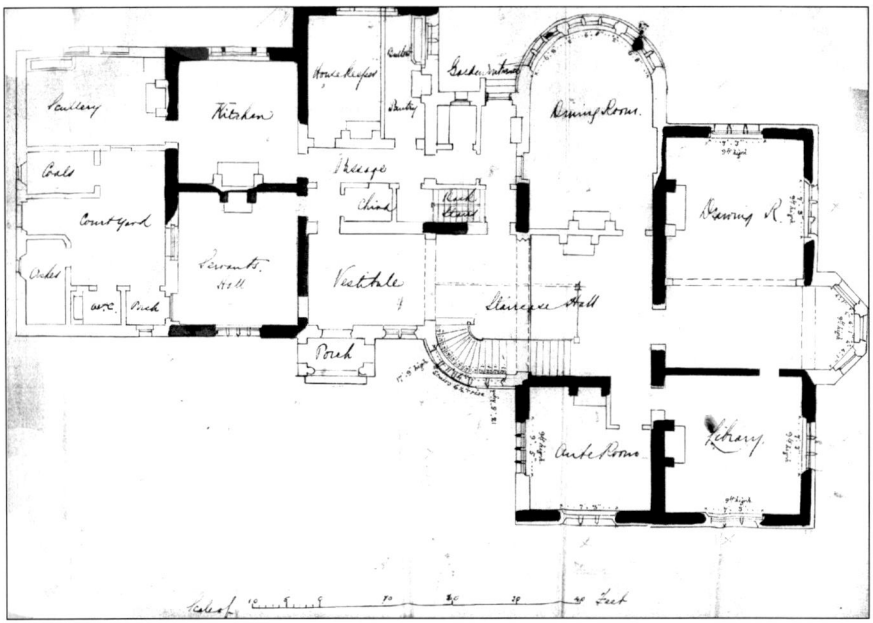

12. Longley Hall after 1873. Ground Plan of W. H. Crossland's hall of 1871–3
WYAS Kirklees, DD/RA/C/27/6.

EXISTING ELEVATION A

13. Longley Hall, (A) North, (B) East, (C) South and (D) West Elevations, 2008 survey by
AHR Building Consultancy Ltd.
AHR Surveys & Project Archive, 2008-10.

LONGLEY HALL: THE HUDDERSFIELD SEAT OF THE RAMSDENS

EXISTING ELEVATION B

EXISTING ELEVATION C

EXISTING ELEVATION D

14. Longley Hall, view of the new south and west fronts from the garden (1871−3), by W. H. Crossland.
Huddersfield Local Studies Library

over the years. Constructed in coursed Crosland Hill stone, the window and door reveals, mullions, sills, heads, dripstones, storey dressings, gable coping and kneelers are all in ashlar. Tall chimney stacks tower above the varied roofscape of blue slate. This includes a conical roof over the dining room bay on the south front. The asymmetrical entrance north front has a finely detailed porch with ashlar reveals and a semi-circular head adorned with the Ramsden arms, to the right of which stands a semi-circular castellated staircase tower with rising windows. Characteristic of Crossland's work, he had included similar details in the Estate Buildings and Rochdale Town Hall. Graham was to claim that as the whole was very plain he had directed the adding of a string course similar to that in the old building and also label moulding over the windows. [94]

Three sheets of plans, showing the alterations and additions to Longley Hall, signed off by Major Graham on 2 October 1871, were submitted for consideration by the Borough Engineer and approved on 24 October.[95] The main contracts had already been awarded to those responsible for the Estate Buildings. There may have been some preliminary work on the site and the first payments are not recorded until December 1871. The eventual cost was £6,364-10-8 including architect's commission of £280.

Sir John was closely monitoring the project. Crossland, who was now working on the Byram Buildings as well as the Holloway Sanatorium at Egham, was sometimes late in providing up-to-date figures. Graham received numerous complaints. Sir John was answerable to his trustees for the £50,000 which had been raised under the terms of the 1867 Estate Act. Until he knew the full extent to which he was committed by the re-building of Longley, he could not raise the remainder of the authorized loan, and to cover the shortfall in the meantime he had no other option but to raise money on his own account.[96] Crossland's clerk, A.J. Taylor, spent a month working on the accounts of the various building projects, allowing Graham to produce a statement of liabilities in November 1873. These included £562-5-10 of ordinary expenditure relating to Longley and extraordinary expenditure of £1,923-6-8 on additions. 'This is nearly double the estimate … and you give no explanation of it', Sir John complained. On a visit in the spring, he had directed that no further expenditure should be made and he now required a full explanation and 'a statement showing the estimate on the faith of which I undertook the building.' Whatever the explanation, Sir John had to accept the increased costs, which were as nothing compared with the overrun on expenditure on Byram Buildings.[97]

The need for economy probably influenced Graham's decisions on the furnishing of the hall. Existing curtains and carpets were re-used as far as possible. In January 1873, Sir John had directed that no new blinds be ordered, but Graham had already had Venetian blinds made for the windows in Sir John's and Lady Guendolen's rooms. New carpets were ordered for the drawing room, dining room, stairs and principal bedrooms. Samples were sent to Byram at Sir John's request, prompting a swift response. He was especially unhappy with the choice of carpet for the drawing room and sorry to learn that it had already been laid. Graham thought the pattern, which he had selected from more than 200 samples supplied by Crossley's, bold and rich, and encouraged Sir John to make a final decision once he had seen it in the room. 'That we should ever like such a carpet is quite out of the question', was his response. Graham found himself in a difficult position. He had been under pressure to get the work on the hall completed as quickly as possible and he had not wanted to do anything to increase costs. He had not expected Sir John to take an interest in the choice of furnishings. He agreed to negotiate with the supplier and, if the carpet could not be returned, he would have it cut-up and re-used in the bedrooms, and he would bear any additional cost. Sir John was insistent that he would pick up the bill. Perhaps with the cost of the carpets in mind, he authorized expenditure on druggets to protect them when the rooms were not in use.[98]

With the house almost ready for occupation, a consignment of furniture arrived on 18 January 1873,[99] and Sir John wrote to Graham setting out his intentions for the use of the rooms:

> The drawing room and the rooms over it & the room over the dining room, I reserve exclusively for Lady Guendolen & myself. The two sitting rooms [that is, the library and ante room] adjoining the Drawing room, I make over to you, and you are welcome to use the Dining room in our absence. I also make over to you the 4 bedrooms over the East end of the House, the two remaining bedrooms at the top of the front staircase, I should wish to have available in case I bring any guests with me, but you are welcome to use them occasionally for any visitors of your own.[100]

Graham does not appear to have raised any objections to these arrangements and since Sir John's visits were fairly infrequent and of short duration, they were of no great inconvenience. With the marriage of Major Graham to Frances Mary Smith in September 1874, Longley became a family home once more. By 1881, the Grahams had three sons and a daughter, and their household included Mrs. Graham's mother, a nurse (the youngest child was only seven months old) and two housemaids.[101] This happy existence was to be short-lived; Major Graham died suddenly, aged 51, on 16 March 1885.[102] Sir John reassured Mrs. Graham that she could stay at Longley for as long as she needed, but in due course she had to make way for her husband's successor. Frederick William Beadon (1853-1933) was appointed in June and was soon taking part in public meetings and fulfilling his professional duties, though this was not soon enough for Isaac Hordern who complained of it being an arduous time for him as the new agent did not get to work soon enough.[103] Previously agent to Sir William Eden of Windlestone Hall, Co. Durham, Beadon was already married. His family was to grow up at Longley where they lived until the sale of the estate in 1920. Major Beadon then moved to Byram where he oversaw the dismemberment and sale of that estate.[104]

During his 35-year tenure of Longley Hall, there were no major changes. Mains drainage arrived in 1889 following a diphtheria scare which the Beadons' second daughter survived.[105] At about the same time, a new and improved heating system was installed, much to Sir John's satisfaction. He found Longley very cold.[106] There were new kitchens and improvements to the servants' quarters.[107] Electricity was installed in 1914, the year that Sir John William Ramsden died.[108] In his later years, he had spent little time at Longley, Lady Guendolen having inherited Bulstrode Park on the death of her father, the 12th Duke of Somerset, in December 1885. Sir John Frecheville Ramsden, who took on the Huddersfield estate in 1910, had little enthusiasm

15. Tudor chimney piece, Tapestry Room, Muncaster Castle, removed from Longley New Hall, 1920.
Muncaster Castle

for Longley – his interests lay further afield – but he did inherit his father's enthusiasm for family history. On one of his infrequent visits he found a portrait of the first baronet which he had removed to Byram.[109] At the time of the sale of the Huddersfield Estate, he expressed an interest in retaining the old mantel piece from Longley Hall for sentimental reasons.[110]

Specifically excluded from the sale was Longley Old Hall, which was considered to be the family's ancestral home, and which his father had 'restored' in 1885. From being the house of one of the richest families in the community, in the words of G. S. Phillips, it had become 'a poor and naked cottage'.[111] By the time Sir John ordered the restoration, it had been sub-divided to form three cottages. Plans prepared by A. J. Taylor restored the porch, mullioned windows, and gables with finials. The pitch of the roof and gables was determined by discoveries when the plain roof was removed during the restoration work.[112] Having consulted some of his older parishioners, Hulbert considered that the hall had been restored to its original form. 'Old oak wainscoating was also found in out of the way places, which, when collected was found sufficient for forming a Dado round the walls of the inner Hall. This together with an old oak Settle and other furniture,' were to give what Hulbert described as 'a most quaint and pleasing appearance'.[113] In the principal ground floor room, Hulbert described a board painted with a biblical text and associated with Longley from the time of the Wood family. The words from the first epistle of St Peter read:

> All flesh is as grasse and all the glory of man as the flower of grasse. The grasse withereth and the flower falleth away. But the Word of the Lord endureth for ever.[114]

The Last Years

A number of options were considered for the Victorian Longley Hall before it was passed to the council's education department to become the home of Huddersfield's second selective school for girls, which opened in 1924. Longley Hall (Girls) Central School was later to become a special school known as Longley School. Since 2016, it has catered for the special needs of children and young people on the autistic spectrum, aged from 3-19 years, and is now known as Woodley School and College. Whilst 'Longley' may have disappeared from its name, the hall would be immediately recognisable to Major Beadon and his family, the last residents. They might notice the loss of some of the elaborate chimney stacks, and would be all too well aware that the rich and colourful interiors had given way to bland institutional gloss and emulsion and that suspended ceilings had hidden decorative plasterwork. Double skirtings, doors, original fireplaces, a black and white ceramic chequerboard floor, an etched glazed screen, and curved baluster staircase survive, which along with the carved Ramsden arms and intertwined ciphers of Sir John William and Lady Guendolen provide permanent reminders of their time at Longley and a reminder of whose wealth caused it to be built.

16. Longley Old Hall, interior, showing the board with the text
from 1 Peter, chapter 1, 24−5.
Kirklees Image Archive

With the death of Sir John Frecheville Ramsden in 1958, the family's direct connection with Huddersfield and Longley was lost. His heir, Sir Geoffrey William Pennington Ramsden (1904-1987), was a 16 year-old at Eton when the estate was sold and would have had little, if any, knowledge of Huddersfield. He sold the freehold of the Old Hall to the long-term tenants in November 1975, thus bringing to an end the Ramsdens' 433 year-long association with Longley. The painted board bearing the words of St Peter, still hangs on a wall in the Old Hall.

Endnotes

1   Cant, D. (2001), pp 58-67. For a full survey by the Yorkshire Vernacular Architecture Study Group see Leeds University Library, Yorkshire Archaeological Society MS 1627 No 1669, Longley Hall (2004).
2   For the Ramsden Family Tree see pp. xxii-xxiii. Not all early dates are agreed and some are unknown.
3   Dennis Whomsley, Unpublished typescripts for an intended history of the Ramsden family. Copies lodged at WYASK, KX486/2.
4   DD/DD/dd/V/30 ff 13.
5   DD/RE/5/1 and KC 311/1/1, Survey of Almondbury, 1584.

6   Hulbert (1882), pp.231-2
7   DD/RE/S/4, Survey and Map of the Manor of Almondbury, Timothy Oldfield, 1716.
8   Giles (1986), pp. 48–105.
9   Redmonds (1982), pp.7–11; Tolson (1929), pp.117–24.
10 Hey (2007), pp. 60, 63–4, 311; DD/RA/F/29/32; Wickham and Lynch (2019).
11 Thrush and Ferris (2011); Ormrod (2000), p.138. The county justices sat at Pontefract.
12 Rushworth (1721), 6 November 1648.
13 Law (1985), p. 23. The original document is to be found in Leeds University Library, Special Collections, YAS MS 751, Journal of John Turner of Hopton.
14 Hulbert (1882), p. 232.
15 Fletcher (1900), vol II, p. 41; Schofield (1883), p. 5.
16 Huddersfield Local Studies Library, Photographic Collection, RH1/13, Yi 1871 BTT Longley Hall, South View; RH1/12, Yi 1871 BTT Longley Hall, West View.
17 DD/AH/92, Philip Ahier Papers, Notes on Longley Hall.
18 Wickham and Lynch (2019).
19 DD/RE/S/13, Valuation of Estate.
20 *Leeds Intelligencer* [*LI*], 12 September 1769.
21 DD/RE/S/13, Valuation of Estate.
22 Sarah Holt acted as housekeeper at Longley. Despite her apparent ill-health, she outlived her two sisters retiring on their deaths in 1862. She received a pension from the estate and died at Shorehead Cottage on 12 March 1873, aged 76 years and is buried at Edgerton Cemetery (*Huddersfield Chronicle* [*HC*], 15 March 1873).
23 *Bradford Observer*, 16 March 1843, p.5.
24 DD/RE/S/11, Survey 1797; Baines (1822), vol. 1; Law (1986), 'John Holt'.
25 *LI*, 2 July 1829. Nevertheless, John Charles Ramsden was an MP from 1812 until his death in 1836.
26 *Leeds Times*, 9 November 1844.
27 DD/RE/3/23, Isabella Ramsden to George Loch, 12 August 1844.
28 DD/RA/C, Box 24, Report on Canal by Mr. Loch, Notebook. See below, chapter 2. pp.56-7.
29 DD/RE/C/4, Isabella Ramsden to Loch, 4 September 1844; DD/RE/C/38, Isabella Ramsden to Loch, 21 July, 1847.
30 DD/RE/C/4, Isabella Ramsden to Loch, 4 September 1844; DD/RE/C/38, Isabella Ramsden to Loch, 21 July, 1847.
31 DD/RE/419, Isaac Hordern, 'Notes Relating to the Ramsden Estates and Huddersfield', 1846, pp. 5 and 7.
32 DD/RE/C/36, Alexander Hathorn to Loch, 24 May 1847.
33 DD/RE/C/36, Hathorn to Loch, 24 May 1847.
34 DD/RE/C/38, Isabella Ramsden to Loch, 21 July 1847; 23 July 1847.
35 DD/RE/C/37, Hathorn to Loch, 8 June 1847; 24 August 1847.
36 DD/RE/C/37, Hathorn to Loch, 23 August 1847; 24 August 1847. DD/RE/C/65, Hathorn to Loch, 10 October 1849.
37 For Wallen, see chapter 5.
38 DD/RE/C/46, Hathorn to Loch, 10 March 1848.
39 DD/RE/C/61, Hathorn to Loch, 4 June 1849.
40 DD/RE/C/32, Hathorn to Loch, 16 June 1849.
41 DD/RE/C/65. Hathorn to Loch, 10 October 1849
42 DD/RA/C/56, Hathorn to Loch, 24 January 1849.

43 DD/RA/C/56, Hathorn to Loch, 30 January 1849.
44 DD/RE/C/72, Hathorn to Loch, 18 May 1850.
45 DD/RE/C/72, Isabella Ramsden to Loch, May 1850.
46 See chapter 3.
47 *HC*, 15 June 1859.
48 DD/RA/C/73, Sir John William Ramsden [JWR] to Loch, 20 June 1850.
49 WYL/109/58/3, Paid Bills, 1850. Duppa & Collins, 25 March 1850. Paid 21 September 1850; DD/RE/C/65, Hathorn to Loch, 10 October 1849; DD/RE/C/72, Hathorn to Loch, 8 May 1850; DD/RE/C/72, Hathorn to Loch, 18 May 1850; DD/RE/C/72, Hathorn to Loch, 24 May1850; DD/RE/C/73, Hathorn to Loch, 8 June 1850; DD/RE/C/73, Hathorn to Loch, 21 June 1850; DD/RE/C/73, Hathorn to Loch, 1 July 1850; and DD/RE/C/75, Hathorn to Loch, 19 August 1850; DD/RE/C/75.
50 Loch to Isabella Ramsden, November 1849 quoted in Dennis Whomsley, 'Sir John William Ramsden, Part I, 1831-1857', unpublished typescript, p. 14, note 6. Copy lodged at KX486/2.
51 DD/RE/C/75, Hathorn to Loch, 9 August 1850.
52 Isabella Ramsden to Loch, 20 October 1851, quoted in Whomsley, 'Sir John William Ramsden, 1831-1857', unpublished typescript, p16, KX486/2.
53 DD/RE/C/77, Isabella Ramsden to Loch, 6 October 1851.
54 DD/RE/C/7, Isabella Ramsden to Loch, 18 December 1844.
55 DD/RE/C/7/40, Hathorn to Loch, 30 December 1844.
56 Phillips (1848), pp.19-20. First published in *Bradford & Wakefield Observer*, 27 September 1847.
57 DD/RE/C/74, Hathorn to Loch, 1 July 1850; DD/RE/C/89, Hathorn to Loch, 7 October 1851; TNA, HO 107/2294/15/23, 1851 Census, Longley Hall.
58 DD/R/dd/VII/187, Hathorn to Loch, 16 December 1850.
59 DD/RE/C/66, Hathorn to Loch, 24 November 1849.
60 CBH/A/32, Huddersfield County Borough Records, Plans of Stables, drawn in Borough Architect's Office, July 1924.
61 Hordern, 'Notes', 1855, p. 40; *HDE*, 12 September 1987; WYK 1628/33, Edward Law Papers.
62 *HC*, 18 September 1852; George Loch to Sir John William Ramsden, 14 September 1852, quoted in Dennis Whomsley, 'John William Ramsden, 1831-1857', KX486/2.
63 *The Times*, 6 August 1877.
64 *HC*, 21 May 1853.
65 See chapter 3.
66 Hordern, 'Notes', 1853, p. 33.
67 DD/RA/C/11/4, JWR to Nelson, 6/11/59.
68 DD/RA/C/28, Alexander Hathorn to Sir John William Ramsden, 18 June 1860. These issues had been discussed at length in an 'interview' at Byram.
69 Hordern, 'Notes', 1861, p. 65; 1864, p. 75. Hathorn's venture was short-lived and the partnership dissolved. He undertook work for the Huddersfield Estate and went on to run a farm at Birkin on the Byram Estate before setting up an agency on his own account in London. He died at Frensham, Surrey, aged 76 in 1892.
70 *Daily News*, 9 April 1860. He was a Captain, and later Major, in the militia.
71 Hulbert (1885), pp. 164-5; TNA, RG 10/4356/94/20, 1871 Census, Longley Hall.
72 For William Burn, see *ODNB* (2004) and Walker (1976).
73 DD/RA/C/33/6, William Burn to JWR, 9 August 1865.

74 DD/RA/C/33/6, Longley Hall, Ground Plan of Principal Floor, 9 August 1865.
75 DD/RA/C/33/6, Burn to JWR, 9 August 1865
76 DD/RA/C/33/6, JWR to Burn, 25 August 1865.
77 DD/RE/C/33/6, R.H. Graham to JWR, 9 September 1865.
78 DD/RA/C/33/6, Burn to JWR, 1 September 1865.
79 DD/RA/C/33/6, Burn to JWR, 18 November 1865.
80 DD/RA/C/33/6, William Colling to JWR, 18 May 1866.
81 DD/RA/C/33/6, Burn to JWR, 12 June 1866.
82 Swindon, Historic England Archive, MD60/00034 – MD60/00038, Longley Hall Agent's House, Plans of Cellars, Ground Floor, Bedroom Floor, Roofs and East Elevation and Sections. The five plans were deposited by the successors to William Burn's practice and remained in the Stratton Street premises.
83 DD/RA/C, Box 24, Report on the Estates of Sir John William Ramsden, Bart, in Huddersfield and Almondbury, 1866, by John Beasley, Chapel Brampton. Beasley had taken Loch's place as the country's leading land agent, a role which he helped to redefine. See Beardmore, C (2016), pp. 172-192.
84 DD/RE/449, Ramsden Estate Acts, 1859, 1867, & 1885; Ramsden Estate Act 1876, pp. 20–1; 40–1.
85 *HC*, 11 July and 7 November 1868.
86 *HC*, 27 August and 10 September 1870.
87 Hordern, 'Notes', 1871, p. 92.
88 For Crossland's career, see Whittaker (1984); Elliott (1996), and Law (2001b), 'William H. Crossland'.
89 KMT 18, Huddersfield County Borough, Building Control Plans, Moldgreen Ward 63, Alterations & Additions, Longley Hall, October, 1871.
90 The crenellation, a characteristic feature of Crossland's work, would have been added at this time. It is not altogether clear whether the single storey extension is from the Wallen estate offices or wholly Crossland's work. Matching crenellation is seen most notably on the staircase tower and other parts of the new building.
91 See Law (2001b) for an account of Longley Hall.
92 DD/RA/C/33/6, Postscript to JWR to Burn, 25 August 1865.
93 Law (2001b).
94 Law (2001b).
95 KMT 18, Huddersfield County Borough, Building Control Plans, Moldgreen Ward 63, Alterations & Additions, Longley Hall, October, 1871
96 DD/RA/27/6, JWR to Graham, 31 March 1873.
97 DD/RA/27/6, Graham to JWR, 4 November 1873 and his reply from Kingussie, 7 November 1873. For the growing costs of Byram Buildings see copies of letters included in Graham to JWR, 10 April 1873.
98 DD/RA/27/6, Graham to JWR, 11, 13 & 15 January 1873, and JWR's reply, 14 January 1873.
99 DD/RA/27/6, Graham to JWR, 21 January, 1873 includes a list of the items received.
100 DD/RA/27/6 JWR to Graham, 14 January 1873.
101 TNA, RG11/4375/14/21, 1881 Census, Longley Hall.
102 KC/592/2/5, Isaac Hordern's Notes and Photographs, Ramsden Estate, Huddersfield, list of agents; WYAS, Wakefield, WDP12, Almondbury Burial Register, 21 March 1885.
103 Hordern, 'Notes', 1885, p. 143.
104 *HC* 13 June 1855; *Northern Echo*, 30 June 1885. Beadon began work on 1 June 1885.

105 DD/RE/C/21/9, F.W. Beadon to JWR, 24 August 1889; 11 September and 16 September 1889.
106 DD/RE/C/21/5, Beadon to JWR, 1 October 1889.
107 DD/RA/30, Beadon to JWR, 3 March 1914 and 3 July 1914.
108 DD/RA/30, Beadon to JWR, 9 April 1914.
109 DD/RF/27, Sir John Frecheville's Historical Notes. '… an immense full-size picture of him [the first baronet] on a prancing grey pony which I rescued from Longley whither it had been banished … He has a big aquiline nose.'
110 During the re-building work in 1871–4, according to Ahier, an 'exceedingly good chimney piece of the Tudor period' was found in the basement (DD/AH/92 Philip Ahier, Notes on Longley Hall). A fireplace in the Tapestry Room at Muncaster Castle, which Sir John had inherited on the death of the 5th Lord Muncaster in 1917, is said to have come from a Ramsden house in Yorkshire.
111 Phillips (1848), p. 22.
112 KMT 18, Huddersfield County Borough, Building Control Plans, Almondbury & District Building Plans, 14 September 1884, 'Alterations & Additions to Longley Old Hall'. A. J. Taylor had been W. H. Crossland's chief clerk.
113 Hulbert (1885), p. 163.
114 Hulbert (1882), p. 219. Hulbert wrongly gives the reference as 1 Peter, chapter 1, verse 29. It is actually from verses 24 and 25 and is taken from the Tyndale translation.

CHAPTER TWO   43

The Ramsdens and the Public Realm in Huddersfield, 1671-1920

DAVID GRIFFITHS

Introduction

TO A WELL-INFORMED visitor standing at Huddersfield's market cross today, a century after the Ramsdens sold their Huddersfield estate, their impact on the townscape remains inescapable. The market cross itself, topped by the family arms, records the grant of market rights to John Ramsden (later the first baronet) in 1671. The four streets which meet there, Kirkgate, Westgate, New St and John William St, were named by the Ramsdens, and the last two were their creation. With New St, dating from about 1770, they initiated a small street grid to the south, dominated by the Ramsden-built Cloth Hall of 1765/6; from there the axis of Cloth Hall St and the early nineteenth century King St ran east to Aspley Basin, the terminal port of Sir John Ramsden's Canal (1775-80). John William St, named after the fifth baronet, opened up a new Victorian grid to the north, with the Palladian railway station (1846-51) as its dominant feature. To the south of the cross is the handsome Georgian row of the Brick Buildings and to the north Waverley Chambers, one of three Queen Anne style office buildings along Byram St (named after the family seat near Pontefract); all four were built by the Ramsden estate as commercial developments. There is, then, a great deal of surviving evidence that in the eighteenth and nineteenth centuries Huddersfield was a 'Ramsden town'.

Such was certainly the claim of the Ramsden estate at the time. In their petition in 1774 for the Canal Act, the trustees of Sir John Ramsden, the fourth baronet (1755-1839) asserted that he was 'the owner of the whole town (except for one house) and of a considerable part of the lands adjoining'.[1] In 1832 the parliamentary boundary commissioners, as they drew up new constituencies under the 'Great Reform Act', noted that 'every house but one in the Town belongs to the same proprietor'.[2] Even after the incorporation of Huddersfield as a municipal borough in 1868, Sir John William Ramsden continued to assert that 'the Town of Huddersfield is almost entirely built upon portions of his estates', and successive Huddersfield Corporation Acts down to 1897 continued to reserve his rights as lord of the manor.

The estate's own claims have often been echoed in the national historiography. In his comparative study, *Lords and Landlords*, David Cannadine suggested that Huddersfield was unique in England in having 'one family in such a position of predominant territorial power'; that the small, single-member 1832 constituency 'amounted initially to a nomination borough'; and that 'local government remained almost entirely in their hands until the passing of the Huddersfield Improvement Act in 1848'.[3] Similarly, Norman Gash claimed that Huddersfield, 'without coming quite into the category of proprietary boroughs ... was sufficiently under the control of ... Sir John Ramsden to defy the efforts of radicals and tories to capture the seat'.[4]

Scholars who have undertaken more detailed local studies have been a little more sceptical. Jane Springett, in her extensive work on land ownership, concluded that 'Contrary to the opinions of many contemporary observers, the Ramsden estate did not at any time enjoy an absolute monopoly in land'.[5] Similarly, Vivienne Hemingway found 'little evidence that Huddersfield was a nomination borough in the hands of the Ramsden family', though that did not mean that early parliamentary elections were free of undue pressure or corrupt practices.[6]

This chapter will assess the Ramsden influence on the public realm of the town. It will identify a succession of periods characterised by different relationships between the estate and the town, and the turning points between these. Within each period, attention will be given to three dimensions: the extent and location of Ramsden land ownership; the institutions of town governance; and the development of public facilities and the role played by the estate in their development, whether directly or through the governing institutions.

The long eighteenth century: developmental fits and starts[7]

In acquiring the town's market rights in 1671, it has been said, 'John Ramsden may have been looking to the long-term development of the town as a trading centre', as well as securing a new source of income for the estate.[8] If so, it was indeed a long-term ambition: it would be the best part of a century before the estate took further initiatives towards economic development and urban planning. During this period, the town remained tiny by later standards – the estimated township population increasing from about 1,000 in 1716 to 3,000 in 1778[9] – and the estate took little interest in the facilities it offered.

THE EXTENT OF THE ESTATE

The claimed ownership of 'all but one house' takes a popular if apocryphal form in a tale related by generations of local historians, and appearing in many versions. The house in question was owned by one Thomas Firth, and the local historian, G. W. Tomlinson, set the tale down thus:

> It would be impossible to speak of Mr [Thomas] Firth without allusion to his sharp, practical shrewdness spiced with a flavour of wit. The story about the cottage at the low side of the church-yard which belonged to him is a case in point. The site of this cottage was the only bit of freehold in the middle of the town which did not belong to the Ramsden estate. The ground was wanted for some improvements, and it is said Sir John offered to cover the land with sovereigns if he might have it. Mr Firth replied, 'Put them edgeways, Sir John and the land is thine.'[10]

A Firth biographer describes the story as 'celebrated and not authenticated', though true to Firth's character.[11] It certainly needs to be contextualised.

The name 'Huddersfield' in the eighteenth and nineteenth centuries could denote any of three nested geographies. The *parish* of Huddersfield extended for a dozen miles along the north bank of the River Colne, from Marsden in the west to Bradley in the east, comprising seven townships. One of these was Huddersfield *township*, which also became the parliamentary borough in 1832. This extended several miles from today's town centre, particularly north-eastwards, and was further divided into five *hamlets*, one named Huddersfield. Even this smallest 'Huddersfield' was far from fully urban – Huddersfield being described as being a 'miserable village' in the late eighteenth century.[12]

By then the Ramsden estate was undoubtedly dominant within the inner hamlet – 'the middle of the town'– and the 1786 enclosure award allocated 286 of 323 acres of common land to Sir John.[13] However, two maps of that period, and land tax returns, reveal the holdings of other substantial freeholders close to the centre, notably those of the Bradleys at Newhouse (Highfields), William Walker at Bay Hall, Sir John Lister Kaye at Greenhead/Gledholt/Springwood and the scattered Hirst & Kennet estates.[14] Although these largely came to market in the early nineteenth century – Kaye's estate in 1804, the Hirst & Kennet estates in 1819, Bradley's in 1820 – none fell to the Ramsdens until mid-century [see p. 58].

Further from the centre were other more substantial landowners. Within the township were the Pilkingtons at Bradley, Whitacres at Deighton and Thornhills at Sheepridge, the last also dominant in Lindley township. Across the river were the extensive Kaye estates at Dalton and those of the Lockwood Proprietors in that township. It remains undeniable, however, that in the central area where Huddersfield's urban public realm developed, the Ramsden estate *was* overwhelmingly the dominant landowner.

GOVERNANCE: THE ANCIEN REGIME

Until 1820, the town was governed by the typical English triad of manor, parish and county magistrates. The estate's direct role was thus through the civil and minor criminal jurisdiction of the manorial court leet. This met at Almondbury at least annually to appoint its traditional officers, including the constable, who was 'head of the town', and to prosecute a range of nuisances. A dozen or more jurors, recruited from the gentlemen and 'middling sort' of the town, were convened by the estate steward, invariably a local lawyer.

It seems unlikely that successive lords of the manor took much interest in this low-level regulatory activity. They did, however, have other channels of influence at their disposal. The parish vestry retained its Elizabethan jurisdiction over highways and the poor law, and the Ramsdens had held the nomination rights to the parish church, St Peter's, since 1546; the vicar, in turn, had the right to appoint one of two churchwardens, whose duties had a significant secular dimension. I have found no evidence of the Ramsdens seeking direct influence in the affairs of the vestry.

At a higher level again, as major landowners the Ramsdens were of course well-connected in county society. Their acquisition of Byram around 1632 was partly prompted by its proximity and ready access to York, and from the eighteenth century successive links by marriage to the Earls Fitzwilliam, often Lords Lieutenant of the West Riding, would have afforded opportunities to influence the appointment of magistrates to the county bench and thus to the Huddersfield petty sessions. There is certainly evidence of such influence being exercised by the fifth baronet later in the nineteenth century,[15] and the opportunity would have been available long before that. The magistrates had the oversight of all local matters, including appointments by the vestry of highways and poor law officials, and would have been an obvious focus for the exercise of influence.

THE ESTATE AND ECONOMIC DEVELOPMENT

With these territorial and institutional powers at their disposal, what part did the estate take in this period in the development of the town's economic infrastructure and social facilities? For a century after they had acquired the market rights, the answer is only a very small part.

Two exceptions should be mentioned. In 1681 land was given for a grammar school at Seed Hill (near Shore Head), which had 20 pupils in 1743, although by 1819 it had been 'allowed to deteriorate into an elementary school of the

National [i.e. Anglican] type'.[16] In 1743 a waterworks was established: water was extracted from the river at Engine Bridge and pumped to a small reservoir at the top of the town, whence it was made available to the town through wooden pipes. The water was of course unfiltered – though the river was no doubt much cleaner than it would be a century later – and the pipes such that on one occasion they were reportedly blocked by a large trout.[17]

The turn towards economic development came in the early 1760s, late in the life of Sir John Ramsden (1698-1769), third baronet. He it was who decided to build the Cloth Hall, a principal feature of the town from its opening in 1766, through enlargements in 1780 and 1864, to its demolition in 1930. It provided a covered market for cloth in place of open stalls in and around the Market Place and parish churchyard. Its economic significance has been summarised thus:

> The Cloth Hall made Huddersfield a mart where business was done not only in wool and cloth, but in all that related to them; and it was done at inns, or up inn-yards, at street corners and in warehouses, as well as at the Cloth Hall. Nor is that all. A market town develops the mercantile side in place of the manufacturing, and it becomes a centre for allied and subsidiary trades. So banks and warehouses clustered around the Cloth Hall … all the many dressing shops and dyehouses were concentrated in the town, and it was the headquarters of the packers and the carriers, by waggon or canal, as well.[18]

When the Cloth Hall opened there was no canal, and carriage was perforce by waggon. During his last decade, Sir John supported the fast-developing network of turnpike roads. In 1759 he invested £300 in the Wakefield to Austerlands (near Oldham) turnpike; in 1765 he became a trustee of the Birstall to Huddersfield trust (towards Leeds); and in 1768 of the Huddersfield to Woodhead turnpike (towards Sheffield). 'Five turnpike roads converged in Huddersfield within the decade after 1759 suggesting that in the West Riding cloth producing region it had entered the same "league" as Halifax, Wakefield and Bradford'.[19]

During that decade, too, in 1766 the first survey was undertaken for Sir John Ramsden's Canal, and this vital link to the Aire & Calder Navigation, and thence to the North Sea, was constructed between 1774 and 1780. After the initial survey, work was not taken forward before Sir John's death in 1769, when the fourth baronet was only 13 years old. Until 1776, however, estate management was under the management of his 'conscientious' uncle and trustee, Thomas Ramsden[20], who resurveyed the line in 1773 and obtained the necessary legislation in 1774. Land acquisition and construction cost some £11,500. As Dennis Whomsley commented, citing contemporary sources,

17. Cloth Hall, erected 1766 and enlarged in 1780 and 1864.
Kirklees Image Archive

this was a remarkably small price to pay for putting the town on a main water highway to Hull 'and all its associated rivers and canals', and being 'the principal means of raising … Huddersfield to be one of the principal marts for woollen goods in the West Riding'.[21]

It was also a revenue-earning venture for the estate, which erected canal warehouses and stood to gain from the tolls paid by carriers. These were limited by the Act to a 6 per cent return on the capital laid out, and the turnpikes to less but, as Whomsley emphasised, if 'the new means of transport in themselves were not so valuable as capital investments, yet they vastly increased the value of the estate.'[22] The estate always did best when it recognised local developmental needs and its own interests were aligned, not in tension.

The fourth baronet came of age in 1776. Surveys of the town and wider estate were made in 1778 and 1780 by William Whitelock, a Ramsden tenant who was soon to be appointed a Huddersfield enclosure commissioner. As noted above, the 1789 enclosure award allocated nearly 90 percent of the newly enclosed land to the estate. It also provided 50 new roads, five quarries for their repair and five public wells. Whomsley suggests that these events should all be seen as 'part of the planned development of the estate to take the fullest advantage of the building of the canal … The plan probably originated with

18. Sir John Ramsden, 4th Bt (1755–1839).
Muncaster Castle

the third baronet, it almost certainly was executed by his experienced brother Thomas'.[23] If he is right – documentary evidence is lacking – then this should be judged a significant contribution by the estate to the public realm.

The 1789 Act's new roads were on open land, but the development of the first town centre grid was soon to follow. This comprised New St, Cloth Hall St and King St, all apparently laid out between about 1797 and 1807.[24] As well as town houses, the development included the Brick Buildings on New St, with accommodation above shops, and the expansion and relocation of a butchers' shambles and slaughterhouse, first established by the estate around

19. Market Place, looking towards Kirkgate/Westgate, with the old George Inn (centre).
Kirklees Image Archive

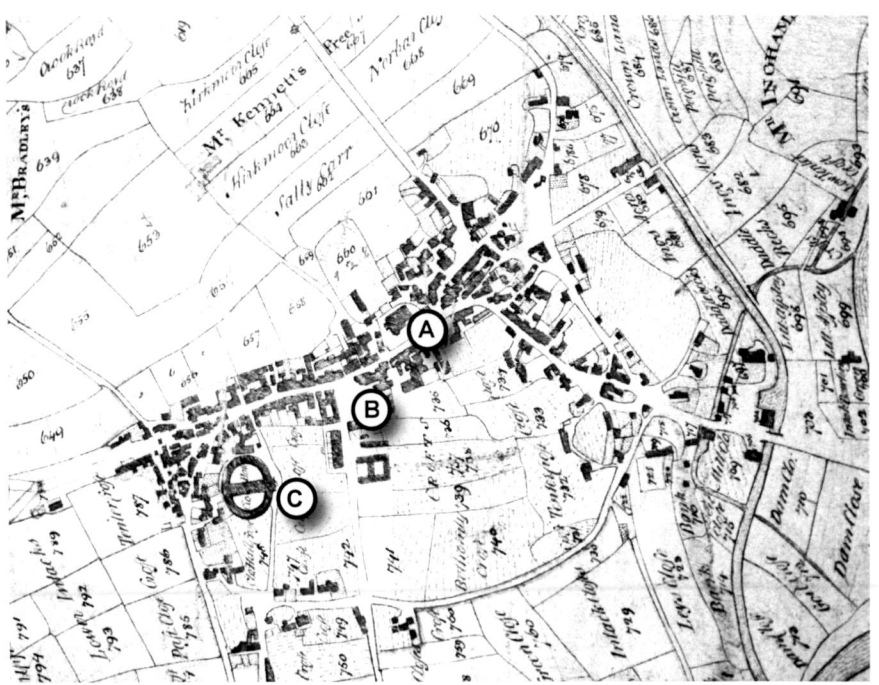

20. Ramsden estate map (1778) – town centre street map of Georgian Huddersfield.

At this time Huddersfield was virtually a one-street town extending along the line of the modern Westgate and Kirkgate. The Parish Church (A) and the Market Place (B) are central and the new Cloth Hall (C) prominent to the left.

West Yorkshire Archive Service, Kirklees

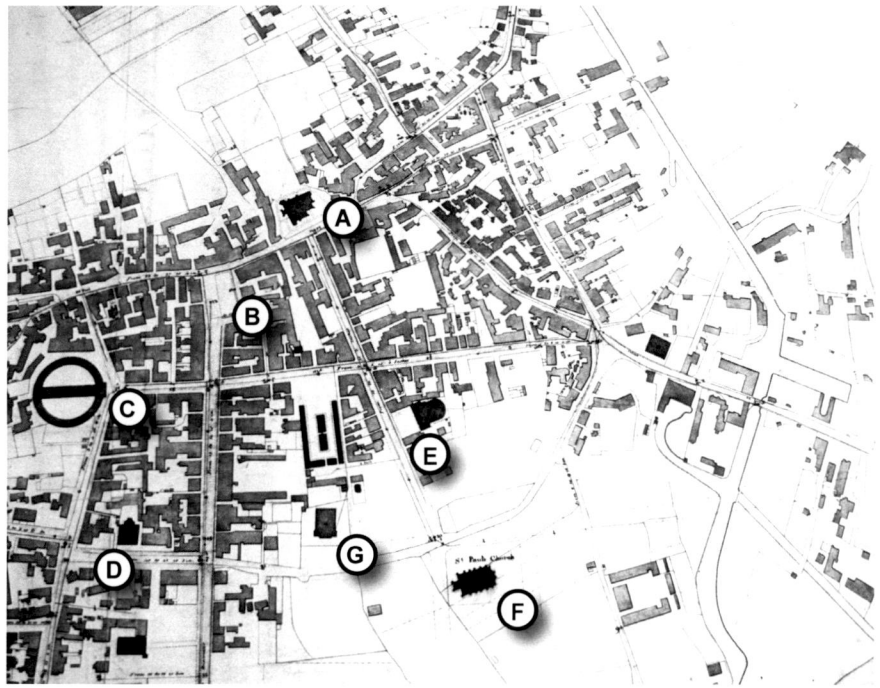

21. Thomas Dinsley map (1828) for the Waterworks Commissioners, showing the later-Georgian street pattern.

The town has now extended to the south of the original development, past the Cloth Hall (C), along Market Street to beyond High Street with its Methodist New Connexion chapel (1815) (D); from the Market Place (B) along New Street, past the Brick Buildings on the west side to beyond King Street; and from the Parish Church (A) along Cross Church Street to Queen Street, with its Wesleyan chapel (1819) (E) and thence to the isolated St Paul's church (1829) (F). Skirting the southern part of the map, Ramsden Street, with its Congregational chapel (1824) (G) is scarcely developed. The building to the north of the chapel was the Shambles.

West Yorkshire Archive Service, Kirklees

1770 south of the Market Place. With an additional axis along Queen St/ Cross Church St, this first grid would continue to develop on Ramsden-leased plots until about 1825, forming a Georgian townscape which partly survives today.[25]

In summary, little was to happen for 80 years after the grant of market rights, but the half-century from 1765 was characterised by a vigorous approach to the development of economic infrastructure and the creation of a small Georgian town centre. This was achieved on the basis of a relatively stable stock of land, and without any formal involvement in town governance beyond the traditional rights of the lord of the manor.

Early 19th century passivity

The next period, from the 1810s until the mid-1840s, was to be quite different, with the estate taking a much more passive approach, to the point of neglect, while urban conditions moved towards crisis point. This was down to the personalities and capabilities of the lord of the manor and his agents. The fourth baronet had deferred to his uncle Thomas's leadership of estate affairs even after coming of age in 1776.[26] Although lord of the manor for over 60 of his adult years until his death in 1839, Sir John visited the town only once, in 1822. This neglect need not have been decisive had he been well-served by his agents after Thomas's death in 1791. To begin with he relied on his father's steward, John Crowder, who had worked closely with Thomas Ramsden,[27] but Crowder died in 1816 and was replaced by John Bower, and this was perhaps the real turning point.

Based at Smeathalls, close to Byram, Bower was not a full-time Ramsden employee but undertook other surveying work, for example as an enclosure commissioner.[28] He was the Huddersfield agent until his death in 1844, five years after Sir John's, but notoriously only visited the town twice a year to collect the rents, and took a *laissez-faire* attitude to what was built on the estate's lands. While the township population grew by over 80 percent between 1801 and 1821, from 7,268 to 13,284, and by a further 89 percent to 25,068 by 1841, the estate's 'entrepreneurial activity during the period of Huddersfield's most rapid growth was limited solely to the provision of wide main streets'.[29] These therefore came to be surrounded by warrens of insanitary and overcrowded premises, largely held on ill-defined 'tenancies at will'.[30] In the year Bower died, the resulting conditions were famously described thus by the Chartist activist and journalist, Joshua Hobson:

> ... there are whole streets in the town, and many courts and alleys, which are neither flagged, paved, sewered nor drained; where garbage and filth of every description are let on the surface to ferment and rot; where pools of stagnant water are almost constant; where the dwellings adjoining are thus necessarily caused to be of an inferior and even filthy description; where disease is engendered, and the health of the whole Town endangered.[31]

This contrasts with Friedrich Engels' superficial observation of the main streets in 1845 [see p. 55].

INNOVATIONS IN GOVERNANCE[32]

There had nonetheless been a modest institutional response to the deteriorating urban conditions. To the traditional institutions were added, in 1820, the Commissioners of Lighting, Watching & Cleansing (CLWC). Established by Act of Parliament, their eponymous responsibilities ran only 1200 yards from the market cross, within the township of Huddersfield – which radius included portions of Fartown and Marsh hamlets as well as Huddersfield itself. For this small tract, the Act named 59 Commissioners to act, including Sir John Ramsden, his four sons and John Bower. Vacancies were to be filled by co-option, subject to Sir John's approval. Presumably he therefore had the right of veto over the initial appointments too, so the CLWC could have been shaped as an instrument of Ramsden control over urban management. In practice this opportunity was not taken. No Ramsden, nor Bower, ever attended a CLWC meeting. Two other men sometimes described as Ramsden agents, Bradley Clay (a canal agent) and James Booth, *were* active early Commissioners, and Sir John took their advice in filling vacancies in 1823 (which happened only twice in 28 years), but there is no evidence in the minutes of any active relationship between the CLWC and the estate.[33] Moreover, the court leet continued to operate in parallel, notably in January 1832 when, at the height of the first cholera epidemic, 22 cases of sanitary infractions were prosecuted.[34]

In 1827 the Huddersfield Waterworks Commissioners (HWC) were established, with a constitution closely modelled on the CLWC although this time with 120 Commissioners, including five Ramsdens and up to four of their local and canal agents. Its genesis is considered further below.

These bodies existed on Ramsden sufferance. From the late 1820s, however, Huddersfield began to regain the reputation for radical politics which it had earned at the time of the Luddite uprising and its after-shocks in the 1810s. It eschewed the opportunity to establish an oligarchical select vestry under the 1819 Sturges Bourne legislation, resolving to retain an open vestry through which the views the town could be expressed. Those views would soon embrace the campaigns for the limitation of factory hours, for a wider male suffrage and against the New Poor Law.[35] By the mid-1830s a vigorous popular politics had developed in the vestry, which took the opportunity of the 1835 Highways Act to establish an elected Board of Highway Surveyors, soon to be a thorn in the side of the increasingly ineffective CLWC.

It was in this context that Huddersfield gained parliamentary representation for the first time in 1832. A petition for a two-member constituency, based on the parish rather than the township and therefore diluting Ramsden influence, was resisted by the family, with the eldest son, J. C. Ramsden, then MP for Malton (a Fitzwilliam-controlled seat), declining to present it to Parliament. In return the town resisted his declared intention to stand as Whig candidate, greeting him with a stormy reception, and he withdrew in favour of a local man Lewis Fenton, who defeated the Radical Joseph Wood by 263 to 152 in a riotous first election.[36] This was despite Ramsden's quite 'advanced' Whig views: he had supported Parliamentary reform and resigned as a deputy lieutenant in 1819 in protest when Earl Fitzwilliam was dismissed from the lieutenancy for supporting an inquiry into the Peterloo massacre. On the other hand, he was for free trade and against the ten hours campaign, setting him against Huddersfield's radicals.[37]

These events illuminate the limits of Ramsden influence. As mentioned earlier, Hemingway's close local study of parliamentary politics led her to challenge Cannadine's judgement that Huddersfield was a 'nomination borough', and the spurning of Ramsden's candidacy bears this out. A similar point applies to local government. Katrina Navickas has argued that 'In many of the towns and villages in Lancashire and the West Riding that were dominated by one or two master manufacturers or major landowners, such as Halifax and Huddersfield, it was much harder for oppositional groups to gain a foothold in local government.'[38] In fact Radicals and Liberals in Huddersfield made good use of the machinery of the vestry to challenge the CLWC on sanitary issues and on the control of policing.[39]

LAND OWNERSHIP IN STASIS

If the estate was failing to manage the land it held, neither was there any drive to expand its holdings. Although Sir John left behind the youthful indiscretions alluded to by Whomsley, he preferred to invest in major enhancements of the house and park at Byram rather than in income-earning assets elsewhere. As noted above, the estate took little or no advantage of the release of several freehold estates in the town around 1820. By 1844, the Huddersfield estate amounted to 1,213 acres, or 30.7 percent of the township by area.[40]

When Sir John Ramsden died in 1839, his eldest son having pre-deceased him, the estate passed to the trustees of his grandson, the fifth baronet, John William Ramsden, who was then only seven years old. The deceased's will put substantial obstacles in the way of the development of the estate. Most of it was to be held in trust for his heirs, rather than being freely disposable to meet changing needs for land. This was not unusual in itself: as has been said, 'In the early nineteenth century the English land system was oriented towards the preservation of dynasties and dynastic dependents, not towards the efficient exploitation of the land';[41] still less of course towards public benefit. The fourth baronet's will further provided, however, that expenditure was to be limited to accumulated surplus income and that proceeds of any land sales had to be reinvested in land, and restricted the terms of lease which the estate could offer.[42] Distinctions between the 'settled' and 'devised' estates added further complexity.[43] As we shall see, these inflexibilities would take some unravelling.

THE DEVELOPMENT OF PUBLIC FACILITIES

Nonetheless this period, and particularly the decade or so from 1827, did see a significant extension of the town's urban facilities. The new waterworks of 1828 was quickly followed by the Infirmary, which opened in 1831 and, in 1837-8, by the Guild Hall and Philosophical Hall. The former became home to the county magistrates, the latter included a news room and lending library, and both offered large halls for public meetings and other events. These were among the buildings which led Engels to salute Huddersfield as 'the handsomest by far' of the Pennine factory towns.[44] Together with the town and county police stations and lockups, and later county court building, they formed a rudimentary civic quarter around Ramsden St.[45] But these were all independent initiatives: the estate was not involved. Moreover, it sometimes actively resisted initiatives from other actors. Two examples concern water supplies in the 1820s and railway proposals in the 1840s.

The pumped water supply from the river had become wholly inadequate to the town's needs. In 1826, 74 inhabitants petitioned Sir John 'that an abundant and never failing supply of pure water might be obtained and conveyed to the town at a moderate expense'. They proposed to activate a scheme, drawn up as long ago as 1819, to capture spring water from Longwood, to raise the necessary capital and to manage it as a not-for-profit utility.[46] The result was the Waterworks Act of 1827 and creation of the first Longwood Reservoir, with water piped to a service tank at Spring St close to that of the previous scheme (and fronted by the 'handsome' Waterworks Office, which survives today). The estate acceded to the plan, but only after insisting that the HWC should buy the old waterworks and make an annual payment of £100 for access to the streets to lay mains. Thirty years later, Ramsden rejected a strong request to waive this payment, which continued until 1868.[47]

The second example was the estate's attitude to the railway.[48] As industrialisation gathered pace, the Lancashire & Yorkshire Railway had opened its Calder Valley line in 1838, linking Manchester and Leeds but bypassing Huddersfield. In 1843 the company proposed a branch from Cooper Bridge, terminating at Aspley. This was opposed from two angles. Bower advised the Ramsden trustees to resist the branch as a threat to their canal revenues, and the trustees concurred in January 1844. By this time the limitation to a 6 per cent return on investment was neglected and the estate's exploitation of its monopoly of eastward transport had become a bone of contention, the celebrated factory hours and Poor Law campaigner, Richard Oastler, taking up the issue in 1834.[49] Moreover, strong voices in the town were insulted that Huddersfield should be placed on a railway cul-de-sac. A petition was raised against the L & Y proposal and a public meeting convened, from which estate steward, J. C. Fenton, reported on 23 February that:

> the Huddersfield people are determined that they will have a railway … great numbers … signed the petition with the intention of throwing out the obnoxious branch but in the expectation that an advantageous railway communication be brought forward without delay.[50]

As the next section sets out, the railway issue would soon precipitate a major turning point in the estate's management, which returned to its earlier developmental activism. Its initial resistance to the coming of the railway, however, typified its position in the last decades of Sir John's and John Bower's lives. Land ownership had remained broadly stable. The estate had abdicated from development, made little use of institutions of governance potentially under its control, and had made no contribution – or even a negative contribution – to the fast-developing public realm beyond the layout and naming of streets.

A decade of activism, 1844-55

All this was to change in 1844, a major turning point for the estate and the town. With hindsight the moment seems strangely delayed. The trustees, who took office in 1839, led by Earl Fitzwilliam with J. C. Ramsden's widow, Isabella, the other leading figure, would transform the estate's policies.[51] For another five years, however, until his death in 1844, Bower's advice seems to have held sway. Then came abrupt change with the trustees' appointment of George Loch as their principal agent, and his appointment of Alexander Hathorn as full-time Huddersfield agent.

Loch's father, James, was a celebrated estate manager employed by several leading landowners; indeed his name 'seems to have been a kind of household word in the highest circles of aristocracy'.[52] His positions included superintendent of the Bridgewater estate in the north-west, where his son George served as his deputy and Hathorn was also employed. In turning to Loch, therefore, the trustees were bringing in a manager of high pedigree.

George Loch spent the last week of May 1844 in Huddersfield, tramping the town, meeting key informants and recording what he found in a notebook.[53] He had been asked to examine canal and railway matters and tenure arrangements. He found strong support for direct railways, both East-West and South via Sheffield to London. Leading business figures told him that the estate's canal-based opposition to the through railway had been a mistake, and that development was being held back by the lack of proper leaseholds. Visiting Bower's putative successor, the canal agent William Alderson, he found that his office 'smelt overpoweringly of snuff and spirits', and that the accounting system was 'very rude and imperfect'. Bower's visits to the town, he was told, had amounted to no more than two to three weeks each year. Within a week of the visit, Loch's conclusions and recommendations were encapsulated in a 21-page report to the trustees; they amounted to a complete reversal of three decades of neglect of the town's potential.[54]

As noted earlier, Whomsley suggested that Thomas Ramsden had pursued an integrated development strategy in the 1780s. Whether nor not that was the case, it is clear that Loch guided the trustees to such a strategy in the 1840s. Its components were tightly inter-connected across the three dimensions of ownership, governance and development.

ECONOMIC DEVELOPMENT AND LAND OWNERSHIP

The starting point was the reversal of policy on the railway. The estate abandoned its defence of canal revenues and any idea of a low-level branch line to Aspley. Instead it released land to make possible the high-level route – essential to through traffic – and the station on its present site, and sold the Ramsden Canal to the railway company, which had already bought the Narrow Canal. Trains first ran to Leeds in 1848, Manchester in 1849 and Sheffield in 1850 when the Palladian station building – a 'stately home with trains in' by noted York architect J. P. Pritchett – was completed.[55] As well as energising economic development through much enhanced connectivity, these transactions brought £87,000 into the estate's coffers and provided new urban and financial opportunities.

In planning terms, the station provided a magnet for the extension of the town northwards from the historic axis of Westgate/Kirkgate. Over the next 30 years, on this formerly open land a new street grid was laid out. The 'Victorian new town', to the north of the Georgian grid, was a bold town planning scheme. To create an approach from the Market Place to the station, the George Inn was demolished to make way for John William Street. Today this leads into St George's Square, in front of the station, and is flanked by the replacement George Hotel which the trustees commissioned from William Wallen, and handsome warehouses erected under the guidance of their consulting architect, Sir William Tite who designed one of them, Tite's Buildings, directly for the estate. The Square did not feature in the estate's initial plans, which centred on 'the erection of new buildings such as woollen warehouses, shops and banking houses etc. etc. … situated in front of the railway station'.[56] But it was strongly advocated by the newly-established Improvement Commissioners [see p. 58], and especially by Joshua Hobson, by now their clerk. With Hathorn's eventual support, they were able to win over Loch and the trustees, and the result was one of the finest public spaces in the north of England.[57]

Financially, the proceeds of the railway sales also enabled the estate to embark on a programme of land acquisition which was to continue for the next 40 years. Within the first decade, acquisitions included several of the estates close to the town centre but not in Ramsden ownership – 40 acres at Bay Hall, beyond the station, in 1844/5; two portions of the former Bradley holdings at nearby Newhouse in 1845 and 1848; and 80 acres at Greenhead/Gledholt, again in 1848.[58]

But there was no point in acquiring new freeholds unless they could be profitably leased, and to do so it was necessary to remove some of the legal impediments arising from old Sir John's will. The 1844 Ramsden Estate Act allowed the estate to renew leases which had lapsed with his death; to create new leases of up to 60 years; and to allot lands on the devised estates for streets and other public purposes.[59] Armed with these new powers (further extended by a second Act in 1848), the estate was able to respond to a vigorous demand for development land. Even before the 'new town' was approved by the trustees in 1849, another warehouse quarter was being laid out from 1846 around the Cloth Hall (the streets all bearing trustees' names – Dundas, Fox and Serjeantson).[60] By 1849, in a review of progress, Loch was able to report to Mrs Ramsden that the town was prospering and much building was going forward.[61] Perhaps responding to Hobson's 1844 report, moreover, the estate was exercising a good deal of control over the *quality* of development. As Springett explains, after Loch's arrival 'New back-to-back houses and cellar dwellings were forbidden, building lines enforced, and materials and building standards rigorously supervised.'[62]

A NEW GOVERNANCE SETTLEMENT

By then, too, there had been a new institutional settlement. By the 1840s the established bodies were struggling, with endemic conflict between the CLWC and vestry, neither of which had the powers or personnel to address burgeoning urban problems. In neighbouring towns, the solution adopted in the late 1840s was to incorporate a municipal borough under the 1835 Municipal Corporations Act. In Huddersfield, after a petition for incorporation had failed in 1842, this seems not to have received serious consideration again for 15 years. Instead the Huddersfield Improvement Commissioners (HIC) were established, replacing both the CLWC and the vestry's Board of Surveyors, and acted as a quasi-municipal authority for the next 20 years. The HIC was brought into being by an apparently unlikely alliance of vestry activists, notably Hobson who became the HIC clerk of

22. Railway Station (1846–51) by J. P. Pritchett, with the statue of Sir Robert Peel in the foreground (erected after 1873, removed 1949).
Kirklees Image Archive

23. George Hotel (1848–1851), by William Wallen. The top floor, above the parapet, is a later addition.
Kirklees Image Archive

works; the local magistrates and other 'principal inhabitants'; and Loch and Hathorn, supported by the trustees.[63]

Loch may well have taken a broad view of the mid-century needs of the town and the inadequacy of the earlier bodies. However, the estate also had a more specific interest in supporting the HIC settlement. Another term of Sir John's will had been the provision of £20,000 to be spent on 'improvements' to the estate, and a further £25,000 was now allowed under the 1848 Ramsden Estate Act. But the intention of these arrangements was disputed and would remain a bone of contention for decades ahead, both within the estate and with the town. As Loch pointed out in his 1849 progress report, this had stood in the way of the continued creation of new streets with paving and drainage. However, this 'great difficulty that has always opposed itself to the Improvement of the Town of Huddersfield by the Trustees has now been removed by the establishment of the Board of Improvement Commissioners': the HIC were empowered to lay out the capital and recover charges from holders of street frontage premises, including the estate and its tenants. [64]

The HIC's urban development role was strictly limited, however. It had no building control powers, leaving this to the estate, but did play a significant part in street works: by 1868 it would boast almost 10 miles of paved streets and eight and a half miles of main sewerage.[65] But the exercise of these powers brought recurrent tension between the HIC and the estate throughout the 1850s over their respective responsibilities for the fabric of new streets.[66]

The HIC was, in fact, a historic compromise between local democracy and the Ramsden interest. The democratic element was limited: of the 21 Commissioners, 18 were elected by ratepayers, but on a property-weighted franchise, while three were to be appointed by the lord of the manor. Although increasingly anachronistic, the CLWC's 1200-yard radius and confinement to the north bank of the river were retained, and while the Act allowed future extension, this was subject to the lord of the manor's agreement and was never pursued.

Unlike nominations to the CLWC, the estate took its three appointments seriously, at least in the earlier years. Over the body's 20-year term, 10 men served as Ramsden-appointed Commissioners. Loch took a seat himself for the first two years; of the remaining nine appointees, four were wool merchants, while only one (serving for two years) was a significant manufacturer. This indicates that the town's power brokers in this period were more often commercial than industrial.[67] Notable among them were Joseph Brook (1787-1858), an architect of the 1848 Act who chaired the HIC from 1849-54, and his son-in-law Jeremiah Riley (1801-65).[68] However, 1859/60 was the last year that three Ramsden appointees were in place, and for the HIC's last six years,

1862-8, only the solicitor T. H. Battye, remained in post; his appointment in 1861 had followed considerable difficulty in finding anyone willing to serve.[69]

The Ramsden appointees were by no means mandated delegates. Riley, for example, reassured townsmen assembled at a New Year municipal dinner that:

> On one or two occasions he had been told he had lost caste by resigning his position as a Town's Commissioner and accepting the nomination of the Ramsden Trustees. He wished to say that before he did this he wrote to know, if he accepted their nomination, whether they expected him to act with perfect impartiality and independence, and he had an immediate answer from Mr Loch stating that they would not offer it to any gentleman under any other condition than that he should be perfectly free.[70]

Conversely, Loch had declined to attend the same event in 1850 after receiving Hathorn's advice:

> … as Sir John Ramsden's coming of age draws on quickly, I think it is desirable on many accounts to cultivate a friendly feeling with the people, but not in such manner as to compromise or affect in any way the perfect freedom and independence of the Trustees.[71]

The dinner itself, drawing together the various institutions, was first held in 1849. It signalled the emergence in 1848 of the kind of self-confident middle-class politics identified elsewhere in the 1820s and 1830s.[72] This had been slow to develop in Huddersfield, compared for example with Halifax, where the Piece Hall and Calder & Hebble Navigation had been established collectively by the town's 'influential inhabitants' in the late 18th century, not 'gifted' by the manor.[73] But the railway campaign and creation of the HIC had now brought a stronger bourgeois civic politics to Huddersfield, albeit in a form which still bore the Ramsden stamp.

NEW CIVIC FACILITIES

Two substantial public realm initiatives flowed from the new nexus of an engaged estate and elective middle-class politics – one abortive, one successful.

The failed initiative at this stage was the construction of a town hall. A ratepayers' meeting back in 1843 had called for suitable rooms to be provided to accommodate meetings 'for every department of the Town's business' and to house all its civic documents.[74] This was revived by the HIC, whose proposals for St George's Square in 1850 included a town hall site east of John William St. This was supported by the *Huddersfield Chronicle,* which continued to press for its inclusion in the improved Ramsden plans.[75] Accommodation was proposed for the courts, HIC, HWC, Board of Guardians and overseers of the poor, all scattered around the town in varied premises, almost none of them purpose-built.[76]

At this point Hathorn and Loch became interested, recognising that it would be in the estate's interest to have a prestigious building with reliable tenants on a vacant site opposite their new George Hotel.[77] The fifth baronet was nearing the age of majority and the trustees and agents were increasingly seeking his views. On this issue as on many others throughout his 60-year 'reign' as lord of the manor, he expressed an ambivalence – or attempt to have things both ways. As reported by Loch, Ramsden 'expressed a perfect willingness to go into it' and indeed wished 'quietly and as a matter of course to take the entire lead, so far as the design and arrangements of the building are concerned'; Hathorn was to inquire what was needed, but be 'very careful not to say anything that will commit Sir John to any pecuniary contribution'.[78] Working with Hobson – with whom he had a fractious but pragmatic working relationship, mirroring that of the estate and HIC – Hathorn moved quickly to collate the various bodies' requirements, now including the Post Office, and his own suggestion for public halls and a dining room with a tunnel to the George! The consultation was complete, and the results with Loch, by early December.[79]

At which point the project stalled: all went quiet until August 1853 when the idea was revived by the newly-established Chamber of Commerce and a joint Chamber/HIC committee was set up. They re-engaged with Hathorn; he approached Thomas Nelson, the London solicitor who had just replaced Loch as chief agent, and a very cool response was received.[80] Faced with seeming lack of interest from the estate, the joint committee nonetheless commissioned a 'suggestive design' from Charles Pritchett, son of the architect of the station. This can hardly have improved relations, as the Ramsden family had fallen out with Pritchett senior.[81] The proposal became embroiled in local discussion about whether the '£20,000 improvement fund' could be deployed in its support, and faded away.[82] Sir William Tite produced a further proposal in 1856, presumably commissioned by the estate, for the Northumberland St site eventually occupied in 1914 by the Post Office, but that too went nowhere[83] – though it was still in play 20 years later when the Town Hall debate resumed [see pp. 74-6].

The second public issue of this period, in contrast, was brought to a successful conclusion by 1855. This was the town's burial crisis. By the early 1840s the parish church graveyard was shockingly full, with the sexton warning that he faced 'the utmost difficulty' in digging new graves without mutilating the bodies already there (said to be up to 19 deep). The vicar, the Revd Josiah Bateman, approached the estate, which owned the ground and appointed the vicars, for assistance – but apparently received no response from Bower.[84] Five years went by, with conditions deteriorating, while efforts to find a solution without Ramsden support made no progress, largely because of tensions between Anglicans and Nonconformists. In January 1847 Bateman tried again and Loch responded immediately. Although he found it 'a matter of wonder and regret that sectarian jealousies and differences should have so long thrown impediments in the way of remedies that have been proposed … [T]he horrors of the Church Yard however are so dreadful that I do think the Trustees would do well to entertain the request now made of them'.[85]

Initially a site at Hillhouse was proposed, linked to the trustees' endowment of St John's Church on the newly acquired Bay Hall estate.[86] This fell through for several reasons, but the vicar took the initiative again in 1849, by which time the HIC was in business. Under Joseph Brook's leadership they vigorously took up the cause of a public burial ground, managed by the HIC and providing for all denominations. Brook and Loch had cordial working relations – they had been allied in achieving the 1848 Act and the railway settlement – and the eventual site at Edgerton was soon identified. But negotiations did not run smoothly, and it was not until 15 September 1852 that Loch handed over the site to Brook; the party then repaired to the George to celebrate Sir John William Ramsden's coming of age. It would be another three years before the cemetery opened on 8 October 1855.

The protracted negotiations of 1849-52 revolved around two issues which went to the heart of the relationship between estate and town in the middle decades of the 19th century, setting a pattern which recurs on other occasions. Whenever the town authorities wished to develop a public facility on Ramsden land, the price of the land and the credit for the initiative came into focus.

Regarding price, the estate usually argued that, as its lands were held in trust for future generations, it was obliged to seek market value for any disposals. This constrained it to operate as a profit-maximising economic agent within the land market. This was often in tension, however, with the sense of 'noblesse oblige' which went with being lord of the manor, and the desire for goodwill from the town. The fourth baronet and John Bower had neglected both aspects, and Loch's approach was strongly commercial: his 'primary concern was always with the improvement of the estate rather than the welfare of the people of the estate … he had no sympathy with the traditional image of the landowner who accepted responsibility for the well-being of his people'.[87] But this was balanced by Earl Fitzwilliam and Isabella Ramsden, who were very conscious of the traditional responsibilities of the landed aristocracy and gentry towards what J. W. Ramsden would often refer to as 'my tenantry'. Once he was in sole charge, this underlying tension ran through Ramsden's own motivation and found expression in his characteristic ambivalence.[88]

In the case of the cemetery, Brook believed he had been offered the land at a nominal price, which Loch denied. When the latter appeared to reconsider the offer of the Edgerton site, Brook suspected this was because the estate had received a higher valuation for residential use – it would certainly have been a good site for villas, for which there was rapidly growing demand.[89] He also played on the estate's divided motives, writing to Loch that 'in the most respectful manner to you and the Trustees [whose nominee he was, of course] I cannot refrain from saying, that considering the immense stake the Trustees have in the town, it is incumbent upon them not to be only passive consenters, but to take an active and leading position'.[90] After considering several 'less eligible' sites, the estate eventually acquiesced in the HIC's strong preference for Edgerton. The land was initially valued at £6,000, but after HIC resistance fresh valuations were undertaken; a figure of £3,554 was agreed; and half of this was then returned as a donation, a model to be followed again in later years.[91] Along the way, estate steward J. C. Fenton, in a different tone from Loch, had given the young Sir John William Ramsden some sound advice on how to handle the town: he should support the proposal 'simply because the Huddersfield people wish for it, for in these cases it is always desirable to gratify them, unless there is (which there is not in this case) some very strong reason against complying with their wishes.'[92]

The decade from 1844 had been very different from the previous 30 years. Land ownership had substantially increased. The estate had contributed, through speculative building and the release of its land, to major developments in public infrastructure, notably the railway, the new town and the cemetery – though much was still lacking. A historic compromise with other forces in the town had resulted in a more effective agency of local government, able to take forward the paving and draining of streets with new vigour, though there was tension as well as co-operation between the estate and the HIC, on which the town hall project foundered.

Seeking a new balance, 1852-67

Sir John William Ramsden's majority in 1852, and Loch's departure in 1853, marked a new turning point. Ramsden was now in charge, but of course utterly inexperienced compared with the retiring trustees, while Thomas Nelson, a lawyer through and through, was no George Loch. The next 15 years are harder to characterise than the previous 10.

Looking first at land ownership, if anything the pace of expansion slackened compared with the previous period, although there were significant acquisitions of the Clough House estate in 1858, Springwood in 1861 [see p. 66] and parts of the Firth estate in 1864 – though still not that 'one house' in the Beast Market. Instead, more attention was devoted to attempts to reform the estate's antiquated tenure arrangements. Even after the Ramsden Estate Acts of 1844 and 1848, it could only grant 60-year leases or tenancies at will, while neighbouring landlords such as the Lockwood proprietors and Thornhills were offering 999-year leases for both residential and commercial development. A further Act in 1859 allowed 99-year leases and also converted tenancies at will to these – a proposal at the heart of the 'tenant right' dispute.[93] Finally the 1867 Ramsden Estate Act permitted 999-year leases, long after their use had become widespread on other urban estates.

These issues of estate management seem to have engaged far more of Ramsden's attention than the development of the town's public facilities. Nor, after the departure in 1854 of Brook from the chair and Hobson from the clerkship of the HIC, was there as much drive for development from that quarter, with the HIC focussing on its day-to-day sanitary and policing responsibilities. But two public realm issues during these years deserve attention – markets and public parks.

The upheavals of the 1840s had left untouched the estate's monopoly of the town's market rights, which embraced the Cloth Hall, the Beast Market and the general retail market in and around the Market Place. Some thought had been given to the creation of a new open market at Fleece Croft, below the parish church; Mrs Ramsden had proposed a covered market for women's domestic produce; and the George Hotel architect, William Wallen, had developed new plans for the Market Place itself; but none of these had come to fruition.[94] Conflict arose in 1852 between the HIC and the estate over whether the latter had the right to collect tolls from stalls placed in public (HIC-maintained) streets. The problem was aggravated by the 'variable and increasing demands for tolls' from the estate's current toll-farmer, James Whitley; by confusion about the rights of the various parties; and by threats of litigation from both sides.[95] As Edward Law explained:

> Whilst the dispute arose from the annual May fair, popular feeling imposed the same objections to the actual Market Place, and whilst the Ramsdens had undoubted rights to market tolls, there were various matters which clouded the issue… The Ramsden estate managers appear to have taken an early decision to extricate themselves from the whole matter as diplomatically as possible.[96]

Their suggested solution, to lease the market rights to the HIC, was eventually achieved in 1864. There was, meanwhile, no further development of the town's market facilities by either party.

The growing town also lacked a public park. Instead Edgerton Cemetery became a place of recreation: the large numbers walking its carefully laid out paths on Sundays in particular necessitated the appointment of keepers to ensure that order and decorum were maintained.[97] However, it emerged in August 1858 that the 32-acre Springwood estate was about to come to market.[98] Adjoining Greenhead, this was a surviving independent freehold close to the town centre, and its potential for residential development was immediately appreciated by Hathorn. But the *Chronicle,* now under Hobson's editorship, was quick to argue that:

> A most favourable opportunity is now presented to secure for the use of the inhabitants of this district a place of public recreation immediately contiguous to the town, in a most delightful situation, and of easy access from every part ... an estate about 30 acres in extent, well fringed with wood, commanding a most extensive and magnificent hill-and-dale prospect, in itself most admirably adapted for the formation of walks abounding with the picturesque, and having on it a good mansion well adapted for a museum, for a public library, and for the accommodation of indoor parties.[99]

The suggestion was immediately taken up by the HIC and also by Nelson, who counselled Ramsden that:

> the opening of such a place for the recreation of the Public would be considered an important acquisition for the Inhabitants and I think that your shewing that you took an Interest in it and were prepared to promote it by a liberal contribution would have a beneficial effect upon the minds of many.[100]

Ramsden took the point and made an offer which drew on the cemetery model. The HIC would buy the whole estate at the offer price of £22,435; he would contribute £3,000 and solicit a further £2,000 from the vendor, Sir Edmund Lechmere; the remainder would be raised by public subscription, not through the rates (which of course fell largely on the Ramsdens and their tenants). These terms were rejected by the HIC on 5 January 1859 when Ramsden's approach was contrasted unfavourably with that of Halifax industrialist Sir Francis Crossley, who had *given* the land for the People's Park to the town in 1857.[101] The committee which considered the proposal had concluded that a public subscription appeal would fail 'especially under the unsatisfactory relations between Sir John William Ramsden and his tenants in the Huddersfield estate', no doubt a reference to the tenant right dispute, which was then at its height.[102]

Springwood was bought by the Ramsdens anyway, for £20,000, in November 1861. This meant that they now controlled a complete arc of largely undeveloped land from the railway at Springwood through Greenhead and New North Rd to their St John's Church at Bay Hall, Birkby, offering ample opportunity for residential development on the favoured north-western slopes of the town. In 1862–3 Ramsden and his agents sought to develop a master plan for the area, taking advice from London architect, William Habershon, and from the London builder (and Lord Mayor), William Cubitt.[103] Had these plans gone ahead they would have been a town planning achievement to rank alongside the Georgian grid and Victorian new town, albeit in a suburban mode. But they did not: still limited to 99-year leases, the estate could not compete with the development of nearby Edgerton as the premier suburb, using 999-year leases from other landlords, especially the Thornhill estate.

A final light is shed on this period by the extraordinary six-page letter from Ramsden to Nelson late in 1859, quoted in chapter 1.[104] The immediate cause was the decision that Ramsden himself, rather than Nelson, should preside at the forthcoming annual rent dinner for his tenants; but a much wider point was made which confirms the view of Ramsden's biographer that

> Jack was not an easy man to work with. Even with members of his team in whom he retained total confidence, he could rarely resist excessive micro-management, seeking to know, record and be involved in every detail of every decision taken.[105]

Reading between the lines, however, it seems unlikely that Nelson had his 'total confidence'; and the vastly experienced Hathorn was to leave in 1862.

In summary, this period was characterised by a slowed pace of land acquisition; limited contributions to the public realm; and a diminished interest in the HIC and town governance. Instead the lord of the manor and his agents turned their attention to the 'micro-management' of residential development, but only at the end of the period cleared away the last of the legal obstacles that stood in their way. The departure of experienced trustees and agents, and Ramsden's own personality and inexperience, played their part in shaping this less 'heroic' period.

1867-70: The world turned upside down?

So far we have examined three major developmental episodes – the 1760s/1770s, the turn of the 18th century, and the 1840s. The first two were entirely Ramsden-led, while the third resulted from a coalition of forces in which they were a leading player. The late 1860s saw a further shift in the balance, with the estate forced to respond to a major upheaval in governance initiated from the 'town'.

THE COMING OF THE CORPORATION

By 1867 there was a gathering consensus that the 1848 settlement was no longer fit for purpose. The town had spread far beyond the 1200-yard radius, but the 1848 Act's power of extension had never been pursued. Instead no fewer than eight local boards had been established in the surrounding hamlets and townships under the 1858 Public Health Act, while Fartown soldiered on with only vestry highway surveyors. The HIC launched a new drive for incorporation of the borough in May 1867 on a wider boundary than the township – and a Charter of Incorporation was gained in July 1868.[106]

The estate's position on incorporation was deeply ambivalent. When he saw the draft Charter in July 1867, Ramsden wrote that 'Now that so much progress has been made towards obtaining the Charter I will no longer delay the expression of my desire to associate myself with a movement affecting so materially the future of Huddersfield' (and indeed the motion for incorporation at the HIC AGM in May had been seconded by T. H. Battye, the remaining Ramsden Commissioner). By September, however, Sir John was seeking a clause in the Charter which would preserve all his manorial rights 'as if the Charter of Incorporation had never been granted'.[107]

As the negotiations continued, Ramsden consulted a range of local and national lawyers and property professionals to establish the full range of his manorial rights. These were conveniently summarised as follows:

- Market rights under the 1671 Charter.
- The appointment of the constable (by the court leet).
- The appointment of four Commissioners under the 1827 Waterworks Act, and an annual payment of £100 as compensation for the estate's previous rights of water supply.
- The appointment of three Improvement Commissioners under the 1848 Act.
- The proviso in that Act that any extension of its jurisdiction should be on the joint application of the HIC and lord of the manor.
- The lord's right to name streets on his land.
- General provisos in the 1845 Waterworks Act and 1848 Improvement Act that nothing therein shall 'prejudice, defeat, lessen or affect' the manorial rights.

At one time or another Sir John sought reassurance of continuity on all these issues, though some proved trickier than others. Market rights were a major bone of contention for the next decade [see p. 72]. The court leet survived until 1896, though latterly with purely honorific functions graced by an annual dinner, and the appointment of a constable continued at least until 1893; a proposal for the Mayor to hold the post *ex officio* was declined by the first incumbent, C. H. Jones, and not revived.[108] The takeover of the HWC by the new Corporation in 1869 was not resisted by the estate, but the nomination rights and general provisos became significant bones of contention.

Ramsden initially sought the right to nominate three councillors just as he could appoint three Commissioners. Asked by R. H. Graham, Hathorn's successor, whether this was really an issue, Sir John characteristically said Yes and No:

> I attach very great importance to the right of appointing three Councillors, though I will not say I attach so much importance to it as to make me an opponent of the application for a Charter, provided the Inhabitants act handsomely by me and do all in their power to have a Similar Right secured to me in the new governing body.

The issue was raised with the Privy Council Office (PCO), which handled incorporations, and Sir John was quickly made aware that there were no precedents for such a 'very unusual' arrangement. The issue having been explored, dignity was satisfied – at least for now – and by 20 June Sir John had stepped back from pursuing it[109] – although one of Sir John's advisers did later discuss with the PCO whether the ward boundaries might be drawn to create a 'Ramsden-owned' ward where Sir John could nominate an alderman!

More troublesome was the quest for a 'general saving clause'. In March 1868, after the PCO had signed off the draft Charter, the matter was still causing delay. Finally after two days of discussions in London on 3/4 April between a deputation from the Incorporation Committee, Sir John and his legal advisors, the clause was withdrawn – but only on condition that, incorporation once granted, the clause would be inserted instead into future Bills extending the powers of the new Corporation, which all knew to be necessary.[110] Although destined to cause future trouble, this cleared the way for the Charter to be promulgated on 7 July 1868 and for the first Corporation to be elected on 4 September. The formal representation of the Ramsden estate in the town's effective governing bodies had come to an end.

ESTATE MANAGEMENT

Alongside the incorporation negotiations of 1867-8, the estate completed the reform of its tenure arrangements through the 1867 Ramsden Estate Act which, by authorising 999-year leases, removed the last barrier to the estate acting as an 'economically rational' property developer. Its role as lord of the manor, by contrast, was becoming increasingly anachronistic. The last annual rent audit dinner for the estate's tenants, which Ramsden had been so keen to attend personally in 1859, took place in 1870. As Ramsden had recognised by then, the dinners

> ... are not suited to the present condition of the estate. In fact that both the Town and the estate have outgrown them. That the numbers of the tenants have become so great that their meeting and dining together has become impossible, and that consequently the original significance of the dinners, as friendly gatherings where the tenants were to meet as their Landlord's guests ... has quite passed away.[111]

The 1867 Act also provided for further improvements to the estate, and allowed borrowing up to £50,000 to achieve these, in addition to the earlier funds. The 'improvements' included the rebuilding of the 300-year old Longley New Hall which had doubled as a residence and estate office, and the creation of the new Estate Buildings, just off St George's Square, as a replacement office.[112] Again this represented a shift of ethos from the antique domestic atmosphere of Longley, secluded from the town, to a purely commercial building in the town centre. Although opened 'without ceremony' on 14 September 1870,[113] the magnificent Gothic edifice of Estate Buildings, designed by the local architect William Henry Crossland, can be seen as a very visible riposte to incorporation: there was a new settlement, perhaps, but the Ramsden estate had not gone away.

PUBLIC FACILITIES

In the coming decades, however, it would be the Corporation rather than the estate that took the lead in the development of the town's public facilities.[114] But there were two pieces of unfinished business where tensions would soon arise between the estate and the new Corporation.

The first concerned markets. In November 1866 the HIC had pressed Ramsden to provide a covered market hall, which he had apparently taken up with alacrity, only to be advised by Nelson that neither the £20,000 nor the £25,000 improvement fund could be used for this purpose, for the usual complex legal reasons.[115] He had evidently chafed at this advice and the 1867 Act included specific powers to erect new markets, authorising expenditure of up to £12,000. Crossland was then commissioned to design a market hall on a site bounded by King St, Cross Church St and Kirkgate (essentially where the Kingsgate shopping centre is today). He produced a block plan and an itemised estimate of £33,244, though no detailed designs have come to light.[116] Clearly the estimate was far more than the authorised funding and the proposal went no further.

The second outstanding issue concerned the town's premier public space, St George's Square. Like almost all the town centre, this was owned by the estate. It had not been adopted as a public street by the HIC. In the 1850s an 'ornamental centrepiece' had been planned, but no designs had been produced to Ramsden's satisfaction, and the space had been left for 'open air meetings at elections and other like purposes'.[117] It was therefore open to the estate to enclose the space, and in 1866 designs to fence it in had been drawn up by Graham but not taken forward. With the advent of the Corporation, Ramsden saw an opportunity for a different solution to what had perhaps become an embarrassment. The state of the Square, Graham wrote at one point, was 'a disgrace to the town', and in April 1870 the land was offered to the Corporation provided that they paved it and on condition that the estate's permission would still be required to erect anything there. The issue remained unresolved in 1872, when it became embroiled in controversy about a proposed statue of Sir Robert Peel [see pp. 73-4].

1870-1910: a long withdrawing roar?

In his comparative analysis of 'lords and landlords', David Cannadine suggests that the last two (of six) phases of the relationship between landed proprietors and 'their' towns in the late-19th and early-20th centuries were 'ornamental impotence' followed by 'territorial abdication'.[118] In the Ramsden case, this latter was reached in 1920.[119] For the post-incorporation period, however, 'ornamental impotence' is too simple a description of the tense relationship between the lord of the manor and the municipal authority.

There were certainly ornamental elements. In his July 1867 welcome to the draft Charter, Ramsden had expressed a wish to present the Mayoral gold chain and badge of office and, after the intervening fraught negotiations, he was as good as his word, presenting them in person to C. H. Jones at a public dinner on 5 February 1869 at the George.[120] Moreover the new Borough's arms, with their rams' heads and castellated 'dens', were closely based on those of the Ramsdens [see back cover]. Over the coming decades, as Brendan Evans has put it:

> There were many examples of deference and respect from the Council to the influential local landowner: for example, when HBC wished to

open a footpath through his land they very respectfully asked Sir John, through his agent, for his permission. Members of the Ramsden family were frequently invited to open a new building or bridge, which would often take a family name, and were always asked in the politest and formal terms, with great gratitude expressed when the family agreed.[121]

But cordiality was accompanied by a hard-headed defence of estate interests and equally by a zealous assertion of the Corporation's independence.

PUBLIC REALM CONTROVERSIES OF THE 1870S

The April 1868 agreement to incorporate a 'saving clause' in future local Acts was activated in 1871 when the Corporation put forward a 463-clause Bill establishing new powers, going far beyond those inherited from the HIC and the local Boards to cover street works, sewers and lighting; building regulations and licensing; smoke control and a fire brigade (established in 1872); parks, baths and libraries; and the erection of a town hall.

The estate's greatest immediate concern was with its market rights. Its motives seem (as so often) to have been mixed. As Graham later recalled to town clerk Joseph Batley, 'Sir John Ramsden himself was averse to alienating the Fairs and Markets, and only consented to do so in order to meet the wishes of the Corporation'. In 1871, therefore, he had renewed his proposal to build a covered market and offered to lease it, with the rights, for 21 years and then to sell the freehold. A corporation deputation to Byram on 7 February failed to resolve the issue, and the Corporation then sought to include compulsory purchase in the Bill before Parliament, which the estate believed violated the saving clause. They prevailed in the Lords and 'even more emphatically' in the Commons, and at the end of June Graham could telegraph Ramsden to report that 'the whole of the Markets Clauses ... thrown out'.[122] Mayor Jones reported back furiously to Council on 19 July without donning the Mayoral chain, vowing that henceforth 'I will not have those bobbing rams' heads stuck around me'.[123]

After this stand-off, however, and with the combative Jones replaced as Mayor by Wright Mellor,[124] negotiations for the sale of the rights were reopened in 1872 and concluded in 1874. It remained to haggle over the price – resolved in 1876 with the Corporation agreeing to pay £39,802, plus interest to reflect the delay since exchange of contracts. Only in 1879, however, was the conveyance finalised, after difficulties over butchers' leases.[125] The new municipal Market Hall, designed by another distinguished local architect, Edward Hughes, opened in 1880 in King St, and a new cattle market and slaughterhouse in Great Northern St in 1881.

The negotiations over market rights were paralleled over the same years by the Corporation's attempts to buy around half of the Greenhead estate in order to create Greenhead Park. Unlike the markets, and despite their opportunistic Springwood initiative, the Ramsdens had no inherent interest in that quintessential piece of Victorian public realm, the public park. The land they held at Greenhead was a prime residential site, which they had owned since 1848 and were now well-placed to develop. Plans to do so were noticed at the estate office by Alderman Thomas Denham in 1869; he resolved that the land should instead be 'secured for the town' and soon persuaded the Corporation to adopt the proposal. From that point it took 12 years of on-off negotiations before the town finally acquired a park of 30 acres, half the size envisaged by Denham, in 1881. Once again, Ramsden was torn between the prospect of more lucrative development and the reputational benefit of a generous gesture towards the town. Eventually, in a reprise of the 'cashback' arrangement adopted at the cemetery and proposed for Springwood, the Corporation paid the estate £27,533-17-6, representing £30,000 for 30 acres, *plus* interest at 5% since 1878, when terms had been agreed, *less* a donation from Sir John of £5,000.[126] The estate then lost no time in capitalising on the splendid residential sites overlooking the new Park. As a report of the opening noted: 'All round the park Sir John owns the frontage, and must gain an immense advantage from a monetary point of view, as the value of the land will be trebled for building purposes.'[127]

Another cantankerous dispute of the 1870s concerned the statue of Sir Robert Peel in St George's Square. Throughout the country Peel was regarded as a hero for the repeal of the Corn Laws and consequent reduction in food prices. On his death in 1850, in Huddersfield as in many other places, gentlemen's and working men's committees had been established to raise funds for a monument, and within a year many subscriptions had been raised. When the time came to choose a sculptor, however, dissension led to years of infighting and committee arrangements became confused. By 1868 there were only 10 surviving committee members, five of whom had left the town. A new committee was formed and a successful new fund-raising drive launched. On 21 October 1869 the committee announced that they had accepted the model of William Theed the younger for a statue which was to be in Sicilian marble.[128] Committee member G. D. Tomlinson, a local artist, invited Ramsden to view the model, which he did, recording that he was 'very favourably impressed with the general effect'.[129]

Over the ensuing two years, as Theed worked on the statue, the Corporation and Ramsden remained at odds about future control of the Square (as noted above). In July 1872, however, Graham found from a newspaper report that the committee had been granted permission by the Corporation to place the statue in the Square. This was a serious *faux pas*. Receiving the news, Ramsden responded that 'I object very decidedly as you know to the use of the Square for such a purpose', that the usage of the Square remained in his gift, not the Corporation's, and that his London lawyer Wynne was to be consulted.[130] The chastened committee now sought permission for an alternative site, perhaps in the Market Place. Initially acceptable to Ramsden provided it did not interfere with the market cross,[131] this was later ruled out too. In the end the railway company allowed its erection on their own land in front of the station, where it was unveiled on 3 June 1873 [see Illustration 22, p. 59]. It stood there until 1949 when, because the stone was deteriorating, it was removed and lost; the empty plinth survives in Ravensknowle Park.

For the estate and Corporation, however, that was not the end of the matter. As its ambitions grew, the Corporation put forward a new Improvement Bill in 1876. This was less voluminous than its predecessor but its 141 clauses advanced many new powers and, as in 1871, attracted a wide range of objections from the estate. Once again matters were closely fought in Parliament, not least the innocuous-sounding Section 69, 'Drinking fountains, &c'. This empowered the Corporation to 'place and maintain in any street or court any monument or statue, ornamental drinking fountain, and troughs as they think fit'. In Graham's words, 'if this clause passes, Sir John … will be driven in self defence to rail in any open space not actually required for street purposes'.[132] The upshot was the addition of a second paragraph, providing

> that no such monument or statue, drinking fountain or trough, shall, except with the consent of Sir John Ramsden, be placed on any part of the public square or open space called St George's Square or of the triangular piece of ground bounded by Spring Wood St, George St, and Upperhead Row ['Sparrow Park'], or of the triangular piece of ground bounded by Ramsden St, St Paul's St, and the public footway running along the north side of St Paul's Churchyard, or of any other ground or open space which Sir John Ramsden may hereafter appropriate or dedicate to public use and which the Corporation may on behalf of the public accept.

Sir John was here reasserting, in no uncertain terms, his intention to retain control of the symbolic features of key public spaces, even where he was willing to concede to the Corporation the right (and the cost) of maintaining them.[133] Moreover, he obtained an *extension* of his street-naming powers from the old 1200-yard 'improvement district' to the Borough as a whole.

It was perhaps for similar reasons that he opposed the erection of the new Town Hall away from the 'new town'. Starting life in the Philosophical Hall, in 1875–8 the Corporation had built modest Municipal Offices in

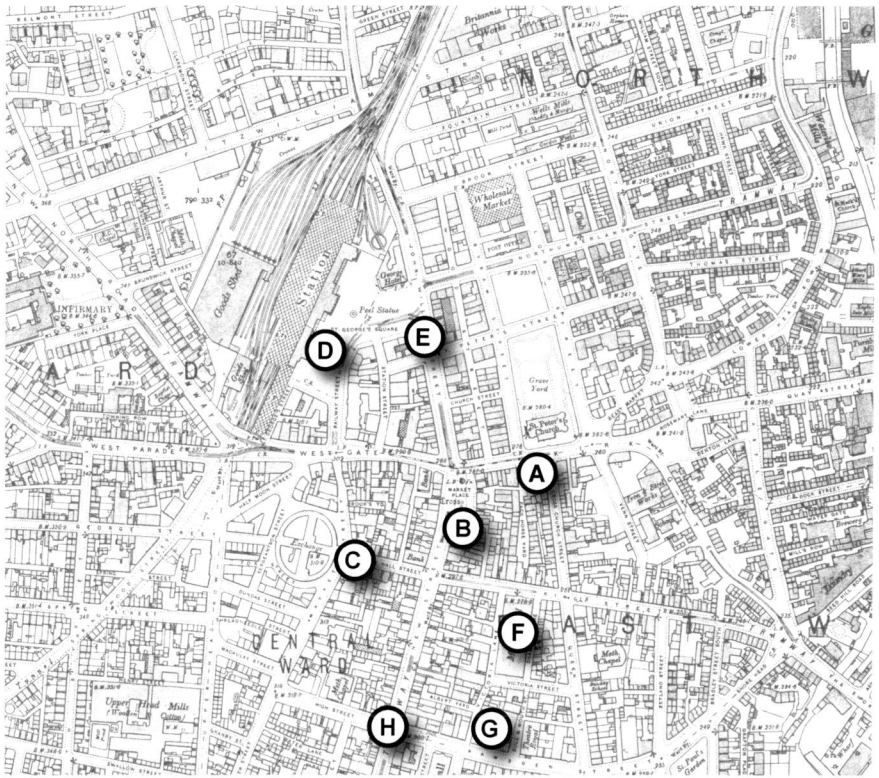

24. 1907 Ordnance Survey street map (1:25,000), showing Victorian development

The central area of the town is now fully developed, with building reaching well beyond Ramsden Street to the south. The Parish Church (A) is still located centrally and the Cloth Hall (C) remains prominent, but the largest feature is now the Railway Station (1846-50) (D). Better-class housing has appeared in West Parade, Trinity Street and New North Road to the north-west, and there is industrial development and lower-grade housing down towards the canal and river to the east. To the north a whole new town has appeared, approached along John William Street from the Market Place (B), past St George's Square and the George Hotel (1849-50) (E), and reaching well beyond Fitzwilliam Street at the top of the map. The Shambles has now been replaced by the Market Hall (1880) (F), and almost opposite the Ramsden Street chapel (G) is the new Town Hall (1875-81) (H).

Huddersfield Local Studies Library

Ramsden St, within the existing 'civic quarter'. In 1877–8 they proposed to add the much larger Town Hall behind the Offices, with concert hall, court and further offices.[134] As Pamela Cooksey writes, Joseph Woodhead, Mayor in 1877/8 had the most acrimonious disagreement with Sir John Ramsden as he and the members of the Town Council sought to build a Town Hall in Princess Street – a site leased from the Ramsden estate. Sir John Ramsden supported by other leading influential local property owners was totally opposed to the proposals and refused to co-operate in any way with the Council. The dispute was so intense that Joseph declared to the Council, 'Gentlemen, this is now not merely a question of Town Hall or no Town Hall, but the independence of the Town Council. We are not representatives of the Ramsden estate but of the burgesses of Huddersfield.'[135]

It is fair to add, however, the burgesses were divided, with a large body of wealthy ratepayers agreeing with Ramsden that the Northumberland St site he had reserved for a town hall since the 1850s would be the 'most eligible' site, in a central position near the station and post office and with room for later expansion of civic facilities.[136] The arguments were practical but also symbolic: a site in the 'civic quarter' versus one half a mile away in the Ramsden-created commercial new town. For better or worse, the Corporation prevailed.

QUIETER TIMES FROM 1880

The relationship between the estate and the Corporation weathered the storms of the 1870s, and by about 1880 settled into a mutual accommodation lasting several decades. This period had several features:

- The estate continued to petition Parliament against aspects of successive local Acts brought forward by the Corporation, for example in 1880, 1890, 1897, 1900 and 1906. But the grounds of objection were increasingly narrow and more technical, usually concerning particular proposed acquisitions of property, for example for street improvements or tramways. The hard-fought saving clause made its last appearance in the Huddersfield Corporation Act 1897.[137]

- As the Corporation continued to extend its functions, however, the estate proved willing to sell land to enable this. In 1880 and again in 1890 land at Deighton and Dalton was sold for the sewage works; in 1887 for the open produce market in Brook St; and in 1892 for 'Fartown Recreation Ground', opened in 1893 as Norman Park.[138]

- The estate, or Ramsden personally, made occasional donations of public facilities apparently without any specific ulterior motivation. He had given £1,200 in 1872 to buy land for an extension to the Infirmary, and in 1887 had offered a floor of Somerset Buildings rent-free for a library and art gallery, though the Corporation – pioneering in many areas but laggardly on this front – had not taken it up.[139]

- From time to time they also brought forward larger schemes which combined commercial motivation with public benefit. Notably, 1876-86 saw the erection along Byram St of three handsome commercial buildings, Waverley Chambers, Bulstrode (now Kirkgate) Buildings and Somerset Buildings, all designed by W. H. Crossland. The estate's outlay of over £120,000 (including nearby Byram Arcade) was undoubtedly a commercial development but, facing the parish church and St Peter's Gardens, these buildings created the town's best public space after St George's Square.[140]

But the Ramsdens' legitimacy as anything more than commercial landlords was steadily diminishing: 'as the century wore on and more and more … local functions transferred to the State, it became progressively more difficult to legitimize the traditional hierarchy in terms of those local functions.'[141]

LAND OWNERSHIP AND MANAGEMENT

After 1868, while the estate faced the necessity of reaching a new accommodation with 'the town', it retained its powers of initiative as a landowner. Perhaps it was no coincidence, then, that the next decade and a half saw the most energetic expansion of the estate's holdings. The years 1868 to 1884 saw over 20 acquisitions. These included large estates in outer parts of the borough, such as the Woodhouse, Fell Greave, Woodside and Sheepridge estates to the north, and the Kaye estates at Moldgreen and Dalton. But there was also a steady stream of smaller purchases in or close to the town centre, in such locations as Newhouse (Highfields), Trinity St, Lord St (Firth's freehold at last!), Shorehead, Spring Grove and Gledholt.[142] It was, in fact, only in this period, that the estate's town centre holdings approached the near-monopoly position often asserted or implied in earlier times. More widely, by 1884 the Ramsden estate held 51.5 percent of the township, and 41.4 percent of the 10,496 acres of the Municipal Borough – essentially the 4,300 acres that would be sold to the Corporation in 1920.[143]

In the absence of public town planning powers before 1909, this made the estate a surrogate planning authority. In 1886 the estate set out its town planning principles to the Parliamentary Select Committee on Town Holdings. In Huddersfield, they reported:

certain districts are set aside for certain purposes. The centre of the Town is devoted to Shops and Warehouses, and the vacant land is reserved for future extensions of these. The lowlying land between the River and the Canal is allotted to mills and manufacturing premises, and their future extensions – other parts are residential and set apart for private houses of various sizes and values.[144]

There is nothing here to challenge David Cannadine's argument that 'for all [the Ramsdens'] tight legal control, the zoning pattern remained primarily influenced by topography'.[145] The real purpose of the submission, however, was to resist proposals for the taxation of vacant land. Considerable land, it argued, had been bought, sewered and paved by the estate for which there was as yet no great demand; but when there was, values would rise and ratepayers would benefit, so there was no detriment from holding it vacant meanwhile.

But perhaps this long-term view had now gone far enough, for it was at about the same time that the estate's 40-year campaign of land purchase came to an end. And while Graham in 1880 had described Ramsden as 'a very reluctant seller of land in any circumstances',[146] the estate was now willing to embark on a number of freehold sales. Once again, a change of personnel may have played a part: Graham died in 1885, to be replaced by Col. Beadon. The estate relaxed its remaining paternalist attitudes, abandoning its resistance to back-to-back housing in 1900 (though new back-to-backs would anyway be outlawed in 1909) and adopting rental policies which favoured a quick return over long-term estate development.[147]

To attempt a summary of this period, including the turning point of 1867–9, is more challenging than its predecessors; indeed there is a case for a division into two sub-periods. From 1867 to about 1880, the estate's relationship to the public realm revolved around the terms of the Borough's belated incorporation and the definition of its relationship to the new municipal authority, which had 'ornamental', pragmatic and conflictual elements.[148] As a landowner, meanwhile – and perhaps in response – the pace of estate expansion was quickened and major developments in the 'new town' asserted that the estate was by no means a spent force. As for day-to-day estate management, the 1867 Estate Act had removed the last barriers to rational landlordism, though the estate continued to take a long-term view of its assets in the 'country estate' tradition. From the early 1880s, however, the balance shifted again. Tension with the Corporation continued but over a narrowing range of issues, very much reflective of 'commercial landlord' rather than 'lord of the manor' concerns. There were occasional philanthropic gestures towards town facilities, albeit sometimes entwined with commercial proposals. Land acquisition was largely at an end by 1885, and by the turn of the century, though still owning half the town's land, the estate behaved increasingly as a rational but short-termist rentier, in a sense returning to its early 19th-century outlook.

1910–20: the last goodbye

On 31 March 1910 Ramsden made over the Huddersfield estate to his son John Frecheville Ramsden (1877-1958) – as he put it, he had 'abdicated in his favour'.[149] It is tempting to see this as the beginning of the end, with John William Ramsden's death in 1914, World War I and the sale of the estate to the Corporation all to come within the next decade.

The son's initial reaction seems, however, to have been a renewed sense of ambition for the estate to take an active part in Huddersfield's development. A series of typed letters from Sir John Frecheville to the agent Beadon shows that several new improvement schemes were under discussion – although only one would come to fruition, and several only reprised earlier ideas.[150]

One was a new proposal to erect a public library and art gallery to the north of the parish church, either on part of the churchyard or on the still-empty 'town hall' site in Northumberland St. Like its predecessor this did not go forward, and the town would wait until 1940 for its purpose-built library in Ramsden St. Meanwhile the Northumberland St site was finally occupied by a new Post Office, which opened in 1914 to replace Crossland's building of 1877 on the opposite side of the street.

This discussion revealed problems with the state of the parish church itself. The Ramsden family had contributed to the rebuilding of 1834-6 but that job had been ill-done by the contractor and the stonework had caused problems ever since (and still does).[151] Sir John Frecheville was now willing to support rebuilding on the same site, with a temporary church in Lord St while the work was undertaken. His letters show a close and intelligent interest in the details of both schemes, but neither went forward.

One project which did come to fruition – unlike the housing proposals of 1890 – was the building of Oldgate tenements. An earlier offer of land for working-class housing down Leeds Rd in 1890 had not been taken up.[152] As Cyril Pearce relates:

> From 1882 to 1909, successive administrations in Huddersfield town hall listened to the calls for more working class housing, whether from the Medical Officer of Health or, after the 1890s, from the local labour and socialist movement, but felt unable to respond. However, new powers made available to local authorities by the [1909] Town and

Country Planning Act encouraged a change of heart. Ironically, at this point, after decades of declining influence, it appears that the Ramsden estate decided to take the initiative and goad the Corporation into action. A site on Oldgate was identified and plans drawn up by K. F. Campbell, the Borough Engineer, acting for the Ramsden estate, were approved by the Council on 15 February 1911. Less than a year later the Ramsden tenements, Huddersfield's first, were completed.[153]

As well as the town centre tenements, Sir John Frecheville was also 'interested to hear that a scheme for a Garden City has been brought forward' – in Dalton – and was 'anxious to do all in my power to help it on'. He was willing to sell land to the promoters at £250/acre (a quarter of his father's price for Greenhead Park 30 years earlier), noting that out-of-town development was good for the estate. Hearing that Beadon was to visit a garden city development in Liverpool, he was keen to come too.[154] Shortly afterwards a plan was drawn up for a new garden suburb on land adjoining Edgerton cemetery, between Highfields and St John's church, in a return to the unrealised residential master plans of the 1860s.[155] Once again nothing came of this and indeed another century was to pass before any part of the site was taken for housing.

Whether Sir John and his agents could have brought more of these plans to fruition, had war not intervened, cannot be known. In the judgement of Meriel Buxton, it seems unlikely:

> There can have been few less propitious moments in British history than 1914 for a business empire, which essentially was what the Ramsden estates had become, to pass from the control of a man who enjoys making money to one whose sole interest is in spending it.[156]

It is, in any event, a matter of fact that, once the war was over, the Ramsdens were ready to sell, and the Corporation was ready to buy. Henceforth the responsibility for the public realm would, for some time, be theirs alone.

Conclusion

The Ramsden family and their agents had an immense influence on Huddersfield's public realm over 250 years, and their impact remains highly visible a century after they sold out. Nonetheless it is an over-simplification to see Huddersfield uncritically as having been a 'Ramsden town'. This chapter has attempted to establish a more nuanced picture, differentiating between periods, geographies and dimensions of influence. Several trends and patterns have been identified:

First, the estate's land holdings in Huddersfield grew substantially from relatively small beginnings to the 4,300 acres sold in 1920. Far from 'owning the town' throughout the period, however, the most vigorous growth was from the 1840s to the 1880s, and especially after 1868.

Second, there is a cyclical pattern to the estate's development of the town's facilities. The market rights were acquired in 1671; the Cloth Hall and Canal established in the 1760s and 1770s, followed by the Georgian town centre; the railway-based new town developed from the late 1840s. Between and beyond these developmental episodes were long periods of retreat from active engagement in town affairs.

Third, there is a long-term shift from a paternalistic to a more commercial relationship to the town, but this was not a simple transition: the elements were intertwined over a long period.

Fourth, these trends interacted to produce a succession of different institutional settlements for the governance of the town. The Ramsdens were always a player in these, and particularly in the case of the 1848 Improvement Commissioners. Paradoxically, however, the HIC's establishment also evidenced the emergence of an independent middle-class civic politics which had been somewhat retarded by the strength of the Ramsden interest, but which now came to challenge it. From 1868 the estate's rise as a landowner was accompanied by its ejection from formal governance, leaving a complex relationship with the new municipal authority.

Fifth, the estate's political grip on the town has been exaggerated. There was always room for independent radical politics, the estate's policies were often strongly contested, and Huddersfield was never a 'pocket borough'. The estate often worked through alliances with other forces, notably the town's leading merchants. These were often Tories: the Ramsdens, Whigs and Liberals themselves (at least until the 1880s), were always pragmatic about their local allies.

Finally, although long-term historical trends were at work, the impact of personalities is striking. The third and fifth baronets had more in common with each other than with the fourth, during whose later years the town languished. Agents were equally diverse in their approaches; and two periods of trusteeship, led by strong family figures, were important in initiating the key developmental episodes. As always, the interplay of personality and circumstance turns out to be the stuff of history.

Acknowledgements

For comments on an earlier draft, I am grateful to Brian Haigh, John Halstead, Cyril Pearce and the editor. Dennis Whomsley's work, much of it unpublished, has been indispensable. Any remaining errors or misjudgements are of course solely my own.

Endnotes

1. *Journal of the House of Commons*, xxxiii, 414.
2. KC311/18/13, Township Papers, Huddersfield: Report on the Borough of Huddersfield; with a Description of the Proposed Boundary.
3. Cannadine (1980), p.42. Huddersfield was not one of his detailed case studies, but his later point, that 'we still await a study which deliberately and self-consciously investigates the position of the Ramsdens in the public life of the town' (Cannadine (1982), p.12), is one inspiration for this chapter.
4. Gash (1953), p.xi.
5. Springett (1982), p.131. She cites other official sources of the 'opinions', e.g. Reports of the Select Committee on Towns, 1887/88/89.
6. Hemingway (1992), pp. 497–8. Hemingway considered the period 1832-53, but Dennis Whomsley records Sir John William informing local agent Thomas Brook in 1859 that 'I have always given strict injunctions to my agents not to interfere in elections' – see Whomsley, 'Sir John William Ramsden and the West Riding, 1859-1867', unpublished typescript, KX486/2.
7. This section relies heavily on the work of earlier scholars, especially Dennis Whomsley. His unpublished work, now deposited at KX486/2, as well as his published papers, are gratefully acknowledged.
8. Law (1992), p.66.
9. Whomsley (1984), p.37.
10. KC174/1/6, Tomlinson papers, Notebook G, press cutting between ff 55–6, G.W. T[omlinson], 'The Firths of Shepley and Huddersfield', *The Watchword*, pp. 77–8. Thomas Firth (1789-1869) was a wealthy Quaker drysalter (f.71). The transaction did not proceed.
11. Dawson (1973), p.181.
12. Phillips (1848), p.1.
13. DD/RE/447 (copy of 1893).
14. WYASK, Ramsden estate plan 1780; WYAS, Wakefield, John Goodchild collection, Hirst & Kennet estate map, c.1780 (copy at WYASK); WYAS, Wakefield, QE13/2/9 & 15, Land Tax returns, 1780-1832.
15. DD/RA/C/27/6, 1873.
16. Ahier (1949), p.81.
17. Woodhead (1939), pp.22-8.
18. Crump & Ghorbal (1935), p.106.
19. Whomsley (1984), p.30.
20. Whomsley, 'The Ramsden family, 1670-1776', unpublished typescript, KX486/2.
21. Whomsley (1984), p.33, citing J. Aikin (1795), p.128 and J. Hewitt (1862-4), p.290. The Ramsden Canal was later complemented by the Huddersfield Narrow Canal, linking to the west. This was not a Ramsden initiative, but Sir John was nominally a director in the company's first year and his steward, John Crowder, represented his interests as an active board member during construction. (T. Ellis, 'Huddersfield Canal Company Committee', unpublished, n.d.).
22. Whomsley, 'The Ramsden family, 1769-1839', unpublished typescript, KX486/2.
23. Whomsley (1984), p. 35.
24. Law (2001a) reports that Cloth Hall St, though misleadingly added to the 1778 town map, 'was not promoted until the 1790s'; George Redmonds notes New St rentals from 1798; the first plot in King St was let in 1802 (DD/R/dd/7/55) and seven properties there appear in the 1807/8 Ramsden rentals (DD/RE/r).

25 Girouard (1990), p.180.
26 Whomsley, '1769-1839', p.15 and (1984), p.35.
27 Whomsley (1984), p.31; indeed Thomas had appointed him, in 1769.
28 In 1818 Bower was involved in 'several overlapping enclosures … which may well have slowed up the process' of the Shipley enclosure, where he was commissioner: Coomber (2017), pp. 357–8. In 1835 he was forced to resign a post with the Duchy of Lancaster because of 'inattention to duties': Hilton (1989), p.26.
29 Springett (1982), p.132.
30 See chapter 3.
31 DD/RA/C/4/1, 'Why should not Huddersfield become one of the best regulated towns in the Kingdom?'. The quotation appears in Friedrich Engels' 1845 *Condition of the Working Class in England* (Engels, 1886), although not verbatim as it has been re-translated into English. The consequences of the tenancy-at-will system have been closely examined by Jane Springett (1979), and the 'tenant right' dispute which brought the system to an end is the subject of chapter 3 below.
32 The governance of this period is fully analysed in Griffiths (2008).
33 The minutes are at KMT98, Huddersfield County Borough records.
34 The court records are at DD/R/M.
35 For details see, for example, Hargreaves (1992).
36 See Hemingway (1992).
37 Whomsley, '1769-1839' pp.19, 26.
38 Navickas (2016), p.175. The judgement is echoed by Roberts (2018), p.53.
39 For details, see Griffiths (2008).
40 Springett (1979), p.16.
41 Moore (1976), p.344.
42 Whomsley (1984), p.48.
43 Springett (1979) gives the fullest account of the legal issues surrounding the Ramsden estate.
44 Engels (1845 [1987]), p.82.
45 Griffiths (2012).
46 Woodhead (1939), p.48.
47 *HC*, 24 April and 1 May 1858.
48 See Whomsley (1974) for a thorough analysis of the Ramsdens and the railway question.
49 R. Oastler, 'A letter to the editor of the *Argus and Demagogue*, on the validity of Sir John Ramsden's title to the sums of money he claims for canal dues, and on other subjects', published as a booklet by Joshua Hobson, 1834. I am grateful to Brian Haigh for this reference.
50 Whomsley (1974), p. 191, quoting Fenton to Fitzwilliam, 1 March 1844.
51 See chapter 1.
52 Spring (1963), p.89. His significant part in the Highland Clearances, on behalf of the Duke of Sutherland, should not go unmentioned.
53 DD/RA/C/24.
54 DD/RA/4 (1).
55 The 'stately home' description was by architectural journalist Ian Nairn ('Football Towns', *The Listener*, 1975) and not, as is sometimes suggested, by Sir John Betjeman.
56 DD/RA/C/36, Hathorn to Loch.
57 Clarkson (1989), pp.7-12.
58 The Bay Hall purchase preceded the canal sale, but Isabella Ramsden advanced the funds until the Trustees could reimburse her.

59 Ramsden Estate Act, 7 & 8 Vic, cap.21.
60 DD/RE/419, Isaac Hordern's Notebook, 1846, pp. 5–6.
61 DD/RA/4, Loch to I. Ramsden, 30 December 1849.
62 Springett (1986), p.45.
63 Griffiths (2009).
64 DD/RA/4, Loch to Mrs Ramsden, 30 December 1849.
65 Joseph Batley's evidence in *Municipal Incorporation of Huddersfield: Report of the Proceedings of the Public Inquiry, 18/19 December 1867* (*HC*, 1868).
66 There are numerous examples in the HIC minutes, KMT18/2/2/1.
67 Thus continuing into the third quarter of the 19th century a pattern identified for earlier decades in Griffiths (2015).
68 The first chairman, John Sutcliffe (1776-1858), was another wool merchant, who corresponded extensively and confidentially with Isabella Ramsden on town affairs (DD/RA/C/4/1-4).
69 As many as nine possible candidates are discussed in Ramsden correspondence, none of them manufacturers: DD/RA/C/38/1, 10 July to 26 September, 1860; DD/RA/C/40/5, 6 September to 16 November 1861. Other membership information has been drawn from correspondence scattered through the DD/RA and DD/RE/C series.
70 *HC*, 25 January 1851.
71 DD/RE/C/78, Hathorn to Loch, 11 November 1850.
72 Chase (2013), p.276; Saville (1988), pp.37-9; Morris (1990); Griffiths (2015).
73 Smail (1994), pp.122-46.
74 KC790/2, Huddersfield Township records, Ratepayers' meeting, 6 April 1843.
75 *HC*, 13 April 1850. Hathorn attributed the editorial to Hobson, who was widely seen to be 'moonlighting' for the *Chronicle* alongside his HIC duties; after dismissal from the HIC, over matters including his attendance at work, he became the editor in June 1855.
76 These are detailed in Griffiths (2012), pp.14-20.
77 DD/RE/C/79, Hathorn to Loch, 12 December 1850.
78 DD/RE/C/88, Loch to Hathorn, 28 September 1851.
79 DD/RE/C/88-91.
80 KMT18/2/3/12/1, HIC Town Hall committee minutes.
81 See chapter 5.
82 See, for example *HC,* 5 November 1853.
83 Linstrum (1978), p.339; Hordern, 'Notes', 1856, p. 44.
84 DD/RA/C/5, Bateman to Loch, 20 January 1847.
85 DD/RA/C/5, Loch to Mrs Ramsden, 21 January 1847. There was more immediate success in relocating the slaughterhouse from the town centre to Aspley, for similar public health reasons and at Loch's instigation, in 1845. (DD/RA/C/2, Loch to Mrs Ramsden, 29 September 1844).
86 See chapter 4.
87 Buxton (2017), p.53.
88 Buxton's judgement that 'Jack's lifelong approach to business affairs … showed an uncanny resemblance to that of George Loch' (Buxton (2017), p.61) is thus perhaps a little one-sided.
89 *HC*, 20 & 27 July 1850.
90 KMT18/2/3/12/1, HIC Burial Ground Committee (BGC) minutes, 15 July 1850.
91 Loch to Hathorn, reproduced in BGC, 28 March 1851.
92 DD/RA/C/4/8, Fenton to Ramsden, 27 November 1850.

93   See chapter 3.
94   DD/RE/C/62, Hathorn to Loch, 27/8/49; Law (1992), p.68, referencing DD/RE/C/90. See also below, p. 166.
95   KMT18/2/3/12/1, Minutes of the HIC Market Tolls (Special) Committee, 16 June 1852.
96   Law (1992), pp.80–1.
97   I am grateful to Brian Haigh for this point. Interestingly HIC Chair Joseph Brook had noted in 1850 a 'strong desire in the public mind for a recreation ground and public gardens', but argued that a well-done cemetery would meet this (DD/RE/C/79, 12 December 1850).
98   The account of this episode summarises Griffiths (2011c), pp.16-25.
99   *HC*, 28 August 1858. Springwood Hall was a Georgian mansion of c.1805.
100 DD/RA/11, Nelson to Ramsden, 1 September 1858.
101 *HC*, 8 January 1859.
102 KMT9/17/1, Draft HIC Park Committee minute, 17 November 1858.
103 DD/RA/C/41/1, 1862.
104 See above, p. 23.
105 Buxton (2017), p.187.
106 These events are detailed in Griffiths (2018).
107 DD/RA/C/35/10 – the source for all quotations in this section unless otherwise stated.
108 *HC*, 14 November 1868, 30 October 1869, 28 October 1893; DD/AH/2. In the 1860s it had become customary for the HIC chair to serve as constable.
109 Ramsden's letter of concession was printed in full in *HC*, 22 June 1867.
110 The agreement is set out in DD/RE/198.
111 DD/RA/C/26/4, Ramsden to Graham, 1 April 1870.
112 S. Chadwick, *HDE*, 23 July 1968. For Longley Hall see chapter 1, pp. 27-34.
113 Hordern, 'Notes', 1870, p. 89.
114 See Pearce (2018) for details.
115 KMT18/2/2/1, HIC minute, 3 October 1866; DD/RE/198, Nelson to Ramsden, 5 October 1866, Ramsden to Nelson, 8 October 1866, Nelson to Ramsden, 13 October 1866.
116 DD/RA/C/26/1, 6/5/69.
117 This and other details in this paragraph are from a memo by Graham and accompanying bundle of correspondence, in connection with the 1876 Huddersfield Improvement Bill (see below), DD/RA/C/vol III. One design was in Gothic style by W. H. Crossland (DD/RE/49).
118 Cannadine (1980), p.59.
119 See Chapters 6 and 7.
120 DD/RA/C/35/10.
121 Evans (2018), p.91.
122 DD/RA/C/33/14, 7 February 1871, 27 June 1871; DD/RE/198, 31 May 1873
123 *HC*, 22 February 1871.
124 Wright Mellor was a cloth merchant and a long-term ally of Ramsden and his moderate Liberalism. In 1860 he had been party to manoeuvres by Ramsden to provide covert financial backing to the *Examiner*, the town's Liberal newspaper [see chapter 3, pp. 103,108]
125 DD/RE/198; DD/RA/C/15/2.
126 DD/RA/1(11), 29 June 1877; DD/RA/15(5). For further details, see Griffiths (2011b).

127 *Huddersfield Weekly News*, 4 October 1884.
128 This summary is adapted, with thanks, from unpublished notes by Christopher Marsden, 'Aspects of Victorian St George's Square and Huddersfield' (2013).
129 DD/RA/C/26/4, Ramsden to Tomlinson, 11 May 1870.
130 DD/RA/C/vol III (1876 Act bundle), Ramsden to Graham, 20 July 1872.
131 DD/RA/C/vol III (1876 Act bundle), Graham to Ramsden, 2 & 3 October 1872; Ramsden to Graham, 10 October 1872.
132 DD/RA/C/vol III (1876 Act bundle), Graham to Ramsden, 2 & 3 October 1872.
133 The exclusion of Market Place from the list is puzzling. In 1888 a Ramsden-gifted Jubilee fountain was erected there, presumably without interfering with the cross. In 1920 the Corporation resolved to move it to St Paul's Gardens, one of the triangles referred to in section 69; it now stands in Greenhead Park.
134 The creation of the Municipal Offices and Town Hall is related in Haigh (2001).
135 Cooksey (1999), pp.21-2.
136 *HC*, 31 October 1877, 11 January 1878.
137 See https://huddersfield.exposed/wiki/Chronology of Acts, for the various Acts.
138 DD/RA/C/20/6, 1880; DD/RE/198, 1886-7; DD/RA/C/21/10, 1890; DD/RA/C/14/3, 1892.
139 DD/RA/C/26/2, 1872; *HC*, 15 February 1898. Nor had they pursued an offer from Ramsden, also in 1887, to provide a new site for the 60-year old Infirmary if the Corporation would buy the existing two-acre site in New North Rd for the erection of a library, art gallery and public baths (*HC*, 11 February 1887). The site in question had been owned by the estate until 1848, when Thomas Firth – the obstinate Beast Market freeholder – had bought it for £1,000 and given it to the Infirmary in order to release them from the estate's rent.
140 DD/RA/C/21/10, 1890.
141 Moore (1976), p. 433.
142 Compiled from various sources, principally DD/RA/C/36, supplemented by deeds and Hordern's 'Notes', 1848, p. 18; 1872, p. 97; 1876, p. 112; 1888, p. 131.
143 Springett (1979), p.16.
144 DD/RA/C, vol III, 19 May 1886.
145 Cannadine (1980), p.406.
146 This was in connection with the sewage works, and in fact Ramsden consented because of the 'urgent necessity' of the case (DD/RA/C/20/6, Graham to Batley, 15 March 1880).
147 Springett (1982), p.141.
148 Trainor (1993), pp. 250–3, identifies a very similar blend in the relationships between Dudley and West Bromwich boroughs, also late to be incorporated, and their former aristocratic 'owners', the earls of Dudley and Dartmouth (the latter also with substantial interests around Huddersfield).
149 Buxton (2017), p.181.
150 DD/RA/2, 1910/11.
151 See chapter 4.
152 DD/RA/C/21/10.
153 Pearce (2018), pp.55-6.
154 DD/RA/2, JFR to Beadon, 15 April 1911.
155 DD/RA/2, Plan dated 25 August 1911.
156 Buxton (2017), p. 214.

CHAPTER THREE

The Ramsden Estate Dispute of 1850-1867

JOHN HALSTEAD

Introduction

THE RAMSDEN TENURE DISPUTE of 1850–67 originated in the lax management of the estate and developed in the response to attempts to modernise its practice. The estate was not alone among landowners in the Huddersfield district during the early nineteenth century who were absentee or took a passive approach to their holdings but action was taken earlier elsewhere. This provided competition to the Ramsden Estate and a model to which its critics and some of its friends from time to time referred. The characters and personalities of those involved were an important element in the dispute, but the human drama sprang from the circumstance that Huddersfield, as an early industrial revolution growth town, experienced a rapid increase in population with an archaic system of local governance. The consequence was poor housing, nuisances and a lack of public amenities, deleterious to the population's health, despite the area's natural advantages. Concern about such matters related to land ownership and tenure and was a factor in the dispute, but the central issue, clearly perceived by some of the parties, was 'betterment'. Who should receive, and in what proportion and circumstances, the increasing value of the estate from the growth of population on the land and its associated levels of economic activity?

The dispute ran through three phases. The first phase refers to the original management of the estate and the interregnum between the death of Sir John Ramsden, the fourth baronet, in 1839 and the majority of his heir and grandson, Sir John William Ramsden, the fifth baronet, in 1852. In this phase Isabella Ramsden, widow of John Charles Ramsden and mother of John William, acting as a Trustee under her father-in-law's will, brought George Loch in to improve estate management. Joshua Hobson, the principal critic

25. Joshua Hobson (1810–76), clerk to the Improvement Commission and editor of the *Huddersfield Chronicle*.
Huddersfield Art Gallery

of the Ramsden family and of sanitary conditions in Huddersfield, emerged in this phase, sometimes to co-operate with the estate but also to sound the tocsin on Loch's moves to secure the landlord's interest on estate tenure.

The second phase of the dispute ran from Sir John William Ramsden's taking full control of his inheritance in September 1852 and the decision the following year to appoint Thomas Wright Nelson, a London solicitor, to succeed George Loch as steward and auditor of his estates. This phase was marked by the passage of the Ramsden Estate (Leasing) Act 1859. This Act, by which the ground landlord obtained power to grant 99-year leases, rather than removing difficulties only exacerbated them. The third phase began with the formation of the Tenant-Right Defence Association [TRDA] on 5 June 1860. This first fully representative body of tenant-right owners was chaired by a solicitor and son of the Thornhill Estate land agent, Frederick Robert Jones, junior, who became alongside Hobson the second principal thorn in the side of the estate. The TRDA started a legal action in the Court of Chancery, *Thornton v. Ramsden*, which was initially successful but was overturned in May 1866 on appeal to the House of Lords in *Ramsden v. Dyson*. The opposition to Ramsden indicated its complete capitulation on 20 December 1866, so concluding the dispute. Sir John William, it seemed, had won complete victory. But there was a coda. Sir John William decided to apply to Parliament for a new Ramsden Estate Act in 1867, which would give him the power to grant 999-year leases.

The Neglect of the Estate

The Ramsdens were absentee landlords who employed absentee agents.[1] The Huddersfield agent to 1816 was John Crowder of Brotherton. Until his first recorded lease issue of 1780 the land would have been let without lease. These early leases were for 60 years, renewable at twenty-year intervals on payment of the renewal 'fine' and regular payment of rent. Such leases, issued by Crowder up to his death in 1816, sharply declined thereafter due to a change in the method for calculating the renewal fine. During this thirty-six year period, however, leases only applied to a portion of the land. The bulk continued to be let without lease, a practice followed almost exclusively by Crowder's successor, John Bower.

After the fourth baronet's death in 1839 Bower continued to serve the Trustees until his own death on 7 May 1844. This then prompted the Trustees to commission George Loch to visit the Huddersfield estate and make recommendations concerning its future management. Loch reported on 6 June, detailing the shortcomings of the previous administration.[2] Bower had visited only twice a year and had more business to attend to than he could get through during his stay. He drew up all the leases, but with charges and delays in completion which sometimes lasted years. Applications had been made to a sub-agent, the surveyor Thomas Dinsley, who set the price of the land, but to get favourable consideration the applicants treated Dinsley to a drink at the public house of Joseph Brook, another sub-agent, who after a year or two fixed the rent. There was no general plan for setting off land for buildings and there was no consistency in requiring leases. People not infrequently erected buildings on land occupied without any lease, or any communication with the estate management. These 'tenants-at-will' trusted this would not be disapproved of and a lease would be obtained eventually, if required.[3] In any case, the rent required for such occupancy was half that applied under a lease. People had great confidence they would not be disturbed from their tenancy at will, and that leases entered into would continue to be renewed. Loch noted several cases had been discovered where the occupiers had not paid ground rent for many years, thereby acquiring a right to claim the freehold! He made detailed recommendations for the setting up of an Estate Office, the keeping of books, the appointment of a competent local agent and reporting to a London auditor.

Loch's actions to secure the landlord's interest

The Trustees responded to Loch's report by appointing him to oversee Huddersfield, while retaining his position on the Bridgewater Estates at Manchester.[4] A fellow Scot, Alexander Hathorn (1815-1892), was appointed under him to be resident at Huddersfield, commencing early in October. Loch's first move on the tenure question – of uncertain date but apparently by mid-June 1845 – was to require *new* applicants for non-lease tenures to sign a paper acknowledging they were tenants-at-will, holding the land at such rents as the Trustees might think proper to fix. The position of the *old* tenants without leases remained a problem which Loch hesitated to address because action to secure the Trustees' legal position might 'arrest the increasing prosperity of the estate and alienate the feelings and goodwill of the whole population'. The remark proved prescient, though this first step did not create alarm.

Loch's second action on land tenure was to make a small addition in April 1850 to the rental of each non-lease tenancy when a transfer was made. Despite Loch's fear in 1845 that further action might have a deleterious effect, by 1850 he appears to have decided that continued hesitation would be dangerous: 'as regards the value of buildings erected', tenants might be successful in establishing a claim in their favour against the landlord in a Court of Equity, because of 'the long usage practised in the management of the property'.[5]

This move coincided with the first appearance of a Huddersfield newspaper, the *Huddersfield Chronicle*. The paper was started by men new to the town, J. J. Skyrme and Robert Micklethwaite, the latter a Tory in politics.[6] Joshua Hobson, who already had a considerable newspaper career with *The Voice of the West Riding* and the Chartist *Northern Star*, was engaged to contribute anonymously, despite still being employed by the Improvement Commission.[7] He drew attention to Loch's innovation in June with an article placed on the page normally used for editorials, noting the anomalous character of Ramsden tenures without a lease. He identified all the interests affected – the tenant, whose hard-earned savings and 'possessions' were involved, the ground landlord, and the general public interested in the prosperity of the town. As money was borrowed and lent on properties, it was incumbent on all parties to refrain from weakening the *confidence* sustaining the system. It had been the custom for the last sixty years to charge half a crown on transfers of ownership or the removal of mortgagees' names from the rent roll when loans were paid off, but Loch's innovation added 2.5 per cent to the yearly rent. Hobson saw this as 'tax of no small amount'.⁸ A further article drew attention to Loch's earlier move, which ensured that new persons applying for a building site signed a document constituting them tenants-at-will. But some old tenants had also been induced to sign without receiving the explanation that it also made them liable to be *ejected* at will!⁹ Hathorn was in no doubt as to the identity of the author and both he and Loch recognised his intellectual grasp of the matter.¹⁰

The shock to confidence that Loch had anticipated and Hobson urged against had arrived. In the subsequent development of the dispute Sir John William and his allies blamed Hobson's newspaper articles for the prolonged disruption to economic activity on the estate, but, as Loch's initial report to the Trustees noted, difficulties had already been experienced and the new move would probably have given rise to some alarm even without the newspaper intervention. In any event, the consequence was a meeting of those associated with the building clubs. Hobson's former colleague, James Brook, was in the chair.¹¹ Thomas Robinson argued that the estate policy of introducing an advance in rents whenever tenant-right property was transferred would affect the willingness of the clubs to extend money in loans against the security of the constructed property. Resolutions were passed about the deleterious effect on enterprise and the building trade, so it was important to meet with Loch.¹²

After the meeting had taken place, Brook reported his satisfaction with Loch's assurances that the addition being made was merely nominal, perhaps not more than one penny in the pound.¹³ Hobson was scornful. It was the position *at present* that a rate of one penny only would be charged on rentals not exceeding one pound, but hitherto the half crown charge had been a fee rather than a rent advance. By accepting the innovation the whole legal position of old tenants-at-will was changed. They would have to accept any increase that was introduced and be liable for ejection at will without full compensation for any buildings they had erected upon the property. Despite Hobson's reaction, Loch's assurances quietened the matter and, as the former later explained, 'the thin edge of the wedge ... was allowed to take effect'.¹⁴

Loch told Ramsden that Hobson saw 'the whole scope of the point at issue' and if his view prevailed it would deprive the landlord of effectual control. While he took no further action on 'this very complicated question', it could not 'long remain in its present uncertain and ill-defined position'.¹⁵ Ramsden was then a student at Trinity College, University of Cambridge, within two years of reaching his majority. He was close to his older sister Charlotte and was particularly influenced by her Scottish husband, Edward Horsman, a father-figure who stiffened the young man's resolve.¹⁶ As Ramsden observed in a subsequent letter to Loch:

in dealing with a community like Huddersfield it will be necessary for me to take a very decided stand against all that is demanded and expected of me by the people.[17]

His 'decided stand' was to be against a large number of people in the community, especially Joshua Hobson.

From Sir John William Ramsden's majority to the Ramsden Estate (Leasing) Act, 1859

Loch, with whom Hobson was even able to claim some friendship, decided to leave the estate's service in 1853. He was replaced by the London lawyer, Thomas Wright Nelson, who recommended a complete stop to the creation of tenancies-at-will.[18] A greater estate income would achieved from leases, especially London-type 99-year leases. Action on the second point did not come before 1858, but measures were taken in 1855 to strengthen conditions for leases granted under the power gained by the Estate Act of 1844. Hobson, editor of the *Chronicle* from June, argued in November that the new agreement required for a lease would double the costs to applicants.[19] Under the old system leases were 'delivered up' when seeking a renewal, but under the new arrangement they would be 'surrendered', requiring preparation of a deed and an abstract of title. These new legal forms prepared by Nelson would triple the costs to lessees. The insurance covenant and repairs and fixtures provisions might be suitable where landlords erected buildings as in London, but at Huddersfield the lessee employed capital and ran the risk.

Further alarm was expressed about a month later. This time it was a question of whether a tenant without a lease should be required to quit. Notice had been served on Frederick Swift, occupying a property formerly owned by his father Samuel Swift, who died in 1842. Swift, an executor of his father's will and only one of its beneficiaries, was summoned to the Huddersfield County Court in October 1854. He survived the action, which the *Chronicle* then reported without comment, but it returned to the matter in December 1855, referring back to its reaction to Loch's second move of 1850. The notice to quit issued for the estate by Alexander Hathorn was now no longer 'a penny - *only* a penny' but "I do hereby DEMAND POSSESSION of the dwelling houses and tenements", which you or those in whose name you act, erected with your own money'.[20] The newspaper continued to address the subject of the Swift property and the interests involved in further issues from 1855 until 1858 while Swift ignored the notice and remained in occupation.[21] The *Examiner* also joined in, distancing itself from the 'spirit of determined mischief' that seemed to actuate its rival, but recognising the existence of a problem.[22] The best course, it argued in February 1856, was to seek a new estate act, the Thornhill Act of 1852 being held up as a good model.[23] It particularly thought in March that it would be proper and just to adopt the 999-year leases issued on the Thornhill estate.[24] The matter was eventually settled in favour of the Ramsden estate at the York Spring Assizes in March 1858 when a jury decided for Swift's dispossession.[25]

The Swift case particularly disturbed confidence in Huddersfield for reasons other than Hobson's journalism. The presiding judge remarked that Swift's attorney was wise not to raise a doubt about whether the tenancy was capable of being determined by notice to quit, since had he done so Sir John 'would have been compelled to serve notices throughout Huddersfield in order to maintain his right'. Could one successful eviction be followed by many more? In any case, Sir John announced in April that he intended to stop transferring tenant-at-will property and to grant 99-year leases in place of the 60-year leases provided for in the 1844 Estate Act. The Swift eviction and notice of the intention to cease transfers of tenant-at-will property created great public alarm, especially among members of the building trade. The builders decided to invite representatives of the building clubs or societies to join them in producing a memorial to address Sir John.[26]

Yet before their work had barely started a sensation was caused by the sale of Thomas Kilner's property by his trustees on 9 June. His freehold and leasehold properties had been successfully sold before the auctioneer startled the assembly by expressing regret that the property could not be offered for sale after all. The estate was only willing to transfer this property on a lease for 99-years, dated from when Kilner came into possession and terminable on Sir John's death. C. S. Floyd, solicitor for the Kilner trustees, pointed out that a purchaser would thereby either take the risk of holding the property for 99 years or one week, should Sir John be called so soon to heaven! The difficulties arising were fully appreciated and outlined in a letter to Sir John William Ramsden by Alexander Hathorn, who had been charged by Nelson with sending news of the estate decision to Floyd and the auctioneer, Thornton. The latter pointed out that he had dealt with 2,691 tenant-right properties since November 1844, including 1,231 since Sir John's majority of 1852. He also pointed out that the latter group included 687 that had the character of new tenancies, even though they were transfers. He felt some personal responsibility, since he had on many occasions assured parties that they would never be disturbed so long as they behaved in an honourable and proper manner. The alarm, want of confidence and fear that had now set in would not be easily allayed. He renewed his advice that only leases for a definite term of years would meet the situation, criticising the intention to offer them just for Sir John's life.[27]

The Kilner property was not the only one affected. Another was that of John Redfearn, who held a plot of land on non-lease tenure that had been transferred in 1842. The land had originally been 'waste', then partially built upon by David Shaw, its original tenant.[28] At the time of Redfearn's purchase from the Ramsden resident agent, Joseph Brook of Bridge End, there were other buildings, occupied for some years from 1832 by Read Holliday as a dwelling house and small chemical works. The ground rent was £1 a year, as at the original letting. Redfearn subsequently added his own buildings at a cost of £2,000, though the estate view was that he had only expended £950.[29] He eventually took an advance of £600 from a bank on the security of the property in order to extend his business. Unfortunately, on Swift's ejectment the lender took alarm about the safety of his security and demanded full repayment or some alternative. Redfearn's response was to transfer the security from the buildings to his stock and machinery, but was forced to sell the latter when the bank pressed for re-payment at a time of intense commercial pressure. The tenant-right property was now principally what he had to pay his debts. What Nelson offered rather than a transfer following a sale was a lease of 83 years for Sir John's life, at a rent of £21-6-0 per annum and subject to appropriate covenants.[30]

Two points should be noted here. The rent was calculated on the assumption that the value of the land at the time of Redfearn's entry on to it was £10 per annum rather than the £1 when Shaw had entered into it. Moreover, the ground landlord was entitled to recover what he would have obtained in rent if he had charged it from 1842 on the £10 valuation. Nelson's offer could be seen therefore as a retrospective re-writing or repudiation of the original contract. The estate was not prepared to waive its previous undervaluation. This raised a question of equity and, as Hobson pointed out, the value of the land had risen because of building on contiguous plots as well as on that of Redfearn's – the capital involved had been expended by tenants rather than the ground landlord. His point about the expenditure of capital here in 1858 applied to tenants as producers, but it was analogous to one made in 1838 in a *Northern Star* editorial that he almost certainly wrote or contributed to. In the latter, the 'Landlord's Title to the People's Share of the Land' referred specifically to Huddersfield, and the growth in the value of the land from the activity of the people on it as consumers, to which the owner of the soil had not contributed.[31]

The alarm arising from Swift's ejectment and the refusal of transfers brought the building trades representatives together at the Pack Horse Inn in April 1858. They were supplemented early in June by the addition of representatives of the district's money clubs. Five times before the end of the month Hobson was at the new joint committee meetings as a building club representative. He proposed nine of twelve resolutions passed, including one inviting the town's principal inhabitants to sign a requisition for a public meeting. He drafted the requisition with the lawyer, John Freeman, as well as the programme for the meeting and the resolutions to be approved.[32] Some 3,000 inhabitants signed the requisition published on 17 July.[33]

The public meeting took place almost two weeks later on 28 July, appointing eight prominent townsmen to a deputation to meet with Sir John. The deputation comprised John Freeman, George Crosland, George Armitage, Bentley Shaw, Thomas Mallinson, Jere Kaye, John Booth and John Rushforth. The last three - Kaye, Booth and Rushforth - were chairman, treasurer and secretary respectively of the Pack Horse building trade committee. John Freeman, the lawyer, had been invited to the committee to advise them and was to figure prominently in the events of the next two years. Interestingly, Thomas Mallinson was not present at the meeting that nominated him to the deputation. He was not a tenant-right property owner and lived off the Ramsden estate at Newhouse. He was a member of the textile firm, George Mallinson and Sons of Linthwaite. Similarly, Bentley Shaw, a brewer of Woodfield House in Lockwood, lived off the Ramsden estate. Both were prominent Nonconformists and Liberals. George Crosland was a woollen manufacturer of Lockwood who employed 342 people in 1851. George Armitage was a woollen merchant of the firm of Armitage Brothers, whose house was then at Edgerton Hill. Neither Crosland nor Armitage were tenant-right owners.

Sir John received the deputation to discuss its memorial at Buckden on 24 August 1858. The memorial was prepared by Freeman. Hobson received the draft and returned it with the comment that 'it was firm and just, a gentlemanly statement of the case'. It was then signed by all members of the deputation. A long discussion ensued at Buckden. Sir John was pressed to obtain new powers from Parliament to grant leases so as to remove the prevailing uncertainty. Ramsden agreed to give the memorial his full consideration. He was unsure Parliament would agree to grant powers, but would make enquiries. After some correspondence, he wrote to Freeman on 30 November that he intended to apply for new powers, though he foresaw difficulties and objections already that might at any time make it necessary to change his mind.[34]

Hobson's reaction was to commend the deputation for its service in the public interest, but he disagreed with its view that no public meeting was now necessary. He noted that uncertainty was not dispelled. At that time only the Free Wesleyan Chapel off New North Road (Mallinson's chapel) and the Independent School in Paddock were under construction, both on the old lease terms.[35] What was promised, an application for a power to grant 99-year leases of an absolute term instead of being terminable on Sir John's death, did not settle the question of the length of the lease. Sir John thought it might commence at such a date as was just with reference to the past length of the holding, so could last for a term of less than 99 years. The 'fair and equitable ground rent' to be charged would be at present value, which implied an increased value over that charged on existing leases. Hobson deplored the fact that one man had it in his power to decide the matter. There were two sides to a bargain.[36] It may have been Sir John who put a pencil lining against a cutting from the *Examiner* editorial of the following week stating that the *Chronicle*

> by its unprincipled attacks upon, and vile abuse of Sir John William Ramsden and his agents, has done more damage to the holders of the property on the Ramsden estate than all the good which its editor in his chequered career will ever counterbalance.[37]

The *Chronicle* returned to the issue twice during December pointing out that it did not say it was wrong to put an end to the tenant-right system. What concerned it was steps of confiscation taken without warning or mutuality; and while it might be that some rentals were inadequate, measured by the value which the occupation and use of the holdings had imparted to contiguous lands, surely that was no reason for refusing all transfers to those who claimed no more than the 'perpetuity' of holding that was promised.[38]

Matters moved forward in March 1859 when Nelson wrote to Freeman suggesting that the tenants appoint a legal representative and a 'committee' to consult with Lord Redesdale about the drafting of a Ramsden Estate bill. As a consequence, Freeman and the eight members of the deputation to Buckden were re-appointed with twenty three additional names, of whom some sixteen persons are identifiable as tenant-right property owners.[39] What proved to be the first version of the bill was presented to the House of Lords in June. The body appointed to the bill found it objectionable. The *Chronicle* published extracts showing that the powers sought were for the lessor to act 'if and when he thinks fit'; and to grant leases 'to persons considered in his uncontrolled judgement and entire discretion' fairly entitled to any benefit. Terms and conditions were that leases would not exceed 99 years, but the actual term could be less since it could be computed from the date of the granting of the lease, or such other time as the lessor thought fit. This could mean from first entry into the holding, which in the Redfearn case was 1842. The rent to be charged would be present value, no matter from whom or from what cause increases in value might arise. Re-valuations would take place at fourteen-year intervals during the term of the lease.

These provisions were consistent with what had been said at Buckden, but a deputation of Freeman and seven others arranged to meet with Sir John at Longley Hall. They most objected to the provision for re-valuation every fourteen years, since the 'continually recurring and unnecessary expense' entailed would make property unavailable for mortgage. Sir John conceded the difficulty of the clause, but if it were to be cancelled payments should be at a silver standard 'to maintain the land at its present value'. He expected gold to depreciate by twenty five per cent within the course of a few years. The deputation agreed that such a clause should be drafted, implicitly conceding that the real value of Sir John's income should be preserved even though there was no similar mechanism for the income of his tenants.[40]

The status of Freeman and the committee appointed to watch the bill is uncertain. Freeman was apparently alone in consultation with Nelson and Redesdale during the early stage of the presentation of the first bill. He reported that Redesdale would not allow the bill to be contested, but there is no doubt that he heard Freeman's objections. Whatever their impact, Redesdale was unhappy with the bill and despatched it to two judges for an opinion. The judges also found it objectionable, though said a properly framed bill should pass. According to the *Examiner*, the 'committee of tenant-right holders' offered to co-operate with Sir John in framing a proper bill.[41] A draft number two bill was prepared with power to grant leases for future building land for either 99 years or 1,000, though in the latter case a lump sum fine would have to be agreed and paid on the granting of the lease. The *Chronicle* thought the inclusion of this more flexible provision in the bill had been prompted by some family connection. Hobson expressed caution concerning the reliability of this information, but commented that if the situation was as represented it was a most worthy attempt to do justice'.[42] But Lord Redesdale objected to the inclusion of the two powers in the same bill. The same lease, whether 99 years or 1,000, had to be available to all tenants-at-will. The draft had to be revised. The completed second bill sought power to grant only 99-year leases. It subsequently passed the Lords, obtained formal assent of the Commons and received the Royal Assent on 16 August 1859. Sir John asked Jere Kaye to requisition the Constable for a public meeting during the passage of the bill so he would know if it was satisfactory to the tenantry.

It should be noted before passing to an account of the public meeting of 8 August 1859 that there are problems with the historical record. The account of the developments from March and the passage of the bill is derived almost entirely from newspaper sources. If Lord Redesdale did not allow the bill to be contested, he almost certainly sat without a Lords' committee and the status of those sent from Huddersfield to watch the bill is rather unclear. Information as to how many of them were in London and what contribution they made to discussions is lacking. The tenant-right owners among them do not appear to have been involved. The file at the House of Lords record office, which might have thrown light on the matter, is empty of any papers except a copy of what was finally approved.[43]

The public meeting of 8 August was chaired by William Moore, the Huddersfield constable. He opened the meeting by apologising for calling the meeting at the early hour of six o'clock, a time chosen so that the results of the meeting could be conveyed to Sir John that same evening. The consequence of this timing was that the meeting could not be attended by many of the less wealthy tenant-right property holders, even if some were present. The first speaker was John Brooke of Armitage Bridge, who admitted he was not a tenant-right holder, even though the meeting had been called for them. He had been invited to propose the motion that the meeting was 'sensible of the honourable and high-minded conduct' of Sir John in applying for powers to grant leases for a longer period than his life.[44] Freeman then read apologies for Bentley Shaw's absence, and gave an account of proceedings since the Buckden meeting of the previous year. Brooke's motion was passed unanimously. Wright Mellor then moved that while the meeting regretted that Sir John did not see it right to make it obligatory on himself to grant 99-year leases to all tenant-right holders from their entry into possession, it appreciated the concessions applied for in the bill and assurances that the powers would be exercised 'in a spirit of liberality', entitling him to the confidence of tenants and Huddersfield inhabitants. This was seconded by Mr W. Keighley, who was not a tenant-right holder, supported by Thomas Mallinson. Suffice to say, despite unanimity, the message conveyed was from prominent townsmen, rather than a representative body of tenant-right owners.[45] The view that the affair was 'stage-managed' is difficult to resist.[46]

In the wake of this apparently satisfactory reception, Sir John took residence in October at Longley Hall. Hobson 'purposely refrained from comment' at the start of the month, but published a letter from 'One Deeply Interested' of Paddock expressing anxiety about the rentals that would be charged on the leases to be granted under the act. He also sought advice on the cost of the new leases. If it was likely to amount to the sum required for leases and renewals under the old system, it would be a 'tax' of a magnitude that owners of small tenant-right properties could not afford.[47] Hobson refrained from adverse comment in November, however, and expressed pleasure at Sir John's behaviour in meeting tenants for the first time at the month's rent dinner.[48]

From the Ramsden Estate Leasing Act to Thornton v Ramsden in the Court of Chancery

The moment of calm was not to last long. In November a 'Tenant-Right Owner' wrote from Marsh to complain about the stage management of the

August 1859 meeting. He noted the bulk of the business was concluded before tenant-right owners were able to attend in substantial numbers; the twenty or thirty there early did not contribute. They received the resolutions in sullen silence and did not raise a hand in support. The author, subsequently to be revealed as John White Moore, also presented information on the cost of constructing his property, the outgoings, and an estimate of his annual return from investment in a stone building. His builders advised it would last for two hundred years, but under the lease proposed Sir John would take the second hundred for free.[49] Moore's was a cottage property. He pointed out in a second letter that this accounted for the bulk of the property held by tenant-right owners and it was not that for which leases were normally sought. Whether the old renewable leases or new 99-year ones, they would generally be sought for plots where the leaseholder expected to make money from commercial activity. Leased land contained shops, warehouses, factories and workshops, excepting plots on which a superior class of dwelling house had been constructed.[50] The implication of this point – though not fully elucidated in discussion of the relative merits of the old renewable lease, as opposed to the 99-year lease – was its irrelevance to the bulk of tenant-right property, especially that not situated in a central location.[51] As Moore noted, cottage property on adjoining estates, including that of Thornhill, obtained leases for 999 years.

The first discussion of the relative merits of the different forms of lease appears in a private letter from Josephus Jagger Roebuck to Sir John William Ramsden during the passage of the bill. He was prompted to write by the appearance of three letters anonymously published in the press early in July.[52] Roebuck wrote from Goderich Villa on New North Road, a superior location in the town and from a better class of dwelling house, but he argued the case on the basis of property held on an old renewable lease in Manchester Road. Sir John agreed that 99-year leases would be more beneficial financially to tenants than renewable ones.

Roebuck subsequently put his argument into the press and it became apparent that he was constructing a warehouse for Thomas Mallinson, whose firm had property on John William Street, a central location. The question of the relative advantage of the two forms of lease and other aspects of the new act was argued in the newspapers from December through to April 1860. Hobson discussed the matter on two occasions. He took the example of the St George's Square Britannia Buildings, arguing that compound interest employed to demonstrate the merits of the one kind of lease applied also to the other. This arcane question was less significant however than the arguments of 'Idem', later revealed as the solicitor Frederick Robert Jones, junior, in a series of seven contributions from December to April 1860. The central point of the series was that Parliament should be approached again for a power to grant 999 year leases as 'the only leases' to be available in Huddersfield.[53] The significance of Jones' entrance into the argument is that his father, also Frederick Robert Jones, was the land agent whose expertise had been employed in producing the varied covenants for Thornhill leases in the Edgerton, Lindley and Hillhouse areas.

Discussion turned to action on 11 April 1860 when a group of tenant-right owners met at the Nag's Head Inn at Paddock. They appointed a preliminary committee to set up a defence association,[54] and by mid-May eight local 'protection committees' had been formed for separate districts in which tenant-right property was situated. A general committee met every Tuesday evening at the White Hart Inn with the object of arranging a meeting on 5 June to consider a memorial for presentation to Sir John.[55] Meanwhile, on the Ramsden Estate, Hathorn was appointed with John Stewart of Liverpool to determine the present value of tenant-right property for the fixing of rents under the new style leases. Tenants wanting a 99-year lease were to apply before 13 August 1860. Applications approved would be dated from the passing of the Act and the revised rents applied at the November rent audit.

The preparatory work of April constituting a tenant-right defence association culminated in the foundation meeting at the Philosophical Hall on 5 June. At least 2,000 were estimated in attendance, including female tenant-right owners in the orchestra part of the hall who were reported as equally earnest as the men in approval of criticism of the estate's policy. A circular had been issued previously by Thomas Mallinson, Bentley Shaw and John Freeman, with the evident purpose of frustrating the meeting, but this only increased attendance.

Frederick Robert Jones, junior, chair of the preparatory committee, presided on the motion of Benjamin Halstead, flanked on the platform by the joint secretaries, Joshua Hobson and Thomas Robinson.[56] John Jebson, president of the Commercial Building Society at the Green Dragon, moved dissatisfaction with the terms of the 1859 Act. He criticised the employment of the valuer, John Stewart, who was to come in from Liverpool as stranger to the Huddersfield tenant-right property and, he suspected, set rents higher than under the old leases. Joseph Thornton of Paddock, whose tenancy was soon to feature prominently in the dispute, briefly seconded Jebson. Benjamin Halstead, seconded by William Smith, moved that a liberal policy would best suit the interests of Sir John and his successors as well as the permanent welfare of the tenants on the estate. The speech contrasted the halted progress on the Ramsden estate with that on its neighbours'.

Hobson delivered the main speech, proposing the memorial to Sir John in favour of 999-year leases, rather than 60 years or 99 years. He was not a tenant-right holder, but his grandfathers and his father had erected buildings on that tenure and he had long taken an interest in the question. He said he had written to the *Leeds Times* 'more than twenty years ago' in support of tenant-right owners on the Moldgreen estate of Sir John Lister Lister Kaye.[57] His friendship with Loch, who had come twice from London to aid him personally in 'matters of considerable moment', had not prevented him from doing his public duty when action was first taken on the tenant- right tenure. The tenant-right owners on the Thornhill estate were originally in a worse position than those with Ramsden, but when leasing powers were obtained there in 1852 the tenants received an 'entitlement' which contrasted with Ramsden's 'sole will and pleasure'. He argued that the valuations in progress would increase Ramsden's aggregate rental income from the £4,000 stated in the 1859 Act to £10,000 or £12,000 per annum. At the rental level of £12,000 he would realise £300,000 on sale of the estate, but after 99 years the whole property would be swept into his lap. The memorial before them should be signed, but it might be necessary for the tenant-right owners to make their own direct appeal to Parliament or to make application to the Court of Chancery.

The motion was seconded by Thomas H. Broadbent, but before it was put to the meeting Hobson delivered apologies from Jabez Brook, who perhaps held the largest amount of tenant-right property. The intervention was used to reassure those who thought their signature on papers at Longley Hall excluded them from an equitable remedy. This was to become a question at issue in Joseph Thornton's case, but here Hobson argued that though the estate's associates said tenants who signed had no course other than to do what was required of them, they were not in that position. They had signed, but Sir John had not. Perhaps there was no agreement in such a transaction? And, Hobson asked, was any solicitor called in to advise the tenant? The intention was clearly to stiffen resistance. The TRDA was duly constituted with instructions to consider and resort to further action should the initial 'moral means' prove unsuccessful. A deputation comprising Frederick Robert Jones, junior, the joint secretaries Hobson and Robinson, with Joseph Thornton, Benjamin Halstead, Jabez Brook, William Smith and John Broughton, was appointed for a meeting with Sir John.[58]

The collection of signatures for the memorial continued into July and Sir John agreed to a meeting at his London residence, 6 Upper Brook Street. The letter of thanks requested a meeting in Yorkshire for the convenience of the working men among the deputation,[59] but London it had to be, and eight committee members met with Sir John in Mayfair on 6 August.[60] The deputation reported back to the TRDA members in Huddersfield on 13 August.[61]

The deputation took a professional short hand writer with them to meet Sir John. It was his account of the proceedings that Hobson presented to the assembled tenant-right owners. When the deputation arrived, Sir John offered to provide lunch after the business had been concluded, but this was respectfully declined. Richard Hird read the memorial. Sir John then said he would read his answer and then the interview must be concluded. A painful silence was recorded. Then Sir John said, 'I shall read it'. Hobson intervened: perhaps Sir John would listen to what the deputation members had to say before reading the answer? Afterwards, the proceedings would have to take their chance: the deputation would probably wish to make some answer or present some counter proposition. Sir John's response was that he must lay it down as a rule that when he had read the answer, he would have nothing to add or detract.

Hobson pointed out that Sir John was taking a rather unusual course and if it was followed the deputation would afterwards have to take its own. Some 1,700 tenants were directly interested in the issue, if one excluded the money and building clubs but took multiple holdings into account; and of these, 1,232 had signed the memorial. A majority of those whose names were not attached to the memorial had expressed strong sympathy with the movement; and each tenant represented a family, which at an average size of five, amounted to 8,500 directly interested in a settlement. He continued with some history of the non-lease tenures, the granting of leases under the 1844 Act to tenant-right owners to facilitate sales of property required for the railway, and the effect on one tenant-right owner being given notice to quit: he took down his building and re-erected it on another estate!

When Sir John was reading his reply to the memorial, his sister, Charlotte Horsman, appeared to say 'it was fully time' Sir John 'was down at the House'. Sir John stood up as if to go, but Hobson proposed that the issue in debate should be put to arbitration, as suggested by the *Law Times*, and nominated Lord St Leonards. A court of arbitration should be held in Huddersfield so as to facilitate the taking of evidence. Would it be possible to have an interview tomorrow to hear the answer to this proposal? The answer was negative and the meeting concluded in some asperity.

It was clear to the TRDA meeting hearing this report that the deputation's arguments had not made any impression on Sir John, as Thomas Haigh, a hosier of King Street, noted in moving a vote of thanks. His conclusion was that the only course was to bring Sir John into a Court of Equity, there to be floored to the ground! Legal opinion was read out to the effect that the tenants were not 'bound' by the provisions of the 1859 Act; they should avoid unnecessary litigation but might try a test case. A resolution was passed unanimously that the tenants would stay as they were and not take leases under the 1859 Act.

A week after this report in the *Chronicle* appeared, its competitor newspaper, the *Examiner*, commented that the ground landlord had been 'held up as a gigantic swindler', but no one was likely to be won over by means 'whose natural tendency is to alienate and sour'. The Buckden meeting had for the most part produced a fair and honourable settlement of differences: all shades of political opinion and the intelligence, enterprise and interests of Huddersfield had been represented in the deputation. The paper included a letter from Thomas Mallinson on the relative value of leases but concluded with comment on the fate of the 1,000-year lease clause. He admitted such a clause was in the bill but claimed Sir John had never intended it for tenant-right property, or only exceptional cases such as the provision of land for public institutions. He did not think he would get it approved.[62]

Thomas Mallinson wrote to Sir John in July 1859, suggesting 'we make use of our local paper with advantage'.[63] He had already had one interview with Joseph Woodhead, editor of the *Examiner*. Sir John had not responded immediately, but following the meeting with the TRDA deputation at Upper Brook Street and clearly upset by the campaign in the *Chronicle*, he invited Mallinson to meet him at Byram on 14 September 1860 to discuss 'the newspaper press at Huddersfield'. At their meeting Mallinson told Sir John about a debt Woodhead owed to Frederick Robert Jones, junior, who was pressing for payment. A meeting of Mallinson, Wright Mellor and Woodhead had elicited the information that Jones and other debts could be paid off with a loan of £500. This would restore Woodhead's position and enable him to enlarge the paper's size without an increase in price.[64] Woodhead subsequently signed an agreement that in return for 'pecuniary aid' channelled through Mallinson and Mellor his paper would 'adequately represent the political opinions of themselves and other persons of respectability', now recognised as leaders of the Liberal party in Huddersfield. It would also promote cordiality and kindness of feeling between Sir John and his tenants to bring about a higher social tone than that hitherto prevailing. Sir John authorised his bankers to draw a draft on Mallinson for £400 so that the business could be 'completed without a day's delay'.

Dispute about the relative merits of the clauses in the new model lease, particularly that requiring payment in silver in the event of a depreciation in the relative price of gold, continued into 1861. Criticism of provisions in the 'new model' caused Sir John to abandon it in March in favour of a new version modelled on that employed by Lord Derby in Liverpool. Wright Mellor argued that the lease was apparently free of objections against the previous version and expressed hope that Sir John had at last solved the difficulty. Even so, the silver clause had not been removed.[65]

26. Wright Mellor (1817–93), leading Congregationalist, Mayor of Huddersfield in 1871–3, 1883–4 and 1886–7.
Huddersfield Art Gallery

The new move was inspired by Sir John's consultations with John Stewart, chairman of the Liverpool Corporation finance committee, which had started in late December 1859.[66] The TRDA response to the new move was to send a deputation of Hobson and James Taylor to meet with Stewart. This gave rise to a public dispute about Lord Derby's 75-year leases in Liverpool. It was maintained on one side that Sir John's intention to grant 99-year terminable leases was more generous to lessees than Lord Derby's; on the other side that they were not comparable since the leases of the latter were conversions of previous leases. These contained unsatisfactory covenants which the new ones improved. Lease holders in Liverpool, unlike tenant-right holders or old-style leaseholders in Huddersfield, had not entered on land with assurances of being undisturbed in possession or of perpetual renewal. It was argued that independent valuation in Liverpool at present value, while increasing Lord Derby's rent roll, provided fair terms for lessees, since rents would be lower for depreciated property.[67]

The merit of the argument on both sides of this public debate is unclear, but Ramsden's patience with the tenant-right agitation came to an end in November. Seven notices to quit were served on the leaders of the TRDA. Sir John wrote some time later that this was 'to terminate an uncertainty which was more prejudicial to the tenants than myself', but at the time there was no end to general uncertainty in the district. The notices to quit did not bring about greater confidence and an increase in construction investment on the Ramsden estates in comparison to its neighbours. The relative uncertainty Sir John had in mind undoubtedly related to his legal position as compared to that of the tenants-at-will, but both sides to the dispute had obtained legal opinion and the issue had not been fully determined in a court. The immediate effect of the notices to quit was to stimulate an action in the Court of Chancery.

Seven bills were filed in Chancery but it was decided to proceed with that entered concerning Joseph Thornton of Paddock. The case entered Vice Chancellor Stuart's court in February 1862, but there was a delay of two years, largely at the behest of Ramsden, to allow for the preparation of a large volume of affidavits, before the hearing commenced on 10 February 1864.[68] The court proceedings lasted for eleven days. Judgement was delivered on 25 May 1864.

The facts in *Thornton v Ramsden*, while distinct in detail from the cases of Swift, Redfearn and Kilner, which had given rise to the collapse of the building trade and insecurity on the Ramsden estate, referred to the same system of letting. Joseph Thornton, aged twenty five, a partner in a cloth-dressing firm, decided to build 'a gentleman's residence' on high ground at Paddock. He applied to the resident Ramsden agent, Joseph Brook, for a plot adjacent to a quarry. This was approved, the land staked out and the ground rent fixed at £4 per annum. Thornton spent around £1,850 building 'Edge House', an access road and surrounding gardens. Brook and Thornton's father, John Thornton, visited the site shortly before completion in 1839, and discussion took place about the granting of a lease. Brook stated that it would be folly to take a lease as Thornton would be equally safe without. The rent would be higher if he took one and it would be available, if ever wanted. Thornton entered the property on completion, was enrolled as a tenant at Longley Hall and remained in possession, duly paying the agreed rent. He applied for a second piece of land in 1845, so as to build a mistal and other outbuildings. Hathorn agreed, but stated the plot was held 'at will'. As Thornton required funds in 1858, he borrowed from the Commercial Money Club, visiting Longley Hall with its president, Lee Dyson, to enter the mortgagee as a joint tenant. Both signed forms saying the property was 'tenant-at-will', although neither read the forms and their significance was not explained.

Vice Chancellor Stuart delivered judgment in May 1864, noting that Chancery had gone very far in many cases to protect the possession of a tenant who expended money on land in good faith and reasonable confidence that his possession would not be disturbed. Chancery would not presume that a landlord had a right to take the immediate possession and enjoyment of a building, without any compensation, as soon as the tenant had expended his money on it. He thought that in this case there was sufficient evidence of an understanding or agreement that the possession of the tenant should not be disturbed. In his view, the language of 'tenant-at-will' was merely used to distinguish those tenants who had a lease from those who did not. He did not consider it a case of specific performance, whereby a specific party would be required to act to fulfil a contract; nor had compensation been argued. As both parties seemed to think the grant of a lease under the terms of the 1844 Act would be the most appropriate relief if he found for the plaintiff, that was the decree. He found for the plaintiff with costs, with the matter to be settled between the parties in chambers.

The telegram summarising the decree sent by Mr Clarke, the London solicitor employed on behalf of Thornton, to Frederick Robert Jones, junior, chair of the Defence Association, 'was read with the greatest avidity' when printed and circulated in the town. In the evening a band of musicians voluntarily paraded the streets; but the tenant-right owners as a body received the good news with discretion and thankfulness, avoiding demonstration or exultation.[69] Nelson sent a copy of the judgment to Sir John with the comment that he thought it would not 'accord with the views of the tenants whose interests were intended to be served by the late agitation'.[70]

From Chancery to the House of Lords and the Ramsden Estate Act 1867

Nelson's comment was not without point, for while Ramsden had to go into chambers to seek agreement with the plaintiff's representatives on implementing the court's decree, discussions about the terms of the lease spread into February 1865. Just as final agreement was apparently being reached, Sir John decided to appeal to the House of Lords.

Thomas Mallinson, who had been Sir John's principal ally at Huddersfield from July 1858 and his agent in assisting Woodhead at the *Examiner* in 1860, had died in April 1863. Sir John had been sorry to hear of his ill health in the previous year when writing to Wright Mellor about the insertion in the *Examiner* of a letter from resident agent John Noble to Wright Gledhill.[71] Gledhill had written on behalf of his mother, Salome, re-applying for a 99-year lease for a tenant-right holding with two cottages and a mistal at Berry Brow. The letter from Noble that Sir John wanted published expressed surprise and grief that so many of his tenants who had expressed gratitude for the Act of 1859 and originally applied for leases under it had been induced to withdraw their applications and make themselves part of an agitation to set aside their own Act. He dreaded more on their account than his own the consequence of them compelling him in self-defence to enforce his rights against them, but he was willing to make allowance for the circumstances under which they had been misled and would treat the application as though it had never been withdrawn. This was on condition it would be made public that Gledhill had openly separated from contesting Sir John's rights.[72]

The correspondence between Gledhill and Noble duly appeared in the *Examiner* which commented that 'the noted failure of many other schemes propounded by Mr Hobson does not augur well for the success of the tenant-right agitation'. It believed Gledhill to be representative of a large class of tenants who were beginning to understand the danger of not taking 99-year leases and clearly agreed with the estate that it had no end in view but the welfare of the tenants.[73] The *Chronicle* reprinted the correspondence a week later, but here Frederick Robert Jones commented that while unsure whether the humility of Salome and Wright Gledhill was sincere, he felt humiliated to see such a specimen of ignominious surrender published and even gloated over. He thought the publication was a breach of faith and had been told that Salome so considered it. Moreover, the Gledhill letter was 'the very echo and counterpart' of two other letters addressed to Noble. Jones's comment was supplemented by two letters from Frederick Schwann, who was away from Huddersfield at North Houghton, near Stockbridge in Hampshire. His first letter expressed support on the tenant-right question, believing in the 'intrinsic justice' of their case. His second letter enclosed £50, remarking that he did not pretend to understand the subtleties of the law that might give the landlord 'the right of demanding his pound of flesh', but he hoped that he would 'meet with no better success than Shylock in a similar case'.[74]

The publicity about the Gledhill re-application for a 99-year lease was part of an attempt to counter the TRDA success in persuading tenant-right owners to not submit or withdraw applications for 99-year leases. It was a detail in the broader measure whereby the estate drew up a draft 99-year lease for every tenant-right holder and sent it to them for perusal and possible signature. It was to be returned at the tenants' convenience but the accompanying letter from Longley Hall assumed they would want a longer rather than a shorter lease. The draft therefore gave recipients the option of accepting or rejecting the silver clause for payment of rent. If they accepted, Sir John would grant a 99-year lease dated from 29 September 1859, but if they struck out the clause it would be 99 years from the date of the commencement of their original tenancy. Frederick Robert Jones claimed that the purpose of this move was to provide evidence 'hereafter' that Sir John had done everything in his power to act justly towards his tenancy. The option should have nothing to do with the term and what it proved was 'the despotic disposition of Sir John in the treatment of his tenantry'.[75]

This activity by the estate and in the press was taking place shortly after Thornton's bill had been filed in Chancery. The co-operation of Woodhead at the *Examiner*, secured in 1860, had been helpful, but as the suit finally entered into hearings at Chancery in February 1864 Sir John decided on further action. He invited Wright Mellor to meet him at Byram to discuss the *Chronicle*.[76] Mellor subsequently met with Woodhead, who was willing to co-operate so long as it involved no additional expense. Mellor's advice was that contributions appear as letters to the editor.[77] Sir John made plain that his primary concern was to have 'the rights' of the Chancery suit fairly stated. Could Mellor please talk to Woodhead again. Sir John was willing 'to help him liberally' and would rather have the thing done well than not at all.[78] The action did not stop there. He was in contact with M. L. Meason about a London correspondent and, most importantly, with William Henry Wills, sub-editor to Charles Dickens on *All the Year Round*.[79] Woodhead went down to London to see Sir John, and Wills was sent to Huddersfield.[80] Wright Mellor was introduced to Wills and they met together with Sir John at Upper Brook Street on Wills' return from Huddersfield.[81] One consequence was the delivery of £100 to Woodhead as the first instalment of a loan.[82]

This activity also included the preparation of a letter for publication in the *Leeds Mercury* as soon as the decree was delivered in Chancery. This was a justification of his position, which may be summarised as follows. The population of Huddersfield was upwards of 30,000 people and the whole town was built on his land. The welfare of such a community was a public concern and discharge of his duties in relation to the property, from the many interests which it might affect, became as much a trust as a private right. He outlined the state of affairs until he came of age in 1852. In 1853, he determined, under legal advice, to create no more holdings at will and only to allow building on lease. The notice to Frederick Swift to quit properties which he occupied as executor of his father Samuel Swift's will was issued because his agents had received complaints from other beneficiaries that their shares were being withheld. His agents had attempted to get an amicable arrangement among the parties, but as they had failed there was no alternative but to issue the notice to quit. Swift's solicitor was informed that it was because of 'his refusal to do justice to the surviving members of his family in the management of the several premises'. When Swift was successfully ejected, the property was divided amongst the family for whose benefit the suit had been instituted. Sir John argued that he had no personal interest in the matter, though the law had been pursued at his expense. The effect of the trial in Huddersfield, however, was very serious. The *Chronicle* had sounded the alarm and its campaign had led to the application for the 1859 Act, which he believed he had obtained on behalf of the tenants and for their benefit, reciting events from the Buckden meeting, involvement in the passage of the Bill and the town's subsequent initial reception of the Act. But the unavoidable delay before conversion to leaseholds could take place, since three to four thousand holdings had to be valued and that took time, allowed agitation to begin. It had had a considerable success in that of 1,482 applications for leases, only 735 were subsequently withdrawn. Sir John believed that he had not been at issue with the general body of tenants in this contest, only that section which repudiated the Act which he had secured at their request. He argued that the benefit he had secured for them was protection from his creditors should he or his successors fall into debt or difficulties. As to Thornton, who had been offered a lease, it was only when he refused to accept or acknowledge himself a tenant-at-will that counsel advised notice of ejectment to try the question. As the judgement in Chancery left the exact terms of a lease to be settled in chambers it was not possible to say until that was done whether Thornton's position would be more favourable to him than if he had accepted that offered under the 1859 Act.[83]

Sir John's letter was followed the next day by a rebuttal from Frederick Robert Jones, junior. He disputed Sir John's account of the circumstances of Swift's eviction, claiming that the property was first sold by public auction and when the parties saw Alexander Hathorn to effect the transfer and complete the purchase, Swift, on the advice of his solicitor, proposed that the proceeds should be put into the hands of Hathorn to distribute in accordance with Samuel Swift's will. How then could Swift's ejectment arise because of Frederick's refusal to do justice? As to the Redfearn case, Sir John could have granted a renewable lease under the 1844 Act. His unwillingness to do so reduced Redfearn 'to absolute ruin and poverty, often wanting even the barest necessaries of life'. Those involved with Sir John in 1858 and the passage of the Act in 1859 were never representative of the body of tenant-right holders. The Act itself had been summed up as the lessor may, if and when he pleases, in his uncontrolled judgement and entire discretion, grant leases for 99 years, or any lesser term, on such rents, covenants and other terms, as he thinks fit. Constant iteration of this created a belief among tenants that they were completely at the mercy of the ground landlord so they rushed to make application for leases under the Act. Legal advice was obtained from men eminent at the equity bar, who advised that tenants did possess rights and they were not at the mercy of one man, as they had been led to believe. The estate resorted to a tactic of refusing the rents of tenant-right owners when tendered in the usual way at the next rent audit, but when dissatisfaction was expressed, they were told their application for a 99-year lease could be withdrawn and the rent paid as previously. The offer was acted upon and 735 withdrawals, as Sir John had stated, took place. Sir John's claim that he was not at issue with 'the general body' of his tenants, only those who 'repudiate the act which he procured at their request', was not borne out by the fact that only 556 leases had been granted on some 3,000 holdings. Jones concluded with comments on the Thornton case. He argued that while Sir John denied any attempt to dispossess any of his tenants of the vast property constructed on his land, he did commence an action which could have no result other than dispossession, unless the Court of Chancery had interfered to restrain such intention.[84]

This correspondence was followed by an editorial in *The Times* criticising Ramsden for attempting to force 99-year leases on tenants on pain of eviction, even if they offered more suitable security than the tenant-right system.[85] A further exchange of often acrimonious letters between Thomas Pearson Crosland, one of the proprietors of the *Chronicle*, and Sir John appeared in the press three days later.[86] Thereafter the discussions about a lease for Thornton dragged on in chambers until Jones informed tenant-right holders that preliminary proceedings for an appeal to the House of Lords against the Chancery decree were underway.[87] The appeal was heard during June and July 1865, before the Lord Chancellor, Lord Westbury, and Lords Cranworth, Wensleydale and Kingsdown. Thornton was stated as a respondent, but he had been declared bankrupt on 19 May 1864, which placed Lee Dyson, mortgagee for the property, effectively into that position. Shortly after the hearing ended Westbury resigned as Lord Chancellor and was replaced by Cranworth, who delivered judgement on 11 May 1866.

A majority of the judges allowed Ramsden's appeal. The Lord Chancellor stated that to succeed Thornton had to prove both that he believed he had an absolute right to a lease and that Sir John knew of that mistaken belief. In his view Thornton had failed to establish with respect to his transactions in 1837 and 1845 that he believed he had an absolute right beyond that of tenant from year-to-year, or that Sir John knew Thornton had the belief he failed to prove. As to evidence that persons taking land without lease would never be disturbed, it meant only that they could rely on the honour of the Ramsden family and that excluded jurisdiction of the court of equity; also, that Ramsden would not disturb their possession, rather than that he could not. The precaution had been taken in 1845 to require signature of an application document on which 'tenant-at-will' was printed in large letters. The expression was used in its proper legal sense and the tenants must be taken to have understood it in this sense. Lord Kingsdown dissented from

Cranworth and Wensleydale, taking the view that on entering possession there was only one class of tenant rather than two, but some subsequently took up leases. More emphasis had been placed on the words 'tenant-at-will' than they deserved since it had a technical meaning in Huddersfield which was equivalent to copyhold, or holding at the will of the lord and according to the custom of the manor. What the majority judgement illustrated was the success of a legal reform movement strongly influenced by liberal political economy, as opposed to the continuance of local land customs and Chancery protection of tenant-right holders. Cranworth would not pass an opinion on whether the tenants had a right to look for more or less from the Ramsden family than what they were prepared to grant, but he thought it indispensable that an end be put to the system that had prevailed.

As a consequence of the House of Lords decision, more tenants came forward requesting 99-year leases under the 1859 Act. But Ramsden, unlike Nelson, did not think matters could be settled by the granting of these leases. Sir John had discussed an intention to dispense with the services of Nelson with Abel Smith in July 1865. He had been persuaded to retain him until delivery of the judgement from the House of Lords appeal, but by autumn 1866 he had decided on a new course. It was, rather than 'a mere question of granting leases' under existing powers, 'a larger question of bitter memories left behind unsuccessful litigation unless other means were taken to efface it'. He was therefore bringing the estate office and his resident agent into town to be more accessible to the tenants, building a new house at Longley so he could be there part of the year, and applying for a new Act of Parliament to provide for larger powers.[88] These larger powers were 999-year leases.

The final meeting organised by the TRDA of tenant-right owners and those holding 99-year leases took place soon after Ramsden's new Bill was introduced in Parliament. Jones remarked that Sir John had offered an 'olive branch of peace', Hobson outlined the provisions of the Bill, and a resolution was passed congratulating Sir John on 'having determined to offer so important and valuable a boon' to his tenantry.[89] The Ramsden Estate Act 1867 was passed on 25 July 1867.

Endnotes

1   For a detailed account of the relative impact of Ramsden family members on the early growth of Huddersfield see Whomsley (1984), pp. 27-56.
2   DD/RA/4/1, For further details, see chapter 2, pp. 56-7.
3   The term 'tenant-at-will' is used interchangeably with 'tenant right'. The terms were contested and opinion differed on the legal position of Ramsden and his non-lease tenants prior to the House of Lords judgement of 1866 in *Ramsden v. Dyson*. Characters

favourable to the Ramsden Estate referred to 'tenants-at-will' while tenants in opposition to the estate preferred 'tenant-right' owner or holder. The expression 'non-lease tenants' was not in use historically, but is an appropriately neutral term of art.

4 The Ramsden Estate Trustee, Lord Zetland, informed Isabella Ramsden on 21 June 1844, after meeting James Loch, that his son George was willing to take on an appointment at a salary of £600 a year. Zetland recommended appointment and urged it strongly again on 11 July: Sheffield City Archives, Wentworth Woodhouse Muniments, G56.
5 Loch to Isabella Ramsden, 4 May 1846 and Loch to JWR, 19 June 1850, cited in Whomsley (1987), p. 16.
6 Skyrme (1825-1858) was originally from Worcestershire; Micklethwaite (1819-1888) from Soyland, near Ripponden. There is no clear evidence of Skyrme's politics but Micklethwaite may have been associated with support for the liberation of Richard Oastler from his debt imprisonment in 1843 and voted for Conservative candidates in the West Riding election of 1868. They were joint proprietors of the paper until the dissolution of their partnership on 31 May 1852. Skyrme continued to be associated with the paper until 4 June 1855.
7 See Halstead (1991), pp. 22-57, and (2018), pp. 83-122.
8 *HC*, 15 June 1850, p. 4.
9 *HC*, 22 June 1850, p. 4.
10 DD/RE/C/71, Hathorn to Loch, 13 April 1850.
11 For Brook and Hobson as colleagues, see Halstead (2012), pp. 91-144.
12 *HC*, 6 July 1850.
13 *HC*, 20 July 1850.
14 *HC*, 22 December 1855.
15 Loch to JWR, 20 July 1850, cited in Whomsley (1987), p. 17.
16 Meriel Buxton (2017), pp. 44-5.
17 JWR to Loch, 21 October 1851, cited in Whomsley (1987), p. 8. The letter is at the Buckinghamshire Record Office.
18 Thomas Wright Nelson (1802-1883), originally from Nottingham, was practising as a solicitor in London. In addition to the Huddersfield appointment, he was agent for Sir John William during his parliamentary election campaign at Taunton in 1853 – *Bristol Mercury*, 25 June 1853.
19 *HC*, 17 November 1855. Hobson became editor for the proprietors, Thomas Pearson Crosland and Cookson Stephenson Floyd, in June when Skyrme left the partnership.
20 'The Thin and the Thick End of the Wedge into the Tenant Right Interest on the Ramsden Estate', *HC*, 22 December 1855.
21 'The Tenant Right Interest on the Ramsden Estate. The Baseless "protectorate"', *HC*, 19 January 1856; 'The Baseless "Protectorate" II', *HC*, 26 January 1856; 'Tenant Right Confiscation on the Ramsden Estate', *HC*, 12 June 1858. While it is customary to speak of people buying land or property, the transactions are in 'interests' or 'proprietary rights', which may be quite complicated. See Ralph Turvey (1957), pp. 2-5.
22 The *Huddersfield Examiner,* which was associated with Nonconformist Liberals and later became the organ of the estate in the newspaper battle during the tenure dispute, was founded shortly after the *Chronicle* in 1851 as the *Huddersfield and Holmfirth Examiner.*
23 'The Lease Question: Fred Swifts' Case', *HHE*, 2 February 1856. Also see *HHE*, 5 January 1856; 'The Lease Question', *HHE*, 12 January 1856; 'The Lease Question. The Estate Acts and the Tenant Right Holders', *HHE*, 26 January 1856; 'The Lease Question. Plan Suggested for the Settlement of the Tenant Right and Leasehold

Difficulties on the Estate of Sir John William Ramsden Bart.', *HHE*, 23 February 1856; 'The Lease Question. Prospective Advantage to the Lessor – the Lessees – and the Public – By the Adoption of Our Suggested Plan of Leasing', *HHE*, 1 March 1856; 'Sir John William Ramsden and the Tenant Right Question', *HHE*, 12 June 1858. Copies are available online only to the end of 1856. The copy cited for 1858 can be found in the Ramsden Estate Cuttings Book No. 1, Extracts 1858–65, which is held un-catalogued at WYASK.

24   *HHE*, 1 March 1856.
25   *HC*, 28 October 1854 and *York Herald*, 13 March 1858.
26   'Management of the Ramsden Property', *HC*, 8 May 1858.
27   DD/RA/C/9/2, Hathorn to JWR, 11 June 1858.
28   The history of the Redfearn tenant-right holding in this paragraph is from Hobson's account in *HC*, 24 December 1858, except where otherwise noted. A statement in the article that Redfearn paid a total ground rent of £333 does not seem credible and has been omitted.
29   According to the Estate's advice Redfearn had expended only £950 on improvements, excluding repairs – DD/RA/28/2, 'Ex parte Sir John William Ramsden. Case and Opinion of Mr Morgan, 17 May 1858'.
30   DD/RA/C/9/5, Nelson to R.W. Clough, 19 May 1858. The offer differs from the 75-year term recommended in 'Case and Opinion of Mr Morgan' – DD/RA/28/2.
31   See Halstead (2018), pp. 97-8 and pp. 105-6 for the possibility of authorship.
32   For Hobson's role, see Whomsley (1987), pp. 18-19, citing 'Minutes of committee meeting of delegates from building and money clubs', Appendix 1 in two volumes of *Ramsden v. Thornton. Appeal by Sir John William Ramsden to the House of Lords against the decision in the Court of Chancery in favour of Joseph Thornton, a tenant-right owner, 1866*.
33   *HC*, 17 July 1858.
34   The full text of the Memorial, a report of the Buckden discussion and the subsequent correspondence with Freeman was published in *HC*, 11 December 1858.
35   See chapter 4, p.123.
36   *HC*, 11 December 1858.
37   *HHE*, 18 December 1858.
38   'The Ramsden Estate. The Equitable Right of Tenant Right Owners to Leases on the Old Terms', *HC*, 18 December 1858; 'The Magnitude of the Huddersfield Tenant Right Interest', *HC*, 24 December 1858.
39   DD/RA/C/9/5, Noble to JWR, 15 April 1864.
40   *HHE*, 25 June 1859.
41   *HHE*, 2 July 1859. The source for *HHE* after 1856 to 1860 is the Ramsden Estate Cuttings Book No. 1 at WYASK.
42   *HC*, 9 July 1850.
43   I was involved in the Local and Personal Acts Bill procedure as an official at the Home Office in 1963-4. In those days we met with the equivalent of Redesdale, Lord Merthyr, who was referred to as the Lord Chairman. He sat and decided alone on bills that were uncontested. A Lords committee was only formed for contested bills. The House of Lords Record Office clerk was as surprised as myself when we found that the file only contained a copy of the final bill.
44   John Brooke (1794–1878), was a Justice of the Peace and Deputy Lieutenant of the West Riding in 1861.
45   *HC*, 13 August 1859.
46   The view of Whomsley (1987), p. 19.
47   *HC*, 1 October 1859.

48 *HC*, 5 November 1859; *HC*, 12 November 1859.
49 *HC*, 26 November 1859.
50 *HC*, 17 December 1859.
51 The supply of urban central land is essentially fixed, but the demand for it was likely to be related to high-value uses. Cf. Richardson (1971), p. 45.
52 As a 'Tenant Right Owner and (what involves a greater difficulty) Mortgagee of Tenant Right', *HC*, 25 June 1859; and as 'Idem', *HC*, 2 and 9 July 1895. Roebuck correctly identified the author as the solicitor Robert Frederick Jones, junior.
53 *HC*, 14 January 1860.
54 *HC*, 24 March 1860; 14 April 1860.
55 *HC*, 19 May 1860.
56 DD/RA/C/9/5, Noble to JWR, 15 April 1864. Thomas Robinson (1799-1861+), plasterer, rather than the Huddersfield solicitor of the same name. He had also been a member of the committee sent to watch the bill.
57 My search for appropriate correspondence in the *Leeds Times* has been unsuccessful so there is some doubt about the accuracy of Hobson's recollection on this point.
58 *HC*, 9 June 1860.
59 *HC*, 21 July 1860; *HC*, 28 July 1860 and 4 August 1860.
60 *HC*, 11 August 1860.
61 *HC*, 18 August 1860.
62 *HHE,* 22 September 1860.
63 DD/RA/C/19/9, T. Mallinson to JWR, 23 July 1859.
64 DD/RA/C/19/9, JWR to Mallinson, 15 September 1860.
65 *HE*, 16 March 1861, Ramsden Estate Cuttings Book No. 2 1860–7.
66 DD/RA/C/28/3, Stewart to JWR, 21 December 1859.
67 *HC*, 4 May 1861.
68 For the Court of Chancery within the legal system see Lobban (2004), pp. 389–427 and 565–99.
69 *HC*, 28 May 1864.
70 DD/RA/C//9/5, Nelson to JWR, 25 May 1864.
71 DD/RA/C/37/3, JWR to Wright Mellor, 21 May 1862.
72 DD/RA/C/37/3, Noble to Wright Gledhill, 20 May 1862.
73 *HE*, 24 May 1862.
74 *HC*, 31 May 1862.
75 *HC*, 24 May 1862.
76 DD/RA/C/9/5, Mellor to JWR, 27 February 1864, accepting the invitation.
77 DD/RA/C/9/5, Mellor to JWR, 15 March 1864.
78 DD/RA/C/9/5, JWR to Mellor, 15 April 1864.
79 DD/RA/C/9/5, Wills to JWR, 12 April 1864; Meason to JWR, 27 April 1864.
80 DD/RA/C/9/5, JWR to Mellor, 20 April 1864; JWR to Mellor, 7 May 1864.
81 DD/RA/C/9/5, 11 May 1864.
82 DD/RA/C/9/5, JWR to Mellor, 12 May 1864; Mellor to JWR, 16 May 1864.
83 *LM*, 30 May 1864.
84 *LM*, 31 May 1864.
85 *The Times*, 1 June 1864.
86 *LM*, 4 June 1864.
87 *HC*, 11 March 1865.
88 DD/RA/C/33/2, JWR to Abel Smith, 15 November 1866; JWR to Abel Smith, 17 December 1866.
89 *HC*, 18 May 1867.

CHAPTER FOUR

Religion and Philanthropy

EDWARD ROYLE

Introduction

THE ORIGINS OF THE Ramsden family fortunes date back to the Reformation and the opportunities it presented to astute landholders and manufacturers to extend their economic and social standing through the purchase of former monastic properties from the Crown. The rectory of Huddersfield had belonged to the Priory of St Oswald at Nostell from the early twelfth century until the latter was suppressed 1539. William Ramsden bought this in 1546, giving him and his heirs the right as lay rectors to the great tithes and the advowson – that is, the right to appoint a vicar to the living – which the family retained until 1920. After William's death in 1580 his brother John continued the process of land acquisition in Almondbury, Huddersfield and elsewhere; then John's son, William, bought the manor of Huddersfield from the Crown in 1599. The manor of Almondbury followed in 1627 during the time of this William's son, another John, who was knighted in 1619. The advowson of Almondbury, though, had been bestowed on Clitheroe Grammar School by Queen Mary, and was not acquired by the Ramsden family until 1857. This they then held until 1920.

The ecclesiastical influence exercised by the Ramsdens was only partly through the right of presentation to the living. Indirectly their influence went far wider. As lords of the manors of Huddersfield and Almondbury and one of the leading families in the district, for three centuries they were able to exercise influence over the restoration and building of churches, chapels and schools for the Established Church and to exert some control over the development of Dissent. This was especially true of the nineteenth century when the population of the township of Huddersfield expanded rapidly, from around 7,000 inhabitants in 1801 to almost 45,000 in 1901. The parish of Huddersfield extended well beyond the township and the Ramsden's manorial jurisdiction. From Cooper Bridge in the east it reached all the way up the northern side of the Colne Valley through Longwood, Golcar, Slaithwaite, one half of the village of Marsden and up into the moorlands of Scammonden, an area of over 12,000 acres. There were two ancient chapels of ease, in Slaithwaite and at Deanhead in Scammonden, each with a perpetual curate appointed by the vicar of Huddersfield, to which was added in 1798 a small chapel at Longwood which had been built by public subscription in 1749. The chapel at Marsden was in Almondbury parish and the curate there was appointed by the vicar of that parish which extended from the village and township of Almondbury through Honley, up the Holme Valley to Holme, and across through South Crosland and Meltham to the southern side of the Colne Valley from Lockwood through Linthwaite and Lingards to Marsden. Here there were chapels of ease in Honley and Meltham as well as Marsden. Though the Ramsdens built up considerable landholdings in both parishes, these were mainly in the lower townships to the east. Among the holders of significant lands elsewhere were, in Almondbury parish, the Kayes of Woodsome, and in Huddersfield, the Thornhills of Fixby. The Woodsome estate passed through the female line to the Legge family, earls of Dartmouth, in 1732. As lords of the manor in both Honley and Slaithwaite, they exercised considerable ecclesiastical influence there alongside the Ramsdens.[1]

There are two instances of Ramsdens holding the living at Huddersfield. Probably related to the Ramsdens of Longley, and the most distinguished, was Robert Ramsden, Fellow of Trinity College, Cambridge in 1565 and University Preacher in 1570. He became a Canon of Westminster in 1571 and was chaplain to Lord Burleigh, the most powerful member of the government under Queen Elizabeth. Rector of Spofforth from 1573 and Archdeacon of York from 1575 until his death in 1598, he was appointed by John Ramsden to the relatively poor living of Huddersfield in 1581. The second Ramsden to hold the post was John, briefly appointed by his cousin, the fourth baronet, in 1790 before resigning after less than two years to become vicar of his father-in-law's living at Arksey; he was also, very briefly, perpetual curate at Scammonden in early 1792 on the death of the previous curate. There were four other clergymen in the extended cousinhood of Ramsdens in the nineteenth century, but none held a living to which the Ramsdens had the right of presentation.[2]

Religious views in the 17th and 18th centuries

The personal religious views of the Ramsdens appear only fleetingly in the family and estate papers, which are most informative for the nineteenth century during the lifetime of Sir John William Ramsden (1831–1914). In the seventeenth and eighteenth centuries the family appears to have been conventionally loyal to the Church of England.

When Henry Venn was appointed vicar of Huddersfield in 1759, Sir John Ramsden, 3rd baronet (1699–1769), made an appointment which for a few years put Huddersfield at the centre of the map for northern Evangelicalism. The background to the appointment, though, suggests less about Sir John's personal views than about the process by which the propertied élite worked together in the administration of their estates. Venn was at the time the curate at Clapham in London and was known in Evangelical circles there for his preaching and his piety. But Ramsden did not know of him and it was the 2nd Earl of Dartmouth (1731–1801), himself a convert to Evangelicalism, who brought Venn's name forward. Dartmouth doubtless wished to promote Venn's career, but Huddersfield was a poor living worth only £100 a year. Dartmouth supplemented this sum, and may have been keen to see Venn in Huddersfield because, as vicar, Venn would have the right to nominate the curate to the chapel in his manor of Slaithwaite.[3] Sir John, the 3rd baronet, died in 1769, leaving a boy aged 13 to be the next Sir John, 4th baronet (1755–1839). When Venn resigned through ill-health in 1771 he suggested to Lady Ramsden that his curate, John Riland, should replace him, but instead Harcar Crook, curate at Bradfield, was appointed – probably because his patron at Bradfield (Thomas Bright, vicar of Ecclesfield) was distantly related to Lady Ramsden through her first husband.[4] This man's lack of Evangelical sympathies prompted a secession from the parish church and led to the formation of the first Independent (later, Congregational) church in Huddersfield with a chapel at Highfield. Crooke, who had also remained curate at Bradfield, died in 1773 but his replacement, Joseph Trotter, who had been his assistant curate at Bradfield and was alleged to be a drunkard, was no better and it was not until Sir John came of age that an Evangelical was once more placed in the vicarage at Huddersfield. With the appointment of John Lowe (later Fitzwilliam's curate at Wentworth) in 1784 and then John Coates, his curate from 1786 and then vicar from 1791 to his death 1823, the Evangelicalism associated with Venn was re-established in Huddersfield and for the next century the living continued in the Venn 'low' church tradition.[5] This was in contrast to Almondbury where appointments in the eighteenth century had usually reflected the old orthodox High Church tradition, though in the nineteenth century under Lewis Jones (vicar 1824–66) Evangelicalism prevailed.

This public face of religion, predominantly male, can be explored by reference to female religious influences expressed in private correspondence. There is a glimpse into this world of female evangelical piety in a letter written by Henry Venn in July 1769, shortly after the death of Sir John Ramsden, 3rd Baronet, in April 1769. Venn recalled a dinner at which he had spiritual conversation on the guidance of the Holy Spirit lasting two hours with the widow and her three daughters – by her first marriage, Mary

Bright (Countess Rockingham from 1752), and by her marriage to Sir John, Elizabeth (Mrs Weddell from 1771) and Margaret (Lady Ducie from 1774).[6] Though Lady Ramsden failed to promote John Riland for the Huddersfield vicarage, as Venn had hoped, it may well have been through the Countess Rockingham's influence that her half-brother, the 4th baronet, appointed John Lowe to Huddersfield (and Brotherton) in 1784.

In the next generation there is correspondence surviving between the Countess Rockingham, her husband's niece, Charlotte Wentworth, and her husband's brother-in-law, John Milbanke.[7] Even allowing for the conventional language of the day concerning religious matters, these letters suggest a deep personal piety which is reflected also in the attitudes and concerns imparted to their wider families – notably Charlotte Wentworth's daughter, Isabella (who married John Charles Ramsden) and her nephew, the 5th Earl Fitzwilliam, both of whom were to be key players in the history of Huddersfield in the nineteenth century.[8] When Fitzwilliam delivered a eulogy on Isabella's son, the young John William, at the opening of St John's Church, Bay Hall, in 1853, he referred to 'the example of his mother' and the son being 'deeply imbued with religious feelings'. It would be cynical not to take from this some insight into the upbringing and character of Sir John William Ramsden.[9]

Public Philanthropy in the time of Sir John William Ramsden

The Ramsdens were absentee landlords and this inevitably led from the later seventeenth century onwards to some disengagement from the local community. Although William Ramsden had been among the petitioners for a charter for the grammar school at Almondbury in 1608, no Ramsden sat on the school's governing body between the next William, who was the last Ramsden to live at Longley and died in 1679, and Sir John William who became a governor between 1867 and 1884.[10] Occasional charitable activities are noted in the intervening years. The Ramsden Charity, which in 1894 was yielding £80 a year for expenditure on clothes for the poor, was started in Venn's day in 1767 with five acres of land from Bay Hall common.[11] In 1818 a new lease was granted for parish schools in Huddersfield. The original lease had been given by John Ramsden in 1681 and this new lease for the balance of 999 years was for an annual rental of 'one red rose in the time of red roses, if the same be demanded'; but it was the 4th Earl of Dartmouth who was available to lay the foundation stone in 1818. While the Ramsdens were beginning to invest in the infrastructure of the town, there was little sign of this in its ecclesiastical buildings until land was granted for St Paul's church in 1829.[12] The parish church itself was rebuilt in 1834–6, and in this Sir John Ramsden played his required part as lay impropriator who was therefore responsible for the chancel (see below), but it was only after his death that the pace of change, including religious change, quickened in the town and parish.

John William Ramsden came into his estates at the age of 7 on the death of his grandfather, the 4th baronet, in 1839 [see Illustration 18, p. 49]. For the next 14 years his affairs were administered by Trustees, the most important of whom was the 5th Earl Fitzwilliam, cousin and brother-in-law of John William's mother, Isabella Ramsden, who was the daughter of Thomas, Lord Dundas. Fitzwilliam, Mrs Ramsden and her brother, the Earl of Zetland, set the tone for the Ramsden approach to religion in the town for the next seventy years, with Sir John William Ramsden playing a full part from 1852 onwards. In this the Ramsdens were served by a series of able agents and their assistants, notably George Loch (appointed overall estate manager in 1844) [see Illustration 6, p. 9], Alexander Hathorn (Huddersfield agent, 1844–61) [see Illustration 7, p. 11], R. H. Graham (agent, 1864–85), and F. W. Beadon (agent 1885–1920) – who advised Sir John William across a range of policy issues, including those relating to religious matters. Sir John William was open to suggestions but also had clear ideas of his own and the agent had to tread carefully, advising but always deferring to his master. The notes of reply which Sir John William wrote on many of the letters he received from his agents and others give some insight into his views on religion and philanthropy.

Sir John William divided most of his time between Byram, the House of Commons, and his estates in Inverness which he began to accumulate and develop from 1865. In 1885 he also acquired through his wife's inheritance the Bulstrode estate in Buckinghamshire, which then became his principal address. He was also an MP for much of the time between 1853 and 1886. He depended on his agents for information and advice and it is remarkable how much attention he did manage to pay to Huddersfield in the light of his other interests and commitments. These latter, however, did determine and limit what he did. Parliamentary sessions could require him to be in London during the Spring and early Summer and by August he liked to be on his Ardverikie estate in Scotland for the shooting season – although he himself did not shoot.[13] If a foundation stone needed laying or a building opening he would usually do it, provided the date were convenient, often accompanied from 1865 by his wife, Guendolen, youngest daughter of the Duke of Somerset. For example, although he had taken an interest in the new church to be built at Newsome, not far from Longley Hall, for which he provided the site and a donation of £850, he declined the invitation to lay the foundation stone on 17 July 1871 as he would be in Scotland at that time. The ceremony was performed instead by Amelia, wife of Thomas Brooke of Armitage Bridge.[14] When he was briefly in Huddersfield his timetable could be overcrowded. After engagements at Byram on 9 and 10 July 1883, he and Lady Guendolen came to Huddersfield on 11

July where she with his assistance laid the foundation stone for the new chancel at St Paul's church, but they then had to go immediately to London, unable to stay even for the luncheon.[15]

It was easier to lend a name as a patron to some worthy cause – though that often meant heading the subscription list with a handsome donation. It was easier still to send a small contribution of £5 or £10. Sometimes, as in the case of a church or a school, Ramsden might donate the land – leasehold – or allow it to be let at a reduced rental. Small donations and favours oiled the workings of community relations; they controlled the mood in a thousand often hidden ways and were essential in the hierarchical and patriarchal social order that the Ramsdens were trying to maintain in the modern, industrial society of Huddersfield on which much of their wealth depended. Even so, Sir John was not a naturally emollient character and, as one contemporary historian noted with reference to the long-running dispute over the length of leases and tenant right between 1859 and 1866, 'relations of the present baronet with his Huddersfield tenantry have not always been of the most cordial description'.[16]

The policy of the Ramsden Trustees on donations was clearly set out in an advice note from Earl Fitzwilliam in 1850 with regard to whether the Trustees should contribute to the organ fund at Paddock church:

> It is very true that an organ is not the most useful thing [on] which 5 or 10£ can be expended, but upon the whole I should advise contributing to it – for two reasons – first, Paddock is not a place where the rich of Huddersfield reside – only poor to be found there – second, I think it desirable that he [Ramsden] should not do anything, either in the affirmative or in the negative line, which may give him a reputation for stinginess – from none to 4 or 5 and 20 is the period during which his character in the world will be stamped – it is in *early* life that the world forms it estimate of man's disposition and character, and the world, having so formed its judgement, rarely, if ever, reverses it, however good reasons may appear subsequently for changing its opinion …[17]

Thus spoke an experienced public figure and politician who had spent a lifetime dealing with such matters. It informed Sir John's thinking throughout his own life: philanthropy in the service of the people of Huddersfield – but best when it also served the purposes of the Ramsden estate.

Running the Ramsden estates was big business requiring careful management and the agent was always frugal with his employer's money. With some exceptions the largesse dispensed by the agents on Sir John William's account was a small price to pay for his reputation. The expenditure account for the year ending October 1881 shows regular expenditure to have been

£26,433-13-0, a few hundred pounds over the estimate; of this sum, £459-18-6 (1.74 per cent) was accounted for in subscriptions. These subscriptions were in support of various good causes, many but not all of which were religious. A further £171 was subscribed annually in support of St John's church [see pp. 134-5]. Extraordinary expenditure amounted to a further £30,124-5-1, well above the estimate of £13,409. Of this sum, £5,099-13-0 was accounted for in donations. This was unusually high because the total included £5,000 for Greenhead Park. The balance (0.33 per cent of extraordinary expenditure and 0.18 per cent of all expenditure) was made up of smaller donations, usually of £5 or £10.[18]

These sums were not insignificant to the recipient and, although small in terms of the estate income, Ramsden was well aware that such donations could rapidly get out of hand, but they had a value beyond mere money in the goodwill that they promoted. As Fitzwilliam had advised in 1850, it was important not to appear stingy. There were several reasons why it was good to give, not least of which was keeping up with the neighbours. The whole point of a public subscription list, headed by the great and the good, was to shame or encourage the reluctant to do likewise. When an appeal was made to fund a memorial to the deceased rector of Lockwood in 1878, Ramsden wrote to his agent: 'I should like to contribute to this Memorial – pray find out what subscriptions are being given, as a guide to the amount of my contribution.' In the end he gave £10.[19] When Sir Joseph Crosland's niece wrote to the agent in 1894, soliciting a £10 subscription for three years to aid the Mission Church which she was supporting at Johnny Moor Hill, Paddock Brow, the agent advised Sir John to agree because 'I do not quite like Sir Joseph Crosland doing so much as he does for the people who live on your property'. Sir John did not like annual commitments, so sent £25 outright.[20] On the other hand, when he sent £10 to the Wesleyan Bazaar at Paddock in aid of their schools in 1894, he asked for his gift not to be 'paraded in public' – perhaps modesty, but more likely so as not to encourage too many expectations elsewhere.[21]

The sort of objects supported by regular small subscriptions were £5 a year for the schools at Cowcliffe (1850), a guinea a year to pay the fee of the independent examiner at the Huddersfield Collegiate School, so long as the examinations continued (1872), and £25 a year towards the salary of the curate at the Swallow Street Mission Church (1878).[22] The Trustees even decided in 1850 to contribute £5 a year to the Catholic schools in the town.[23]

In small matters Sir John could afford to be generous. Donations were usually preferred to subscriptions as they could be controlled year by year. Appeals for money in support of worthy religious objects were usually met with a donation, irrespective of the denomination. When Charles

Drawbridge, curate at Honley, appealed for funds for a parsonage but had not yet launched an official appeal, Fitzwilliam advised Loch: 'if you find a loose £5 note in your pocket I should think it might very properly find its way with Mr Drawbridge'.[24] When the clergyman at Holy Trinity, serving the north of the town, appealed for donations of over £250 towards the liquidation of debts, he was sent money – but only £10.[25] In 1890, Ramsden sent 15 guineas for the fund for new Church of England Sunday schools at Moldgreen; and in 1905 he gave £10 to the new Sheepridge Providence Church United Methodist Free Churches building fund – as the Methodists pointed out, 'we are only a working class congregation' and the chapel was being built on Ramsden land.[26] Though Ramsden's sympathies were with the Church he was alive to the strength of Nonconformity in the town and the prudential as well as charitable reasons for a relatively even-handed approach. When, in June 1875, the local Baptist minister appealed for aid for the new Baptist church in New North Road, Ramsden was inclined to refuse on the grounds that he had already granted a favourable lease and the Baptists 'have no claim which is not equally possessed by every other chapel built on the Estate'. Nevertheless, the estate cashier, Hordern, recorded a donation of £50 in 1877.[27] Only occasionally was an appeal rejected outright, as in 1891 when an appeal for a donation to the Queen Street Wesleyan Schools was rejected because in giving to them Ramsden would be 'open to the charge of partiality if I did not also give to many other schools of the same class to which I do not now give'.[28] But two years later he was prepared to give £50 to the new Catholic Schools being opened in Commercial Street, one of the least desirable parts of the lower town.[29] Such open-handedness was, of course, liable to abuse. When John W. Moran sent a printed appeal to Sir John William on 13 July 1878 soliciting a donation for the extension of the altar nave at St Patrick's Catholic Church, to which had been added in manuscript the names and generous sums already promised by leading gentlemen in the town, Graham was suspicious, and was able to report ten days later that on 22 July Moran had appeared before the magistrates charged with obtaining money under false pretences.[30]

Donations and favourable leases sometimes had clear ulterior motives. During the Tenant Right agitation of the late 1850 when T. W. Nelson, was ruffling a few feathers with his less than diplomatic handling of leases, [see pp. 92-111], the Ramsden Street Congregational Chapel was reminded that their lease had been for an annual rental of sixpence a square yard. They had in fact paid only fourpence but had no paperwork to justify this, so the full sixpence was insisted upon. However, an annual payment of ten guineas to the Ramsden Street Schools was also authorised – the equivalent of a rebate on the annual rent of about 1½d. a square yard.[31] The Unitarians were not so successful when they claimed that they were not obliged to pay for the drainage and paving of the street outside their new chapel in Fitzwilliam Street,[32] but the Free Wesleyans did better. They had acquired a site for their new chapel in what was to become Brunswick Street and found they needed extra land for the caretaker's house. The going rate was 4d. but they hoped for the usual discount down to 2d. as with the chapel site. Nelson advised 'having regard to the state of public feeling at the present moment and to the fact of Mr Thomas Mallinson the principal party connected with the chapel being one of the deputation on the Tenancy and [sic] Will question, I think it may be best policy to let them have the whole 209 yards at 2d per yard' – in effect an annual subscription of about £1-15-0 towards the rent. Sir John approved. Perhaps it was this dubious decision which prompted the generous resolution of the Ramsden Street case – and may have earned for Nelson both promotion to be steward of the manor of Almondbury, and the dislike for him felt by the estate cashier, Isaac Hordern [see Illustration 8, p. 11].[33]

The Ramsden policy of benevolent neutrality was felt to be both prudent and appropriate, which meant that, on the one hand, requests from Nonconformists for financial assistance were always considered on their merits, and on the other that the Church of England did not always get its own way. When the Rev. Josiah Bateman, appointed to the Huddersfield living in 1840, kept coming back to the Trustees for more money, Loch cautiously advised 'against concurring in some of Mr Bateman's applications'.[34] There was indeed considerable friction between the vicar and his patron. Bateman later recalled his brush with Sir John William over pew rents. Ramsden controlled sixty-five pews in the parish church which his agent let out at 10 guineas each a year, the income going to the Ramsden estate, not the church. Bateman arranged for a lawyer to rent a pew and then refuse to pay the Ramsden agent. This challenge was successful, securing for the church all the pew rents previously due to the Ramsdens and other private pew owners.[35] Bateman also drove a hard bargain over the sale of vicarage land to Ramsden which raised £7,000, paid into Queen Anne's Bounty to augment the income of the vicar.[36]

Occasionally there were outright refusals of assistance even for the Church of England. Sometimes this was for a good reason: in 1875, in the middle of heavy capital expenditure on Almondbury parish church, there was nothing left to augment the living at St John's church.[37] Sometimes the refusal expressed Sir John William's disapproval. When the vicar of St Paul's appealed for a donation towards improvements to his church in 1890, Sir John rejected his claim. The agent, F. W. Beadon, attempted to persuade him, re-iterating the sorts of considerations a benevolent landlord had to bear in mind, but Sir John was not a man to change his mind easily on subjects dear to him.

As well as the site for the original church, St Paul's had had £50 in 1856 for general repairs, £5 for additions to the schools in 1868, £200 for the chancel in 1883, and £25 towards the liquidation of the schools' debt in 1889. The grounds for his hostile reaction to the appeal give an insight into Ramsden's personal religious views:

> To establish "a surpliced choir", to alter "antiquated" pews, to put new heating apparatus, and gas standards, and windows are all very well if the congregation have a mind for these changes and like to spend their own money in effecting them. But they certainly constitute no sufficient justification for appealing to those who are not members of the congregation, and when a clergyman applies such language as "earnest effort" and "renewed zeal and usefulness" to such trivialities as these, the effect is only to destroy my confidence in anything the same clergyman may say on graver matters.

It was left to the agent to communicate this more diplomatically. Ramsden's reaction to the idea of supporting 'a surpliced choir' and his scathing comment on 'trivialities' are evidence of his prejudice against the 'modern' trend towards clericalism in the Church of England and any signs of ritualism in worship.[38]

Ramsden's overriding concern was to protect his freehold and to maintain a reputation for open-minded generosity while balancing the estate books at the end of each year. Sometimes he made larger donations. In 1849 the Trustees gave £200 towards the Mechanics Institute building fund; and the following year they refunded as a donation half the £3,554 they received for the site for the new cemetery in Blacker Road; in 1872 Ramsden bought land from his own Trustees in order to release £1,200 to give to the fund for the enlargement of the Infirmary; and in 1881 there was the £5,000 for the new public park, though this was paid as a rebate on the purchase price of £27,533-17-6 that Ramsden received for the 30 acres from his Greenhead estate, in an arrangement similar to that reached concerning the cemetery thirty years earlier.[39]

The preferred way of giving regular support to smaller causes was through reduced rents, and several appeals from Nonconformists were met in this way. An application from the Independent minister at Highfield, Dr Robert Bruce, for a free site and a donation for an Independent chapel at Paddock might have been thought a cheeky try-on had Bruce not been such a well-respected figure in the town. Ramsden – who only in the most unusual circumstances would agree to convert leasehold into freehold land – offered instead to discuss a lease at a reduced rent, 'as I have granted in similar cases': 1½d instead of 3d a yard rent plus a donation of £50 or £100 was suggested. It was expected the Wesleyans would ask the same for a chapel they wished to build just down the road.⁴⁰ An equally chancy request came from the Berry Brow Methodist New Connexion Salem Chapel in 1885, asking for a donation for their new chapel and a conversion lease at no increase in rent. The advice was to withhold any donation until the matter of the rent had been settled.⁴¹ An appeal for funds to reduce the debt on Hillhouse Free Wesleyan chapel had been rejected earlier that year on the grounds that they were already paying a reduced rent.⁴² Rarely was a request turned down out of hand, but when J. E. Willans, leading Congregationalist and Liberal politician, applied for a site for a new Independent church and school in 1881, he was informed that rents could not be reduced in the desired part of the town because available land there was scarce and so prices were high. Instead Ramsden suggested he look at cheaper sites not far away; Milton Chapel duly appeared in 1884 in Queen Street South, next to the new Technical School which had been opened the previous year.⁴³

Religious toleration

As these and many similar transactions with the Nonconformist bodies of the town suggest, though the bulk of the Ramsden philanthropic support went to or was administered through the Church of England, Ramsden and his agents were acutely aware that in Huddersfield they were operating in a strongly Nonconformist town where many of the most prominent individuals, including tenants of the Estate, were Congregationalists, Baptists or Methodists. It was therefore necessary to appear even-handed in approach, as Fitzwilliam had advised in 1850. A few months after this advice the vicar of Paddock had urged the Trustees not to permit a Wesleyan, Edward Brooke, to convert a disused water house opposite his church into a Dissenting chapel. Loch suggested that it would be dangerous for Sir John not to be neutral in religious matters: it was desirable in a town where at least half the inhabitants were Dissenters to avoid stirring up religious jealousies, 'always more formidable and less controllable than those springing from any other sources'. He went on to observe, wrily, that 'In a town … it must constantly happen that the Dissenting Meeting House will be near the Church'.⁴⁴ This advice came when religious tensions could be close to the surface, only three years after the final attempt of the vicar to raise a Church Rate for the maintenance of the churchyard had been defeated by the Nonconformists.⁴⁵

Though Ramsden was a loyal member of the Church of England, his commitment was to the whole community of Huddersfield – which therefore included the Nonconformists and even, to some extent, the Catholics. He was wary of anything which might suggest he was partisan. On one occasion the local YMCA invited him to be their president for the year.

Beadon advised that the local YMCA 'is rather sectional [meaning sectarian] in its managing staff – and you might appear to uphold Nonconformists against Church people'. Accordingly, Ramsden politely declined, citing 'many considerations' why he could not accept.[46] But when in 1884 he suspected his new vicar, James Bardsley, of attempting to side-line the Nonconformists at an important civic occasion he attempted to steer him towards a more neutral stance. The occasion was the visit to Huddersfield of the new Bishop of Ripon, William Boyd Carpenter. Bardsley had asked Sir John Ramsden to preside over a meeting to welcome him in the new Town Hall on 11 December 1884. Ramsden had agreed, having been assured that the Mayor, Wright Mellor, who was a member of Highfield Independent chapel, would also be present and would be invited to speak [see Illustration 26, p. 104]. Sir John 'was greatly pleased to hear this and expressed to him [the vicar] my satisfaction and the importance I attached to inducing as many as possible of those who did not belong to the Established Church to join in the welcome to be offered to the bishop.' But a week before the meeting Sir John realised that since the invitation there had been a change of mayor and that the new mayor, John Varley, was a Churchman, thus making the Town Hall gathering an exclusively Church of England affair. Half suspecting that the vicar was pleased about this, Sir John now urged his agent to ask the vicar to try to remedy the situation by inviting Mellor and other leading Nonconformists and even adding another Resolution to the agenda so one of them could speak. 'That the clergy and laity of the Church should welcome the Bishop is all very right and proper ... If however he could receive a welcome from the whole community, irrespective of sect, the occasion would be full of hopeful meaning'.[47] What Sir John did not admit at the time was that Wright Mellor was in fact one of his 'oldest and most valued friends at Huddersfield'.[48]

Such progressive views, however, had their limits. In December 1871 T. McGregor Miller, a draper from Hillhouse, applied to the Ramsden estate on behalf of the Huddersfield Secular Society to lease land on which to build a Hall and School. Graham refused so Miller approached Sir John directly to appeal the decision. At first Ramsden ignored their letter but the Secularists wrote again. As Graham explained to Sir John, 'The Secularists, as you suppose, avow hostility to the Christian religion, and they do everything in their power to discredit the teaching of the Bible'. A reply was sent stating that Sir John had ignored the appeal at first 'to avoid a painful refusal' but now spelling out clearly the limits of his forbearance: 'Sir John does not consider he would have acted rightly in giving facilities for such a purpose' ['disseminating doctrines hostile to the Christian religion']. The Secularists were to try again in 1886, with the same result. 'Freethought,' commented G. W. Foote, one of the national leaders of Secularism, 'is thus boycotted in Huddersfield by one man, who holds the mental life of the town in the hollow of his hand'[49]

Church Patronage

Next to atheists, Sir John William disliked ritualists the most. This becomes clear in the way he set about choosing new incumbents for those churches where he had influence. The Ramsdens' principal ecclesiastical patronage lay with the two ancient parish churches of Huddersfield and (from 1857) Almondbury, and the new church of St John, Bay Hall, opened in 1853. There were also two other new churches where he was a trustee – St Andrew's on Leeds Road, built in 1870 for which Ramsden gave £1,000 towards the £5,000 building cost; and St Mark's, also on Leeds Road but closer to the poorer bottom side of the town centre on Lowerhead Row, built in 1887.

Possession of the advowson of a church could be a source of great influence in a parish, which is why Sir John paid £3,500 for the Almondbury advowson in 1857. The first time Ramsden was asked to exercise his right of appointment there came when Lewis Jones, vicar since 1824, died suddenly in 1866. During his long tenure at Almondbury (1824–66) he had succeeded in staffing the parish's increasing number of churches with clergy who shared his Evangelicalism – several of whom were fellow Welshmen.[50] As his successor, C. A. Hulbert, noted with satisfaction in 1882, 'The Churches [of the parish] have been favoured with an unbroken series of devoted Clergymen of sound Evangelical views'.[51] As soon as Jones's death was announced there was a rush to succeed him, with applications from clergy in the ancient parish and beyond. Some parishioners and clergy wished to ensure an Evangelical succession. Others were equally determined to break with recent tradition and supply a more 'modern' – that is, Oxford-inspired – style of churchmanship. There were, in all, 41 applications. As Sir John William noted, 'The Living is a very important one, especially from the large Patronage it carries with it, and the selection of a new Vicar will be a very onerous and difficult duty. I am already overwhelmed with applications.'[52] The churchwardens helpfully arranged a canvass of the parish with five names on the slate and put two names forward as the parishioners' choice. A second anonymous canvass was made for only one of the candidates, Edmund Snowden, first vicar (and nephew of the foundress) of St Thomas's church, Longroyd Bridge, the first High Church in Huddersfield. Although supported by 11 former churchwardens, the current churchwardens refused to endorse him, pointing out that the Snowden cavass had been unofficial and fraudulently conducted. Letters came in both for and against his candidature, and there developed an Evangelical fear that Snowden might be appointed. A deputation comprising two clergymen from the parish and the vicar of Kirkburton waited upon the agent to urge their belief that 'the clergy throughout the parish would, without a single exception, unfavourably regard his nomination'. Such opposition to a High Churchman accorded with Sir John William's personal views and after some delay he made an offer to one of the more experienced clergymen within the parish, Thomas Bensted, who had been vicar of Lockwood since 1848. When he declined the offer, Ramsden turned to Charles Augustus Hulbert, the long-standing moderate Evangelical clergyman at Slaithwaite, whom he knew only by reputation and who accepted. The delighted Evangelical Bishop of Ripon congratulated Ramsden 'upon having made such an excellent appointment'.[53] What none of the candidates and lobbyists appears to have known is that Snowden and Ramsden had been at Eton together and Snowden was 'a very old friend'.[54] Ramsden was clearly prepared at times to put his own preferred brand of churchmanship above personal friendship when it coincided with the wishes of a majority of parishioners; just as in the case of Wright Mellor he was prepared to put personal friendship when it coincided with the needs of the wider community above narrow churchmanship.

Other cases were less arduous and contentious but, in contrast to the earlier Sir John's style when Venn was appointed in the mid-eighteenth century, Sir John William always showed a keen personal interest in who he was appointing to his livings. Sometimes this involved no more than approval of a proposed exchange of livings between likeminded clergymen, though even then in each case careful enquiry was made, either in person or through a reliable contact. When Canon W. B. Calvert, vicar of Huddersfield since 1866, sought retirement to a quieter parish through a three-way exchange of livings in 1884, James Bardsley came to Huddersfield – but only after Ramsden had received the reassurance that he was not a Ritualist.[55] The same concern was expressed when Charles Edward Story was permitted to succeed the Evangelical G. S. Wilson at St John's, Bay Hall in 1891, but only after Ramsden's local clergyman at Bulstrode had made the necessary enquiries to assure Sir John that 'There is no hint of Ritualism about him'; it also counted to Story's credit that his wife was the daughter of Canon Garratt of Ipswich, 'and therefore clerically trained and she is an excellent helper of her husband'.[56]

The procedure which was followed and the patron's contribution to it when there was no obvious candidate – and no queue of candidates as at Almondbury in 1866 – is well illustrated by two well-documented instances, both in 1905, when by coincidence Ramsden had to deal with vacancies at both Huddersfield and Almondbury.

Folliott G. Sandford, vicar of Huddersfield since 1903, resigned after only two years to become vicar of Doncaster. The procedure adopted by the agent, F. W. Beadon, was to seek 'advice and recommendations' from the Bishop of Wakefield. Sir John concurred with this but added, 'You know my wishes so well that I need not tell you. I should consider I acted wrongly if I appointed any clergyman with the slightest tendency towards High Church or "Ritualism".' Beadon considered six names and his reasons for rejecting them all tell us as much about him as they do about Sir John. Edgar Boddington, vicar of Swinton, was ruled out, despite being educated at Repton and Jesus, Cambridge, because of his family connection with Boddington's brewery of Manchester and because 'he is described to me as not being a gentleman nor his wife a lady'; no references could be obtained for a second, a third was considered 'vox et praeteria nihil'[57] and another was unlikely to accept; a fifth was a poor preacher who had almost emptied his church; the final one, Thomas Rawlinson Sale (Marlborough and New College, Oxford), rector of St Mary's Crumpsall, was ruled out because, wrote Beadon, 'I am afraid his views would be considered too Evangelical by the Huddersfield congregation'. But the bishop was not so hostile and Sir John noted on a letter from the latter with reference to Sale: 'in my opinion a strong recommendation, and I am quite prepared to offer him the living'. He drafted a letter to this effect. At this stage in the negotiations, the agent was clearly set against Sale as much as the patron was in favour. So Beadon produced another candidate, Albert Victor Baillie, rector of Rugby, whose wife was the daughter of Lord Boyne, but he refused on the grounds that Huddersfield would not suit his wife. Beadon also came up with Cecil Henry Rolt of Holy Trinity, Darlington. The Bishop then reported of Sale and Rolt that both were moderate Evangelicals. Sale was, the bishop assured him, 'a liberal Evangelical, and I understand he would not be likely to upset any existing arrangements of church worship.' Sir John then got out the draft letter, re-dated it to a fortnight later, and invited Sale. To attract Sale he pointed out that the vicar would have seven other livings in his gift – the old chapels and the new district churches in the ancient parish – and he repeated his desire that 'his views should be in harmony with those of his parishioners, to whom anything savouring of Ritualism or High Churchmanship in any of its forms, would be most unwelcome.' We may assume that by 'parishioners' Sir John included himself. Sale assured him that he was no party man, adopting neither medieval ritual nor the narrow dogmas of hyper-Calvinism. Sir John got his man. He stayed five years and was then succeeded by C. H. Rolt.[58]

At the same time, in May 1905, a vacancy occurred at Almondbury when Owen Thomas Lloyd Crossley resigned to become Archdeacon of Melbourne. Beadon at first tried putting forward the son of Bishop Gott of Truro, but Ramsden sought and took the advice of John Brooke of Fenay Hall, the most influential member of the local gentry, and he recommended Charles Dixon Hoste. The Bishop was happy with either Gott or Hoste and so Sir John invited Hoste, whom the Bishop described as 'a very moderate

Churchman – perhaps not so advanced as they have been accustomed to at Almondbury'. Again Sir John had shown himself prepared to get involved in the detail of the appointment, to make his own enquiries and to follow his own preferences to secure a sound, moderate Evangelical clergyman for his church, even when this meant overruling his agent.[59]

Ramsden may well have got clergy of his own choice but sometimes they could still annoy him and he may well have come to regret approving the appointment of James Bardsley. The matter of the visit of the Bishop of Ripon [see p. 126] was not a good start. Then, in 1890, Ramsden had cause to suspect Bardsley of deceitful practice when the vicar approached Sir John as 'patron paramount' to sign a form agreeing to the incumbent at Slaithwaite borrowing £145 to repair dilapidated farm buildings on the glebe land to increase the rental income of the chapelry. Ramsden did not believe the rental value would be increased, and so refused. Bardsley then tried a second time, not admitting this was still for the same purpose. Ramsden, who had clearly read the paperwork, was furious and declared that had Bardsley not been a clergyman he would have called his actions 'dishonest'.[60] Bardsley nevertheless survived until 1901, but the next two vicars each stayed only two years. When Canon Sandford left in 1905 the usual testimonial fund was set up. Sir John gave £5 to this and to a similar fund set up for Crossley who had been at Almondbury for four years. Sir John was incensed then to be asked for £44 to pay the balance of a ten-year debt incurred by Sandford in repairing the vicarage: £44 was not much, he thought, and Sandford had received a very generous testimonial considering the short time he had been vicar; he was refused.[61] Sir John William Ramsden may have become more acerbic and assertive with age and experience, but he was never in doubt that he was the (benevolent) master in his own house and was careful that none should forget it.

Church buildings

Buildings were and remain highly visible evidence of the public support given to religion. Places of worship and attached schools needed large funds for building, extending and running costs, and the landlord and lord of the manor was expected to play his part in this, not only by granting a lease on a site but also by allowing his name to go forward as a patron, heading a subscription list with a handsome donation, and setting an example to others to make their own contributions to the worthy cause.

Before the start of the nineteenth century, the Ramsdens had only two church structures to consider, the ancient parish churches of Almondbury and Huddersfield. In both places they were lords of the manor and owned an increasing amount of the freehold.[62] The chapels of ease, though, even in Huddersfield parish, were not on Ramsden land. The rebuilding of Slaithwaite chapel in 1789 fell to the Earl of Dartmouth who granted the land.[63] Three new churches were opened in Huddersfield parish in the early nineteenth century: Holy Trinity, built in 1819 by Benjamin Haigh Allen of Greenhead, a wealthy banker and Evangelical, at a cost of £12,000; Christ Church, Woodhouse, built by Allen's brother-in-law, John Whitacre, in 1828 at a cost of £6,000; and St Paul's in the town centre, built with the aid of a parliamentary grant in 1829. The land for St Paul's at the end of Queen Street was given by the Ramsden estate.[64] Two further new churches were erected just outside the town centre in the 1850s: St John's, Bay Hall and St Thomas's, Longroyd Bridge. This latter, designed by George Gilbert Scott and consecrated in 1859, was built for the widow and brothers of the local mill-owner, Thomas Starkey, who had died of typhus in 1847;[65] St John's was closely associated with Ramsdens, particularly Isabella Ramsden and her son Sir John William.

The Ramsden papers show involvement in several projects for new churches in the later nineteenth century. In addition to St Andrew's in Leeds Road [referred to above, p. 127], and St John's [to be discussed in more detail below, pp. 134-5], Ramsden gave sites for new churches at Newsome (1871) and Primrose Hill (1904) and was greatly concerned that a new church should be erected in the Somerset Road area near to Longley Hall [see pp. 138-9].[66] He also gave land and money for parsonages and supported schools in connection with churches on his estates. In this he was not unusual – many local landowners did the same in their own areas, according to their means. For example, a chancel was added to Lockwood church in 1848 at the expense of James Crosland Fenton, a local solicitor who also acted for the Ramsdens, and the chancel at Paddock (1879) was paid for by the local industrialist and banker, Sir Joseph Crosland; the site for St Stephen's, Rashcliffe (1864) was given by Bentley Shaw, the Lockwood brewer; and St Paul's, Armitage Bridge (1848) was entirely funded by the Brooke family for the workers in their adjacent woollen mills. These men were visible and active in their communities.[67] The largely absentee and not always popular Ramsdens had to maintain their reputations and influence alongside and in competition with these local families – a fact of which Ramsden and his agents were well aware in offering their support for the Church.

In 1890 the Bishop of Wakefield launched an appeal for Church Extension in the diocese, in which he listed a number of building projects, some of which were in the Huddersfield area. Sir John William offered £1,000 to the appeal but then stipulated conditions which the Bishop was unable to accept. Ramsden did not wish his donation to disappear into the general fund; it was to be used only for projects of his own choosing, some but not all of which were on the bishop's list. For example, the priority in Huddersfield was for new churches in Marsh and Crosland Moor but Ramsden was interested in promoting a new church for Moldgreen, nearer to Longley Hall. As he explained to the bishop:

> I will devote a thousand pounds to the extension of churches in the Borough of Huddersfield, including under the term "extension" the improvement of existing as well as the building of new churches. I do not however wish to hand the money over to a Committee, but to give it direct from myself in each case to such churches and in such amounts as the strength of their respective claims upon me may seem to me to warrant.

He added, 'My difficulty about making any Committee the channel of a gift is that for all objects at Huddersfield application is made direct to me and those interested expect a direct response from me.'[68] In other words, for the gift to serve its function within Ramsden's way of managing his reputation, people and estates, specific gifts were what counted. Perhaps he was recalling the way that his £5,000 gift to Greenhead Park had been 'lost' in 1881 when in the public accounts the price paid for the land was shown net of his gift with no separate acknowledgement of the gift and so no public credit for it.[69]

Four Ramsden Churches

The parish church of St Peter, Huddersfield, last rebuilt in 1503, was in a poor, neglected condition by the 1830s. It was, recalled Bateman, 'very dear, very old, very long, very low, and very badly ventilated'.[70] The Ramsdens recognised their responsibility as lay impropriators and patrons of the living to repair the chancel, but apart from £36-15-8 spent on chancel repairs in 1772–3, the only sum over £10 given by them in any one year between 1774 and 1829 was for the churchyard (£85-15-3 in two instalments, 1786 and 1787). The only other expenditure of note was a small annual sum, usually 10 shillings, for the repair of the chancel windows. In 1805 consideration was given to providing a new church, for which Sir John Ramsden subscribed £25 towards expenses; two years later an assessment was laid for repairs, with a Ramsden contribution of £56-10-0; in 1811 he gave £47-19-7 to balance the account for pews; and the following year he subscribed £50 for an organ. These were not inconsiderable sums but they did little to secure the long-term future of the old church. A Faculty for taking down and rebuilding the tower in 1814 was not acted upon, and in 1829 Sir John had to give another £33-15-0. for chancel repairs.[71]

The situation was becoming critical. When the York architect, J. P. Pritchett, was called in to advise on repairs in 1831 he found that part of the roof had

27. Huddersfield old parish church, rebuilt 1503.
Kirklees Image Archive

28. Huddersfield new parish church (1834–6), by J. P. Pritchett.
Kirklees Image Archive

fallen in and was being propped up on long poles: this would cost £500 to £750 to put right. A proposal to levy a church rate for £500 was rejected and one for £250 was never collected. Pritchett next proposed rebuilding the nave and chancel, leaving the tower, at a cost of £2,000. Then it was decided to raise the chancel floor, so Pritchett proposed raising it sufficiently to create a crypt; then it was decided to replace the tower; this meant that the nave could be extended to increase the accommodation. So, Pritchett ended up designing a new church. Even by taking the cheapest quotation (which turned out to be a costly error) the total bill came to £9,869-14-5. The work was completed in October 1836. Sir John Ramsden and his Trustees' contribution over the years from 1834 was £650. Large though this sum was, it is put in proportion by the £218-17-6. spent in 1842–3 on a monument to Sir John placed in the new church by his Trustees after his death.[72] There is little sign that Sir John himself took much interest in this rebuilding: he was in his late seventies and played little part in the affairs of the town – the foundation stone for St Paul's church had been laid in 1828 by the vicar of Huddersfield and that for the Infirmary in 1829 by his heir, John Charles Ramsden.[73] There may have been some Ramsden influence over the choice of architect. Although Pritchett was a leading Congregationalist, and had designed the Ramsden Street chapel in 1824, he had also worked on projects for the Fitzwilliam estate, including Norton church (in the classical style) in 1816, and Greasbrough (in the Gothic style) in 1828. Though Mrs Ramsden was to lose confidence in Pritchett when Brotherton church, which he designed for her in 1842, suffered subsidence, Fitzwilliam persisted with him and he was to become most celebrated in Huddersfield as the architect of the railway station (1848).[74]

It was only after Sir John's death in 1839 that the Ramsden Trustees, and then Sir John William in person, became more active in the development of Huddersfield, including its churches. The church which most expressed the Ramsdens' religious commitment was St John's, Bay Hall. The original architect considered was Edward Blore (1787–1879), an enthusiast for the Gothic whose commissions had included several cathedrals and Oxford colleges and churches, and – in Yorkshire – the restoration of the choir of Ripon Minster. Mrs Ramsden thought his a 'beautiful but too expensive plan'.[75] The second architect, considered in the summer of 1846, was William Butterfield (1814–1900) and a drawing and plan were submitted by him in the autumn. The Trustees wished to build somewhere in the Hillhouse area and eventually settled on the Bay Hall estate which was purchased for them by Mrs Ramsden.[76] There was some delay while this estate was transferred to the Ramsden Trustees who then gave the site for the project. By 1850 both Mrs Ramsden and the local inhabitants of Hillhouse were growing impatient, and she urged the agent, George Loch, 'Pray take this matter into immediate consideration'.[77] Progress was then rapid, and the correspondence shows the personal involvement of both Mrs Ramsden and her son in the detailed arrangements. It was, for example, she who sent the cheque to pay for the silver trowels to be used at the laying of the foundation stone by her son, which took place on 16 October 1851.[78] The construction was undertaken by local builder, Joseph Kaye, and completed in 1853 [see Illustration 29, p. 136]. This church, which cost £7,000, twice the original sum discussed, was the gift of the Ramsdens to the town in memory of John Charles Ramsden, who had predeceased his father in December 1836. They continued to support it financially, not only with an annual subscription of £171 for the clergyman but also with further gifts and grants for the vicarage and schools at Cowcliffe and Hillhouse.[79] Philanthropy, though, conveniently merged with self-interest. The siting of the church, it has been suggested, was part of an estate policy to open up Bay Hall to development and the style of the vicarage, funded entirely by the Ramsdens, was meant to serve as a model for villa development in the area.[80]

There was a marked difference between the earlier Ramsden attitude towards the restoration of Huddersfield parish church in the 1830s and that adopted by Sir John William Ramsden when plans were developed in 1871 for a thorough restoration of the medieval church of All Hallows, Almondbury, parts of which dated back to the fourteenth century [see Illustration 30, p. 137]. Ramsden gave his consent as lay impropriator and patron to alterations to the chancel and an appeal was launched, headed by Charles Brook of Meltham and Thomas Brooke of Armitage Bridge, each of whom gave £300, and by Lord Dartmouth who undertook to fund the restoration of the family's Kaye chapel. Sir John William held back during the first phase, which was the restoration of the nave and the tower, but then became involved and even enthusiastic once the vicar, C. A. Hulbert, had convinced him that until 1691 there had been Ramsden burials in the chancel. He then agreed to fund the restoration of the chancel, not as a matter of duty but as one of family pride with an antiquarian interest in tradition – a characteristic also displayed in his 'restoration' of Longley Old Hall (1885) [see Illustration 2, p. 3].[81] In this as in other matters, Sir John William showed a keen, detailed interest and was determined to have his say. So, when the old medieval screen, which had been serving as a reredos, was moved back to its original position, he wished to ensure the pulpit and reading desk would be situated within the nave. The reseating of the church was to be in oak, as was the chancel roof, to match the medieval nave roof, and not in cheaper pitch pine. The architect's plan to replace the three lancet east windows with 'a large and handsome East Window' was abandoned on the advice of members of the Yorkshire

29. St John, Birkby (1851-3), by William Butterfield.
Kirklees Image Archive

Archaeological Association [sic]. Ramsden was consulted and deferred to at every stage because he was paying for it. He showed himself sensitive to the fabric of the medieval church which housed the burial place of his ancestors, and was doubtless reassured by Hulbert's promise that 'I am equally watchful that nothing Scriptural and Protestant should be left out, any more than anything leaning to Popery introduced' – but one wonders, in view of his later comments, what he thought of the 'new Surpliced choir' present at the re-opening of the chancel and chapels in November 1876.[82]

30. Almondbury parish church before restoration.
Kirklees Image Archive

31. Almondbury parish church after restoration in 1876.
Kirklees Image Archive

The fourth Ramsden church, St Michael's, is the church that never really was – certainly not in the form that Ramsden had intended – but the discussions about it tell us something about Sir John William's attitudes and priorities. They also illustrate two of his principal weaknesses: a propensity to micromanage and a well-meaning indecisiveness.[83] The Moldgreen area straddled the parishes of Almondbury and Kirkheaton, from the edge of Longley Park to Dalton. A new church was proposed for this rapidly-growing district in 1859. Ramsden offered £1,000 if matched by £2,000 from other sources but only for 'a building of sufficient size and creditable appearance'. He clearly had in mind another church like St John's for this part of town. Various sites were suggested: Lewis Jones, the vicar, wanted a church at Longley, but Ramsden was opposed to this as he was set on one large church for the whole of the Moldgreen district, not just a village church, but when Sir John Lister Kaye gave a site in Moldgreen which left all but 200 of Ramsden's 1,690 tenants living nearer Almondbury parish church than the new Moldgreen church, Ramsden's plan collapsed. A church for the Kirkheaton side was opened in 1863 at a cost of £3,000, leaving nothing for the Almondbury side.[84] Other developments intervened: the restoration of Almondbury parish church, the building of a new church at Newsome (1871); and in 1888 the former Primitive Methodist Sunday School at Longley was acquired to become St Mary's Mission Church.[85] But there was still no church for the area below Longley Park except the Aspley Mission room in St Paul's parish, rebuilt in 1890 on the Huddersfield side of Somerset Bridge. Sir John persisted with his dream for a church to occupy a prominent position at the bottom of Somerset Road.[86] The problem was that, even if the additional £2,000 were forthcoming, Sir John William's offer of £1,000 would not pay for the kind of church that he was wanting, for which the estimate was £7,500. His mother's St John's had been pared back as far as possible and had still cost £7,000. The Starkeys had spent £11,000 on St Thomas's.[87] The Bishop of Wakefield's fund had not prioritised the area, except for a mission room on Mulberry Street next to Ramsden's proposed site. The new vicar of Almondbury, W. Foxley Norris (appointed in 1888) wished to revive the scheme, beginning more modestly with a temporary wooden or iron mission room on the site given by Ramsden, and then proceeding in stages, first building a basement floor of vestries only, and then adding the church proper on top as funds became available, but Sir John wanted all or nothing: in particular he wanted a spire which would create a vista on the road from Huddersfield to Almondbury.

Plans were sought from Charles Hodgson Fowler, one of the leading exponents of ecclesiastical Gothic in his generation. Ramsden did not like his Perpendicular design: 'I cannot think that any architect would of his own choice copy from Gothic in its decrepitude, when it would cost no more to

32. St Michael, Somerset Road (1913—15), by Oswald White. Became St Joseph's Catholic church, 1953.
Kirklees Image Archive

copy from it in the time of its full vigour and beauty'. The design compared unfavourably with that of St John's. But Ramsden was clearly muddled in his ideas, saying he wanted 'a really handsome church' whilst also maintaining that the most important thing was to have a church, 'the appearance of a building is quite a secondary consideration'. The result of this indecision and lack of funding was that nothing was achieved beyond Norris's iron mission church, replaced in 1913 by a pleasantly modest building with a schoolroom beneath and church above – and no spire – designed by local architect, Oswald White [see Illustration 32]. The corner stone was laid by Mrs J. F. Ramsden in the presence of her husband and other dignitaries. In his final years Sir John William was unable to match his mother's earlier achievement at St John's.[88]

Conclusion

The Ramsdens were not unusual in their approach to religion. The Church of England represented their values across the centuries and they loyally supported it. A comparison with the earls of Dartmouth would suggest many similarities in their patronage of schools, churches, and other worthy causes on their estates, though without showing that degree of personal piety and religious commitment exhibited in the life of the second Earl of Dartmouth. While the Ramsdens' religious beliefs were undoubtedly sincerely held, the estate papers unsurprisingly bring little of this out beyond communicating Sir John William Ramsden's deeply conservative moderate Evangelicalism, his conscientious support for tradition, and his abhorrence of 'medieval' Ritualism and other such un-Protestant innovations.

What is clear is that the religion of the Ramsdens, whatever it meant in private, had a public purpose and a part to play in the management of all who lived and worked on their estates. It helped determined the Ramsdens' influence and upheld their local power. This re-enforced their Whig predisposition towards religious toleration, something they shared with their Rockingham and Fitzwilliam relations. In a predominantly Nonconformist town, they were even-handed in their treatment of the various denominations while giving their principal support to the Established Church. Though absentee landlords since the later seventeenth century, they maintained their presence by patronage and paternalism, with many small ceremonial and financial gestures which have now left little trace, punctuated by occasional acts of significance which are still remembered and acknowledged. Chief among these are the appointment of Henry Venn to the Huddersfield living in 1759 – something for which Sir John Ramsden can actually take little credit – and the building of St John's church by Isabella Ramsden in memory of her husband at the time when Sir John William Ramsden, her only surviving son and heir, came of age. This chapter has focused on his life and activities partly because the surviving sources are so rich, partly because the expansion of the town during his lifetime created many new needs for charitable activity and opportunities for church and school building, and partly because, in an age of improved communications – the postal service and railways – it was easier than ever before to be an absentee landlord who at the same time could be in active and even daily contact with the affairs of his Huddersfield estate.

Endnotes

1. These 8 churches had become 25 by 1858 and over 40 by 1914. For a brief survey of religion in Huddersfield, see Haigh (1992), chapters 5 and 6.
2. Foster (1874), vol. 2, 'Ramsden of Longley Hall and Byram'; Venn (1924), p. 417 and (1953), p. 240
3. Venn (1836), p. 68; ODNB (2004), 'Venn, Henry (1725–1797)'.
4. Venn to Mrs Riland, 17 November 1770, in Venn (1836), pp. 164–5; Foster (1874), vol. 1, 'Bright of Badsworth'.

RELIGION AND PHILANTHROPY

5 Information from the Clergy of the Church of England Database 1540–1835 (http://theclergydatabase.org.uk/, accessed 7 July 2017).
6 Venn to James Kershaw, 8 July 1769, Venn (1836), p. 154–5.
7 DD/RA/F/3a, Letter Book, 'Correspondence between Lady Rockingham, Mr Milbanke and Lady Charlotte Wentworth, with other writings chiefly on Religious Subjects'.
8 Foster (1874), vol. 2, 'Wentworth of Wentworth-Woodhouse'.
9 Richardson (1903), p.15 reproduces the speech in full.
10 Hinchcliffe (1963), pp. 147, 358–61.
11 Lawton (1842), p. 137; White's *Directory* (1894), p. 396; Ahier (1950), pp. 112–17.
12 DD/RA/C/21/10, 'Huddersfield Parish Schools', special supplement to the Parish Magazine for July 1881; Taylor Dyson (1932), p. 231.
13 DD/RA/C/26/4, JWR to Calvert, 11 June 1870.
14 DD/RA/C/26/3, Rev. T. B. Bensted to JWR, 12 June 1871. Hulbert (1882), pp. 280, 285.
15 DD/RA/C/20, Henry Barker to JWR, 8 June 1883.
16 See chapter 3; Sykes (1898), pp. 219–27.
17 DD/RA/C/4/8, Fitzwilliam to [Loch?], 4 January 1850.
18 £5 adjusted by the RPI would now be worth about £500.
19 DD/RA/C/15/1, JWR to Graham, 9 and 13 February 1878.
20 DD/RA/C/34/1, Sophie Crosland Robinson to Beadon, 6 April 1894 and Beadon to JWR, 9, 19 and 24 April 1894; JWR to Miss Robinson, 25 April 1894.
21 DD/RA/C/34/1, W. Dawson to JWR, 4 January and 12 February 1894; Beadon to JWR, 9 January and 16 February 1894.
22 DD/RA/C/4/8, Rev. J. W. Grane to JWR, 15 April 1850; DD/RA/C/3, Graham to JWR 30 May 1872; DD/RA/C/15/1, Rev. W. M. Calvert to JWR, 21 October 1878 and Graham to JWR, 25 October 1878.
23 DD/RA/C/4/8. Loch to Mrs Ramsden, 3 January 1850.
24 DD/RA/C/4/8, Fitzwilliam to Loch, 29 November 1850.
25 DD/RA/C/4/8, N. Maning to Mrs Ramsden, and Loch's notes, 13 and 17 May 1850.
26 DD/RA/C/8/1, Ben Walshaw to JWR, 20 November 1905.
27 DD/RA/C/27/7, note by JWR, dated 26 June 1875 on letter from Rev John Hanson, 2 June 1875; Hordern, 'Notes', 1877, p. 114.
28 DD/RA/C/34/3, note on C. H. Bates to JWR, 21 May 1891.
29 Hordern, 'Notes', 1893, p. 173. JWR had refused to grant a 999 year lease on a better site at the bottom of Kirkgate because this would prevent further improvement and mean 'I hand over this central position for ever to the lower class of Irish' – DD/RA/C/34/3, note dated 12 May 1891 on Beadon to JWR, 4 May 1891.
30 DD/RA/C/15/1, Moran to JWR, 13 July 1878, Graham to JWR, 23 July 1878.
31 DD/RA/C/28/2, William Willans to JWR, 12 March, 19 May and 10 November 1858.
32 DD/RA/C/28/2, Memorial from Thomas Ibbetson and other, 29 March 1858.
33 DD/RA/C/28/5, Hathorn to JWR, 21 October 1858; T. W. Nelson to JWR, 8 October 1858; Nelson to JWR. 12 October 1858; Hordern, 'Notes', 23 August 1883, p. 138; see also above, chapter 2, p. 23.
34 DD/RA/C/4/8, Loch to JWR, 9 July 1850 and 31 January 1850.
35 'Senex' [Josiah Bateman] (1880), pp. 101–3; the Ramsden cashier, Isaac Holdern, recalled only 34 Ramsden pews – Hordern, 'Notes', 23 March 1855, p. 39.
36 [Bateman] (1880), pp. 99–100; DD/RA/C/14/8, Loch to JWR, 31 January 1850; DD/RE/C/62– 73, esp. Hathorn to Loch, 27 July 1849 and Fenton to Loch, 5 and 20 June 1850.

37 DD/RA/C/27/7, Graham to JWR, 14 July 1875.
38 DD/RA/C/21/10, Beadon to JWR, 19 and 28 April 1890 and JWR's reply, 23 April 1890.
39 DD/RE/C/67, Mrs Ramsden to Loch, 10 December 1849; DD/RA/C/4/8, Loch to Fitzwilliam, 18 and 27 November 1850; White's *Directory* (1895), p. 394; DD/RA/C/26/2, Graham to JWR, 20 March 1872; Griffiths (2011b), p. 10, and above, chapter 2, p. 73.
40 DD/RA/C/26/3, JWR to Graham, 12 May 1871; for Bruce, see I. Schofield (1999), pp. 89–101.
41 DD/RA/C/22/1, W. Yeoman to JWR, 18 October 1884.
42 DD/RA/C/22/1, Graham to JWR, 8 February 1884.
43 DD/RA/C/20/2A, JWR to Willans, 21 December 1881; DD/RA/C/21/10, Appeal for new Independent Chapel, May 1884.
44 DD/RA/C/4/8, Loch to JWR, 9 July 1850.
45 Sykes (1898), pp. 390–1.
46 DD/RA/C/21/10, T. R. Porritt to JWR, 24 December 1890, Beadon's advice, and JWR's draft reply dated 1 January 1891.
47 DD/RA/C/22/1, Bardsley to JWR, 28 September, 2, 3, 4, 5 December 1884; JWR to Graham, 5 December 1884.
48 DD/RA/C/34/3, JWR's reply, 22 May 1893, to Thomas K. Mellor on hearing of the death of his father. For Mellor and the Tenant Right dispute, see above, chapter 3, pp. 98, 103, 108.
49 DD/RA/C/26/2, Miller to JWR, 26 December 1871; Graham to JWR, 26 January, 6 and 26 April 1872; Wadham Powell to Miller, 27 January 1872; *Freethinker* vol. 6 no. 33, 15 August 1886, p. 258 and *Secular Review* vol. 19 no. 7, 14 August 1886, pp. 106–7. For the Secularists, see Royle (1996), pp. 205–7.
50 Brown (2001), pp. 6–12. Jones was president of the Association of Welsh Clergy in the West Riding for 30 years. The new churches were Lockwood (including Rashcliffe and Newsome), Honley (including Brockholes), Meltham, Milnsbridge, Linthwaite, Holmbridge, Netherthong, South Crosland and Marsden; the vicar was also joint patron of Armitage Bridge and Helme – DD/RA/C/34/4, Beadon to JWR, 9 September 1892.
51 Hulbert (1882), p. 272.
52 DD/RA/C/33/9, note dated 1 September 1866 on Graham to JWR, 27 August 1866.
53 DD/RA/C/33/9, various letters dated 27 August 1866 to 28 February 1867. Although Slaithwaite was in Huddersfield parish the chapelry also served Lingards township in Almondbury parish.
54 DD/RA/C/34/4, note dated 1 November 1893 on W. J. Kaye to JWR, 31 October 1893.
55 DD/RA/C/22/3, various letters, 1 November 1883 – 4 February 1884, esp. Wadham Powell to JWR, 22 November 1883.
56 DD/RA/C/34/3, Rev. Alfred Kennion from Gerards Cross to JWR, 16 March 1891, enclosing a letter from R. I. Knight dated 14 March 1891.
57 'a voice and nothing else' – a Latin translation from the Greek of Plutarch's *Moralia*, section 233A, no. 15.
58 DD/RA/C/10/3, Beadon to JWR, 2 March, 26 April, 15 May, 18 May, 29 May, 30 May, 2 June, 1905; Bishop of Wakefield to JWR, 16 May 1905, 30 May, 2 June 1905; JWR to Sale, 30 May changed to 13 June 1905; Sale to JWR, 14 June, 26 June 1905.
59 DD/RA/C/10/3, Brooke to JWR, 6 June, 9 June 1905, Bishop of Wakefield to JWR, 10 June 1905; Hoste to JWR, 19 June and JWR to Hoste, 20 June 1905.

60 DD/RA/C/22/3, W. Powell to JWR, 22 November 1883; DD/RA/C/21/10, Bardsley to JWR, 1 May 1890 and subsequent correspondence between Beadon and JWR, 5 and 8 May 1890.
61 DD/RA/C/10/3, Beadon to JWR, 26 June, 5 July and 28 August 1905.
62 In 1859, excluding recent purchases totalling nearly 620 acres, the Ramsden estate held 1,213 acres in Huddersfield and 1,603 in Almondbury – DD/RA/C/28/3, Memorandum of estates in 1859.
63 Hulbert (1864), p. 103.
64 Weatherhead (1913); *White's Directory* (1894), pp. 394–5. There were six other churches built by parliamentary grant in 1829–31: Golcar, Lindley and Paddock in Huddersfield, and South Crosland, Lockwood and Linthwaite in Almondbury. For subsequent support given to St Paul's, 1856–1889, see DD/RA/C/21/10, JWR to Beadon, 19 April 1890.
65 *The Church at Longroyd Bridge, 1859–1899* (1899).
66 DD/RA/C/28/3, 26/1 and 26/4, correspondence about St Andrew's, 15 November 1859, 3 June 1869 to 21 July 1869 and 1 June to 23 November 1870; for Newsome church, see DD/RA/C/26/3, Bensted to JWR, 12 June 1871 and Hulbert, *Almondbury*, pp. 279–86; DD/RA/C/10/9, correspondence about the site for Primrose Hill, 31 March 1902 to 23 December 1904.
67 See *White's Directory* (1894), pp. 397–9, and Hulbert (1882), pp. 270 (Lockwood), pp. 275–8 (Armitage Bridge) and pp. 387–90 (Rashcliffe).
68 DD/RA/C/21/10, correspondence between Bishop of Wakefield and JWR, 31 May to 11 June 1890.
69 Hordern, 'Notes', 1881, p. 130; D. Griffiths (2011b), pp. 8, 10, 65.
70 [Bateman] (1880), p. 198.
71 A detailed list of Ramsden expenditure on Huddersfield parish church between 1768 and 1843 was provided by Graham for JWR in 1874 – DD/RA/C/27/5, 9 February 1874; Lawton (1842), p. 137.
72 Ahier (1950), pp. 207–30; DD/RA/C/27/5, Graham to JWR, 9 February 1874.
73 *LM*, 15 November 1828, 4 July 1829.
74 See chapter 5, p. 161; *ODNB* (2004), 'Pritchett, James Pigott (1789–1868)'; also Colvin (2008), pp. 834–7; Broadbent (1956); DD/RE/C/3/26, Isabella Ramsden to Loch, 20 August 1844; Gibson and Booth (2005), pp. 44–54.
75 *ODNB* (2004), 'Blore, Edward (1787–1879)'; also Colvin (2008), pp. 128–34; *ODNB* (2004), 'Butterfield, William (1814–1900)'; DD/RA/C/20/3, Isabella Ramsden to Loch, 9 July 1850.
76 DD/RE/C/27, Butterfield to Loch, August 1846. For the proposed plan, see DD/RE/C/28, 12 September 1846 and DD/RE/C/29, 24 October 1846. For the Bay Hall estate transaction see chapter 2, p. 58 and chapter 7, p.197.
77 DD/RE/C/74, Memorial to Mrs Ramsden, July 1850; DD/RA/C/4/8, Mrs Ramsden to Loch, 9 July 1850; DD/RA/C/4/8, Loch to JWR, 17 July 1850.
78 There is an extensive correspondence concerning the building of the church in DD/RE/C/74 – 91, July 1850 to December 1851. The speeches at the various ceremonies are reproduced in Richardson (1903).
79 DD/RA/C/15/1, correspondence 13 and 25 September, and 3 October 1878; and printed leaflet, 'St John's Bazaar', 7–9 November 1878.
80 Springett (1992), p. 475.
81 For Longley Old Hall, see above, chapter 1, p. 36; Gibson and Booth (2005), pp. 15–16; and Redmonds (2003), pp. 118–20.

82 Hulbert (1882), pp. 33, 88–91, 115–18; DD/R/dd/VII/165; DD/RA/C/26/2; 27/2, 27/4, 27/6 and 27/7, various papers and letters, July 1873 – March 1875.
83 See chapter 2, p. 67
84 DD/RA/C/28/3, Rev. C. Alderson to JWR, 13 December 1859, Hathorn to JWR, 14 December 1859; DD/RA/C/28/6, correspondence between Hathorn, Jones, Alderson and JWR, 8 January–21 February 1860; Jenkinson (1963).
85 Jenkinson (1988).
86 Completed in the early 1870s; Somerset Bridge was opened in 1874 by Lady Guendolen and her father, the Duke of Somerset – see Illustration 44, p. 203.
87 DD/RA/C/34/2, Beadon to JWR, 10 June 1893.
88 DD/RA/C/21/10, Norris to JWR, 17 September and 2 October 1890 and JWR's reply, 24 September 1890; 34/3, Norris to JWR, 16 April 1891; 34/4, JWR to Norris, 26 May 1892; 34/2, JWR to Norris, 6 February 1893; *HE*, 28 June 1913. The Church of England sold the building in 1953 to the Catholics (who rededicated it to St Joseph), and built a new church nearer the new Fernside housing estate.

CHAPTER FIVE 145

Architectural patronage in early-Victorian Huddersfield: the Ramsdens, William Wallen and J. P. Pritchett

CHRISTOPHER WEBSTER

Introduction

AS THE WEST RIDING manufacturing towns prospered in the first half of the nineteenth century on the back of the rapidly developing textile industry, there was a corresponding growth in the provision of professional services necessary to support the manufacturers. Thus, in Bradford there were twelve firms of attorneys in 1822, but thirty-five by 1853;[1] Halifax, with three firms of accountants in 1822, had seventeen 31 years later[2] and there were also substantial increases in the provision of banking, insurance and transport services. It is all clear evidence of a thriving economy in the 'clothing district' towns. A not inconsiderable part of the new-found wealth was devoted to building. And this was not just utilitarian construction, but *architecture*, implying ambition and vision on the part of the patron and a project that required the services of a professional architect, not just a superior builder. It was often through its public buildings that these expanding towns competed with one another for status and were to be judged by visitors. In Leeds, a lone architect's office in 1809 had increased to eighteen in 1851[3] and in Bradford, the two firms in 1822 had grown to thirteen in 1853.[4] It is thus surprising that Huddersfield, well populated by other professionals, had no resident architect before 1838 when William Wallen chose to move from London, bringing to the town the benefits of his metropolitan training, experience and knowledge of current fashions there.[5]

The absence of a resident architect is not an implication that, before 1838, Huddersfield lacked dignified buildings – far from it. Indeed there was already a range of stylish churches, chapels, public buildings and mansions, but all were designed by architects from outside the town including, among the churches,

Holy Trinity church (1816-19), by Thomas Taylor of Leeds; Emmanuel, Lockwood (1828-9), by R. D. Chantrell, also of Leeds; St Paul's (1828-30), by John Oates of Halifax; and the rebuilding of the parish church of St Peter (1834-6) was supervised by J. P. Pritchett of York [see Illustration 28, p. 133]. Meanwhile, the Congregationalists built the Ramsden Street Chapel (1824) to a design of Pritchett's [see Illustration 33, p. 149] while the Roman Catholic St Patrick's (1832) was by John Child from Leeds. Among the public buildings, Oates was responsible for Lockwood Baths (1827) and the Infirmary (1829-31) while Pritchett designed Huddersfield College (1838-9) and would soon be responsible for the magnificent railway station (1846-50).

Did it matter where these architects had their offices? On one level, perhaps not and the absence of a group of resident architects did not stop Friedrich Engels, in 1845, from concluding that Huddersfield's 'modern architecture' helped make it 'the handsomest by far of the factory towns of Yorkshire and Lancashire' – high praise indeed from a well-travelled commentator.[6] However, having a resident architect was one of the signifiers of a town's confidence and its aspirations, and at a time when there was much civic pride among these expanding manufacturing communities, image and status mattered. As these towns sought to present a refined image to sceptical visitors, elegant, fashionable buildings were of crucial importance; it was the means by which the stigma of 'industrial wealth' might be mitigated by claims to culture and sophistication. The erection of the Philosophical Hall in 1836-7 (here attributed to Pritchett[7]) – a fashionably elegant exterior and a succession of worthy, 'improving' events within – was a crucial marker of such ambitions. The early-nineteenth-century historian Dr T. D. Whitaker wrote that Leeds 'had through its public [buildings] emerged from barbarism to a very high degree of elegance';[8] no doubt Huddersfield had similar ambitions.[9]

William Wallen, then aged thirty-one, arrived in Huddersfield in 1838 and established what quickly became a thriving architectural practice, the town's first. Over the next sixteen years he enjoyed considerable success and contributed a number of important buildings to the town. However, the story that follows is more than just architectural history. An examination of architectural patronage reveals much about how the town saw itself and the image it wanted to present; about the establishment of professional services in the town, an essential concomitant to industrial enterprise; and the significance of religious allegiances. It also tells us a good deal about the role played in the town's development by the Ramsden Estate during Huddersfield's physical transformation from 'a miserable village'[10] to the 'spacious' and 'elegant'[11] town centre that still largely exists today. This chapter focuses on two architects, J.P. Pritchett (1789-1868) and William Wallen (1807-88). Together they reveal much about the town in this seminal period of Ramsden influence.

Where does this assertion that the town had no resident architect before Wallen leave Joseph Kaye, a master builder in the town and a man apparently capable of producing a sound design when one was needed? Kaye began his career as a builder around 1800 and over the next sixty years, according to Edward Law, erected a substantial proportion of the town's buildings and at one time employed over 1,000 men.[12] Among the many building for which he contracted were several of those listed above including the Infirmary and St Paul's. The late-Georgian period witnessed the publication of a range of books illustrating, in straight forward terms, the principles of contemporary Classical architecture aimed at ambitious builders and joiners seeking to reinvent themselves as architects, and Kaye was one of them.[13] But everyone in Huddersfield knew him as the owner of a huge and successful building firm and they knew he was not a *proper* architect, despite styling himself as one in the *Directory* of 1834[14] and in several later ones. So, what precisely, at a time when there were no formal qualifications to be achieved prior to opening an office, did being a proper architect imply? Crucially, it was an independence from the building trades, the one issue that bedevilled Kaye's ambitions. As early as 1788, the eminent London architect John Soane had set out a vision for modern practice.

> The business of the architect is to make the designs … and direct the works … ; he is the intermediate agent between the employer, whose honour and interest he is to study, and the mechanic [builder], whose rights he is to defend. [He is to oversee the builders, correct their mistakes and check their bills.] If these are the duties of an architect, with what propriety can his situation and that of the builder, be united?[15]

Initially, it was a radical idea, but slowly, through the first half of the nineteenth century, it took hold and gradually the services of an architect both to design and manage a project were seen as indispensable. And employing a well-known architect brought prestige to the client as well as a stylish building.

Among the 'proper' architects, Pritchett secured many important commissions in the town, despite his York address; perhaps worried that Wallen was encroaching on his territory, he opened an office in Huddersfield in 1843, overseen by his son, Charles Pigott Pritchett, but the York office was always the principal one. Pritchett senior's employment in Huddersfield tells us much about how architectural patronage might operate. During the 1830s and 1840s Earl Fitzwilliam of Wentworth Woodhouse, near Rotherham, exerted extensive influence on the Ramsdens' management of Huddersfield, initially as an informal advisor during the final years of Sir John Ramsden's long life and then, between 1839 and 1852, as a Trustee for Sir John William Ramsden. Pritchett was Fitzwilliam's estate architect for over fifty years, from around 1815, and seems to have been well-regarded by the earl.[16] It is known that Fitzwilliam insisted Pritchett be appointed to build the new railway station in the town in 1846,[17] 'the most splendid [station] façade in England', according to John Betjeman [see Illustration 22, p. 59]. No doubt Ramsden/Fitzwilliam support assisted him to gain other important jobs. One came in 1834 with the decision to rebuild Huddersfield's decaying parish church of St Peter where the Ramsdens were the patrons, and as the lay impropriator Sir John Ramsden was obliged to pay the full cost of the work on the new chancel. This he did grudgingly and, no doubt, to maintain oversight of costs, promoted Pritchett for the whole project, despite his having only limited experience of this sort of work. The new building opened in 1836 [see Illustration 28, p. 133]. And it was Isabella, widow of John Charles Ramsden, who appointed Pritchett to rebuild the old church at Brotherton, near Pontefract, as a memorial to her husband in 1842.

Also useful as Pritchett's career developed were his Nonconformist associations. Despite having a father who was an Anglican rector, Pritchett was a prominent Congregationalist and in a town like Huddersfield, where Nonconformity was strong, his religious allegiance was undoubtedly useful. His first known commission in Huddersfield was the Ramsden Street Congregational Chapel (1824). With clear Nonconformist links of his own and Fitzwilliam promoting his interests in other respects, Pritchett was destined to prosper in the town.

The other prominent architect working in late-Georgian Huddersfield was John Oates from Halifax who added the impressive Infirmary and several Anglican churches in and around the town, including St Stephen, Lindley (1828-9); All Saints, Paddock (1828-9); and St Paul, Huddersfield (1828-30). His premature death in 1831 left a vacancy for a committed Anglican and it was into this void that Wallen stepped. The town would have struggled to find any young architect better trained or connected to welcome as its first resident architect. What made him seek his fortune in Huddersfield? The answer lies in his 1830 marriage to Frances Gill (1804-95), daughter of Richard Gill, Esq. and his wife, Mary, from Notton,[18] a village between Barnsley and Wakefield, and twelve miles from Huddersfield. No doubt it was one of her relatives who alerted him to the opportunities offered in this expanding town with no architect of its own, and perhaps arranged some useful introductions. Given the way Wallen quickly cornered the market in Church of England projects – churches, schools and vicarages – it seems unlikely he did not have an influential ally.

Huddersfield certainly provided a sound base for Wallen's career as well as useful commissions for Pritchett, but in one respect it was a highly unusual town in the context of architectural practice: the normal relationship between

33. Ramsden Street Congregational Chapel (1824), by J. P. Pritchett, demolished 1936.
Kirklees Image Archive

client and architect was complicated by the involvement of the Ramsden Estate, intent on overseeing the town's physical changes. This was especially true from 1844 when the diligent George Loch was appointed estate steward; Loch, assisted by Alexander Hathorn, the local agent, carefully controlled both the overall development of the town and the individual new buildings within it. And Isabella Ramsden, a woman of 'strength and intuition',[19] and uncompromising opinions on a range of topics, regularly expressed her thoughts on architectural matters. The trio certainly kept architects on their toes even when it was not Ramsden money paying for the buildings.

Wallen's early life and training

We know a great deal about Wallen's pre-Huddersfield life thanks to the eminent men to whom he was related or with whom he associated. Wallen was certainly better trained and connected, and more talented than most, but as an ambitious young architect seeking to establish an office in a developing provincial town, he was far from alone.

Wallen was born in 1807, the son of the London architect John Wallen (1785–1865). The family lived in a series of elegant houses in Spitalfields, London, from where John ran his practice. John had been a pupil of Daniel Alexander, a brilliant and successful architect for whom Pritchett had once worked, who excelled at the design of large industrial buildings, warehouses, prisons and dockyards which often involved staggeringly large budgets and provided an essential component in Britain's world-wide industrial and mercantile supremacy. They were looked on with amazement by informed foreign visitors to the capital. John had several pupils who went on to enjoy notable careers and it seems that the training he offered was of an exceptional standard.[20] William Wallen thus enjoyed an unusually thorough architectural education in his father's office. The formal part of his pupillage is likely to have been completed around 1828, by which time he would have been 21. There is then a ten-year gap before he began independent practice in Huddersfield. His activities in this decade, and the men with whom he was associated, give a clear picture of his energy and ambitions, and reveal a young architect of outstanding ability. He became a partner in his father's firm in 1831.[21]

Wallen's antiquarian interests

Wallen was also acquainted with many of the leading antiquaries of the period, especially through the Topographical Society of which he was secretary in the 1830s.[22] His antiquarian interests had already been brought to the public's attention when, between 1828 and 1833, he exhibited a total of eight works of art at the Royal Academy, mainly depictions of medieval buildings.[23] In 1835, he was elected a Fellow of the Society of Antiquaries,[24] an impressive attainment for a twenty-eight year old. The following year he published *The History and Antiquities of the Round Church at Little Maplestead, Essex*.[25] It is an important piece of research from a writer who had adopted the very highest standards of contemporary scholarship and it received a positive review in the *Architectural Magazine*;[26] it was illustrated by eight accomplished plates by Wallen. There were 510 subscribers of which 106 were architects, including most of the eminent, London-based practitioners. Twelve subscribers came from Huddersfield and its immediate surroundings, including a 'Mrs Gill' and a 'Miss S. Gill' of Huddersfield, presumably his in-laws. That Wallen had these contacts is a likely explanation for his hitherto unlikely arrival in the town two years after publication.

On 30 January 1838, at the very beginning of his independent career, Wallen delivered a paper at the Architectural Society's meeting in London. It was titled 'On Prejudice as to Style in Architecture'. Conveniently, it was printed.[27] In the lecture, he cautioned against adherence to a single style: 'this unhappy perversion has swayed alike the mere tyro and the consummate master'. Instead he urged a more catholic approach: no styles 'are deserving of utter condemnation.' He proceeded to deliver a brief history of architecture from the Greeks onwards, taking a swipe along the way at the 'ignorant' use of Gothic by Inigo Jones and Christopher Wren. He urged a careful study of whatever style a patron requested, a philosophy soon to be borne out by his own career in Huddersfield.

Wallen in Huddersfield

Nationally, the first half of the nineteenth century contains many examples of London trained architects identifying an opportunity in an expanding provincial town and relocating in order to exploit it. Thus, both Thomas Taylor and R. D. Chantrell moved to Leeds and Richard Pope went to Bristol, while G. T. Andrews settled in York. Usually, these practices developed relatively slowly. However, in Wallen's case he seems to have established himself with remarkable rapidity. His known early commissions were almost all concerned with Church of England projects – churches, schools and vicarages – suggesting the town was on the look-out for not just a talented architect, but a talented one with solid Anglican credentials.

His earliest known job in the Huddersfield area was St David's church, Holmbridge, in the parish of Almondbury where the Ramsdens were lords of the manor. The project gives some idea of the complexity of church building in this period, especially where there was reliance on a grant from the London-based Incorporated Church Building Society, as many projects did. A church for this isolated community was deemed desirable and a grant was successfully applied for in 1832.[28] A design was solicited from Henry Ward, then in Wakefield[29] – although soon to move to Hanley, Staffordshire – but no suitable site could be found. When, in 1837, a site was found, tenders for the scheme exceeded Ward's estimate. He could not be contacted, or perhaps had lost interest in the project, and in June 1837 new designs were provided by Chantrell. Although an experienced church architect who had successfully undertaken a number of jobs part-financed by the ICBS, the Society's Surveyor objected to the closeness of the galleries. Chantrell made revisions approved by the Surveyor in July, but the Society withheld final approval for some unspecified reason.[30] On 3 March 1838 Almondbury's vicar, Lewis Jones, again asked the ICBS what was causing the delay as he was keen to start building. He went on to enquire whether the ICBS would return Ward's plans, claiming – rather disingenuously – they 'might suit another design for a church on a large scale in this neighbourhood'.[31] These plans were duly returned.

Jones, having retrieved Ward's plans, already approved and for which a grant had been secured, then abandoned the Chantrell scheme and sought an architect to supervise the erection of Ward's design. On 18 March 1838 he asked Chantrell to oblige but the latter declined believing such a course to be 'unprofessional' and had *already* been told that some other person was 'going to execute Ward's plan'.[32] This is confirmed by a letter from Wallen to the ICBS, dated 7 March 1838, only four days after Ward's plans were requested, stating 'the Building Committee had appointed me to carry into erection the church at Holmbridge, relinquishing all the plans previously to this date, and have determined upon erecting the original design of Mr Ward to which the [ICBS's] official seal has been attached … the committee have appointed me to act as surveyor of the works and superintend the erection of the church … .'[33] Clearly, early in 1838 Jones must have had discussions with Wallen and lined him up to take over the Holmbridge project. Other than the chancel, added by Edward Hughes in the 1880s, the design is largely as shown in Ward's *c*.1832 plan. The obvious difference is that a much more substantial tower was built. The foundation stone was laid on 28 May 1838 and the church was consecrated in July 1840.[34]

Wallen must have impressed as, soon after securing the Holmbridge job, he was asked to survey the medieval parish church of Almondbury. His report, of 29 June 1838, identified several problems with the roof – rotten timbers, collapsed trusses and missing slates – and concluded 'immediate attention' was required. He estimated the cost at £107-13-6.[35] Chantrell, the area's most eminent church architect, had undertaken work in the church in 1829-30 and might have anticipated securing this commission. However, the real crown for Wallen in the late-1830s was his victory in the competition for designs for the new Church of England Collegiate School in Huddersfield. The *Leeds Intelligencer* of 27 October 1838 announced his triumph in its 'Local Intelligence' section and the same edition carried an advertisement stating Wallen had moved from his London address – listed as Great Marlborough Street – to Buxton Road, Huddersfield, where he would welcome potential clients. However, he must already have been spending significant amounts of time in the town. Construction of the school began early in 1839.[36]

Perhaps nothing better illustrates the religious divisions in Huddersfield than late-1830s educational provision for the children of the town's middle-class elites. It also reveals something of the rivalry between Wallen and Pritchett, as well as the bases for their support. The area already had several long-established grammar schools – Almondbury, Longwood and Fartown – which offered a traditional classical education, but by the 1830s 'there was felt to be a need for a secondary school … where the sons of woollen magnates and wealthier trades people might be educated … [with] a more modern curriculum than the grammar schools could provide. Furthermore, the Nonconformist elements in the town resented the interest of the established Church in the older schools.'[37] Thus in 1838, the Revd W. A. Hurndell of Ramsden Street Congregational Chapel was instrumental in founding the Huddersfield College Company, floated with 300 shares at £20 each. The college opened in temporary premises on 21 January 1839 and moved to its handsome new building on the fashionable New North Road in 1840, designed by Pritchett. It followed closely behind Wakefield's Proprietary School which opened in 1834, which was also independent of Anglican influence, was aimed at a similar clientele, and also offered a 'modern' curriculum including European languages and mathematics.

It is no coincidence that 1838 also saw the establishment of Huddersfield's Collegiate School, adopting the best name available after its rival had already settled on 'College'. It also proposed a modern curriculum, but one based 'upon the doctrines and practices of that Protestant Church of England to which the Headmaster belonged'.[38] The Archbishop of York and Bishop of Ripon headed the list of its patrons, confirming its Anglican affiliations. It also opened in January 1839 in temporary premises,[39] and moved into the building designed for it by Wallen in 1840.[40] What better credentials could he have had for securing future Anglican patronage in the town? Indeed, through the 1840s, Wallen received a significant amount of it. In addition to the church at Holmbridge, he was responsible for four new churches in West Yorkshire: St John the Evangelist, Farsley, Leeds (1842–3);[41] St Luke, Milnsbridge (1843–5);[42] Christ Church, Oakworth, near Keighley (1844–6);[43] and St Paul, Shepley (1845–8) [see Illustration 36, p. 157].[44] There was also the chapel of ease at Aspley, 'attached' to St Paul's church (c.1853–4), sometimes referred to as the Aspley Lecture Room.[45] His other work for the Anglicans included repairs in 1839 to St Stephen's, Lindley (designed by John Oates, 1829)[46] and the redecoration of St Lucius, Farnley Tyas (designed by R.D. Chantrell, 1838-40) in 1843.[47] After damage caused by the 'great Holmfirth flood' in February 1852, Wallen supervised the 'Restoration, Alteration and Additions' to Holmbridge church and the restoration of the churchyard wall and gate piers.[48]

Associated with the Anglican churches was a series of new schools, schoolmasters' houses and parsonages. He built Holy Trinity school, Portland Street, Huddersfield (1840),[49] a school and parsonage to complement his church at Holmbridge (1841–2),[50] a National School and schoolhouse at Almondbury (1844–5),[51] a National School and master's house at Kirkheaton (c.1844–5),[52] a school 'attached' to St Bartholomew's at Marsden (1846)[53] and a parsonage for Milnsbridge (1846).[54] To put these successes in context, Pritchett's Anglican employment in the Huddersfield area during the 1840s

34. Huddersfield Collegiate School (1839–40), by William Wallen.
Kirklees Image Archive

35. Huddersfield College (1839–40), by J. P. Pritchett.
Kirklees Image Archive

was limited to the completion of the church, school and houses at Meltham Mills, a project started before Wallen's arrival in the town, and the new vicarage for Huddersfield parish church, erected near Greenhead in 1842.[55]

Despite all the newly-built churches, the 1840s was a turbulent time for Anglicans. The rapid advances of the Cambridge Camden Society – often referred to as the Ecclesiologists – formed in 1839 and intent on pushing the Church of England in a 'Higher' direction, caused serious turmoil among Anglican church-builders as well as worshippers. The society was intent on reviving decoration and liturgy banished by the Puritans, and encouraged the building of new churches that more faithfully followed pre-Reformation models; 'preaching box' layouts were soon deemed repellent by its supporters and 'Gothic authenticity' was the new imperative. Impressive support for the Cambridge Camden Society came quickly. After only four years of existence, it could boast the patronage of both archbishops and twelve other bishops. Low Church Evangelicals – and one of their strongholds was Huddersfield – must have felt decidedly marginalised. The society claimed the moral high ground and there was little room for those who merely wanted to maintain the *status quo*.[56] Of central importance in spreading the Ecclesiological message to the provinces were the 'diocesan' societies that sprang up around the country from the early 1840s. The first was the Exeter Diocesan Architectural Society, founded in 1841, quickly followed by the Yorkshire Architectural Society, founded in 1842. The agendum of these groups was, ostensibly, the study and restoration of medieval churches in their areas, but there was certainly a more subversive one: to influence the design and layout of new churches to make them suitable for Ecclesiological liturgy.

Yorkshire Architectural Society and some publications

Wallen was a founder and, initially, very active member of the Yorkshire Architectural Society, the objective of which was

> to promote the study of Ecclesiastical Architecture, Antiquities and Design, the restoration of mutilated architectural remains and of Churches or parts of Churches which may have been desecrated, within the County of York; and to improve, so far as may be within its province, the character of Ecclesiastical Edifices to be erected in future.'[57]

Like the other societies, the Yorkshire group was dominated by the clergy, but at its first formal meeting after formation, it was agreed: 'Those architects who really understand the principles of Gothic architecture and of ecclesiastical design, and only want room, and liberty, and a just appreciation of their talents to distinguish themselves will, we are persuaded, find in the Yorkshire

Architectural Society a very effective ally.' Indeed, Wallen, as the first architect member, was present to hear these words, and over the next few years he would be joined by most of the leading Yorkshire architects who specialised in church work, including Chantrell. It was at this first meeting, on 29 September 1842, that Wallen was elected to the committee.

During its early years, he appears to have been a diligent supporter and a regular attender at committee meetings, despite these initially being held at a variety of locations round this very large county. He also sat on various sub-committees – for instance those overseeing the restoration of Howden Minster in 1842, and the Chantry Chapel, Wakefield the following year. At the first AGM in 1842, he presented the society with 'an illuminated copy' of *Little Maplestead*, possibly the first item acquired for the library. At the second AGM, held in York in October 1843, he read his paper on 'The Geometrical Principles of Gothic Architecture', and after the committee meeting in Halifax in November he repeated it.[58] He – and Chantrell – were re-elected to the committee at the October 1844 meeting, but neither attended any meetings during the year and they were not re-elected to the committee at the annual meeting of October 1845. Were they just too busy elsewhere to continue? Possibly, but having initially been such active members, one is left wondering if there had been some falling-out.[59] Perhaps Wallen found it increasingly difficult to defend the modest, box-like churches his Low Anglican congregations desired. He remained an ordinary member until at least 1850.[60]

Wallen's *Two Essays Elucidating the Geometrical Principles of Gothic Architecture*, the basis for his YAS lectures mentioned above, were initially delivered to the Geological and Polytechnic Society of the West Riding of Yorkshire late in 1841 and were published in Leeds in 1842.[61] They were, no doubt, a significant means of bringing him into the orbit of the YAS's clerical founders. Identifying the principles of proportions which had guided the architects of the great medieval cathedrals, abbeys and churches was a subject that exercised many a Gothic scholar during the nineteenth century.[62] Through his 'personal investigation of our ancient edifices' he developed a persuasive 'system' to explain the use of proportions in the Middle Ages.[63] Although theories like Wallen's are now generally dismissed, exploration of these themes in the 1840s placed him within an elite group of London-based researchers and must have brought him significant prestige.

Wallen's churches

Given Wallen's work with the YAS and his publications, it would be hard to imagine an architect setting out on a church-building career around 1840 who could boast better qualifications for the task or who had more impressive

36. St Paul, Shepley (1845-8), by William Wallen.
Leeds University, Special Collections MS 78.

external interests. He might have been expected to be a torch-bearer for the Ecclesiologists, yet his churches suggest quite the opposite. Specifically, while the Ecclesiologists urged architects to specify long chancels, steeply pitched roofs and clerestoried naves, and never to incorporate galleries, in many respects Wallen's designs of the 1840s remained firmly wedded to pre-1840 ideals: box-like naves undivided by arcades, shallow roofs and always a gallery, sometimes on three sides of the nave, as at Milnsbridge. And several of his churches – for instance Whitehaven and Shepley – have no chancel at all while others are modest in length.[64] Clearly Wallen was not an enthusiastic Ecclesiologist. His apparent reluctance to fully embrace the group's thinking is surely bound up with patronage: the Huddersfield area was a stronghold of Low, Evangelical Anglicanism where a revival of High Church practices was initially mistrusted and treated with deep suspicion.[65] Crucial in Evangelical worship was the congregation's ability to hear and see, and nothing hindered the transmission of sight and sound more than arcades of columns, while galleries brought the maximum number of worshippers close to the pulpit.

Many historians of the early Victorian period have become somewhat blinkered by the pervasive propaganda of the Ecclesiologists to the extent that what was deemed a failure in their eyes continues to be marginalized. But if we can accept that Wallen and his clients had little interest in faithfully reproducing medieval churches, we are liberated from the highly subjective confines of Ecclesiological 'success'. As we have seen, Wallen certainly had an academic interest in the architecture of the Middle Ages[66] but, it seems, his approach to the design of modern churches was much more pragmatic, especially when budgets were small as was invariably the case with his commissions. A particularly revealing passage from his *Essays* is this: he condemns those who believe 'every pointed building must be a cathedral or nothing; nor shall we attempt to *copy* some vast church within a twentieth part of the space, and with a hundredth part of the money.'[67] Evidence that Wallen took a consciously anti-Ecclesiological stance – or, indeed, any stance – is frustratingly elusive, although there are one or two hints in that direction. Crucially, his *Essays* include his opinion that in all but the largest churches, 'the width does not justify the inclusion of aisles': they spoil the proportions and mask the pulpit from parts of the congregation.[68] In the heady days of the Ecclesiological revolution, this was a refreshingly independent and rational idea. And the inclusion of west galleries in all his churches in order to produce a satisfactory level of accommodation was equally reactionary.[69]

Wallen has left few comments about style, although his *Essays* include his belief that 'late-Gothic' was 'gorgeous'.[70] However, rather than adopt this, or Decorated – the Ecclesiologists' favourite – his churches are either Norman or Early English, a stylistic selection probably informed by the limited budgets. Yet even with modest funds, these churches are not dull or bare. Indeed, the combination of a Norman chancel arch with over-sized decoration, supported by debased Corinthian half-columns at Milnsbridge or the incorporation of the *vesica piscis* as a decorative motif at Holmbridge and Oakworth, suggest Wallen had little interest in archaeological fidelity but was, perhaps, a pioneer in the drive to develop Gothic as a modern idiom, a concept subsequently promoted eloquently by Beresford Hope and his circle.[71]

How well were Wallen's churches received? The simple answer seems to be, enthusiastically. At their openings, Holmbridge was described as 'pretty and commodious'[72] and Milnsbridge as 'elegant'.[73] Wallen gave his clients precisely the form of church they required, ones in which all could hear and see the preacher. And it should also not be overlooked that to build as the Ecclesiologists wanted to build was usually very expensive, while Wallen's clients were, in almost every instance, pitifully impecunious. The edition of the *Leeds Intelligencer* that reported the opening of Milnsbridge church in 1845 also noted the completion of J. M. Derrick's St Saviour's, Leeds, an early model of the new Ecclesiological thinking.[74] The latter had cost around £17,000 and even then, was without its intended tower; it held just 600 worshippers.[75] Milnsbridge had required a mere £2,500, including 'all its fittings and hot water heating system' and provided places for 945.[76] The 'neat and picturesque' Gothic chapel at Aspley cost only £500.[77]

Wallen's secular buildings

Archives concerning the building of secular structures rarely survive on the scale of that devoted to Anglican projects, and what was recorded of Wallen's secular work is, almost certainly, only a fraction of what he actually did. Nevertheless, what is known reveals engagement with a range of building types and demonstrates Wallen's competence with a number of styles, but especially with the Italian Renaissance Revival which placed him absolutely at the forefront of fashion in the 1840s.

The first notice of a commission unconnected with the Church of England came in 1840: the interior design for the 1840 Huddersfield Exhibition, held at the Philosophical Society's premises: 'The rooms will be beautifully decorated in the Saracenic order under the direction of Mr Wallen';[78] sadly, no images survive. It was a modest project, but one useful in promoting Wallen among the town's elites. The patrons included Earl Fitzwilliam and the Earl of Zetland, both Trustees of the Ramsden Estate, and the list was headed by the Archbishop of York and the Bishop of Ripon, underlining Anglican support, although David Griffiths stresses the exhibition's non-sectarian philosophy. The organising committee's chairman was Joseph Brook, partner in the Meltham Mills company whose family we will encounter below.

Also in 1840, Wallen surveyed the roofs of Fixby Hall for Thomas Thornhill.[79] It was another minor job, but it was through these mundane appointments that useful contacts might be made. In this instance, just two years later, in 1842, Thornhill, in his capacity as lord of the manor of Calverley, donated the site for the new church of St John, Farsley, near Leeds, which Wallen designed. Did Thornhill promote Wallen for the job; it seems unlikely to have been merely coincidence? And in 1844, Wallen was appointed to survey Calverley's parish church.

More significant architecturally, in 1842 or 1843, Wallen was engaged to build Eshold House at Woodlesford, near Leeds, for Henry Bentley, owner of the nearby Eshold Brewery.[80] Completed in 1844, it is a substantial mansion with a huge service wing. The stylistic and planning similarities between Esholt and Meltham Hall, Huddersfield, erected c.1841–3 for William Leigh Brook who inherited Meltham Mills on the death of his father in 1845, make it highly likely that Wallen designed both. Brook had a life membership of the Yorkshire Architectural Society which would have provided a convenient link to Wallen and, like the rest of his family, Brook was a committed

37. Riding School, 1846–7 (subsequently altered, left) and Zetland Hotel, 1846–7 (right), Ramsden Street (now Queensgate), Huddersfield, both by William Wallen.
Kirklees Image Archive

Anglican although his father, James (d.1845) employed Pritchett to design his ecclesiastical projects, beginning with the tower for St Bartholomew, Meltham, in 1835. Other known projects by Wallen for major families in the Huddersfield area included the new estate office at Longley Hall for the Ramsdens in 1848 [see Illustration 9, p. 15].[81]

In 1846, Wallen was responsible for the Riding School and Druid's Hotel – later the Zetland Hotel – in Ramsden Street. Although adjacent, it seems they were discrete projects.[82] The hotel is an elegant design which looks back to an earlier Palladian tradition, while the Riding School reflects cutting edge 1840s Classicism: Italian Renaissance Revival. Grecian – as exemplified by Oates' Infirmary of the early 1830s – was increasingly seen as *passé*, replaced by the new Renaissance style in fashionable circles. The deeply overhanging cornice supported by substantial brackets are clear references to the style, popularised by the publication in Paris of Paul Letrouilly's *Édifices de Rome Moderne*, (3 volumes, 1840-57). It quickly became the standard textbook of examples and perhaps Wallen owned a copy.

St George's Square

The Riding School was a modest-sized building, but it was only a small step, stylistically, from this to the design for the George Hotel (1849-51), the crowning achievement of Wallen's years in Huddersfield [see Illustration 23, p. 59]. The scheme seems to have originated in September 1845 when Alexander Hathorn, the Ramsdens' local agent, wrote to George Loch, the estate steward, setting out what he saw as the opportunities the arrival of the railway offered. He was keen that the Ramsdens, not the railway shareholders, should be the principal beneficiaries. Fitzwilliam was enthused, securing the station commission for Pritchett and laying the foundation stone himself in 1846.[83] The outcome of Hathorn's initiative was a dignified new street leading from the town and an impressive new 'square' in front of the station surrounded by an outstanding set of buildings, the work of a number of mainly local architects. In terms of both the acreage covered and the architectural magnificence of the new buildings, it was a scheme almost without parallels among the northern industrial towns. Only the development of Newcastle upon Tyne in the second quarter of the century could rival it. William White, publishing in 1853, concluded 'St George's Square and the new streets opening into it, are the handsomest parts of Huddersfield, being spacious, and lined with elegant stone buildings.'[84] The *Huddersfield Chronicle* enthused, not unreasonably, 'from the front of our noble station … Huddersfield is one of the most splendid towns in the kingdom'[85] and it praised Wallen's new hotel.

This was, indeed, a remarkable piece of town planning in terms of scale and ambition. Absolutely central to the successful completion of the project was that the land was in single ownership: the Ramsdens. In, for instance, Bolton, Bradford, Leeds or Manchester, land ownership was so fragmented that development on anything other than a modest scale was impossible. But in Huddersfield, with a combination of long-established ownership by the Ramsdens, and a series of astute recent purchases masterminded by Loch and Hathorn, it was indeed possible. In terms of scale, it was a town centre development almost without precedent in England, but what was equally important was the Ramsden determination to have only buildings of the highest order. It was a commendable vision, overseen from 1851 by the eminent London architect, William Tite.[86]

Wallen's design for the George was accepted in January 1849; despite the admiration generated by Pritchett's station, the latter had, by then, annoyed Isabella Ramsden, which perhaps precluded him from being invited to design the hotel. Significantly, it was 'the only building in the square for which the Trustees had to pay', suggesting Wallen was held in high regard. Indeed, Loch judged it 'the most substantial and best constructed edifice I know anywhere' – praise indeed. It cost £10,470-14-2.[87]

The station is, indeed, magnificent: majestic in scale and perfectly sited. But it is also an old-fashioned design: Palladianism tricked out with a few Grecian details.[88] The George Hotel – 'one of the largest and handsomest hotels in England', according to White[89] – is, on the other hand, ultra-fashionable Italian Renaissance, a stunning development from Wallen's earlier, more modest essay in the style, the Riding School in Ramsden Street. It is by comparing the station and the hotel that the approximately two decades that separated the architectural education of Pritchett and Wallen becomes noticeable. The George really was cutting edge Parisian fashion brought to Huddersfield *via* Letrouilly's books. The style is typified by quoins marking the corners of walls, deeply overhanging cornices supported by brackets, an absence of an architrave – usually an essential component in a Classical entablature – and a rusticated ground floor. All these details can be found in Letrouilly's illustrations. It was a style to be found in London, but was one that largely escaped West Yorkshire until much later. The refinement and subtleties of the style are clear if one compares the George with slightly later buildings in the square. Britannia Building (by William Cocking, *c*.1858), reflects Tite's fondness for a somewhat ostentatious species of Classicism with exuberant sculptural decoration and a heavy parapet; Pritchett's Lion Building (1852–4) remained a clumsy design, despite Tite's best endeavours to correct it.[90]

Wallen's final landmark contribution to central Huddersfield was six shops and attached warehouses on the corner of Westgate and the new John William Street (*c*.1852–3).[91] It is another sophisticated, thoughtfully proportioned Classical composition, but deliberately more understated than the George as befitted the buildings' function and street location. The block was important in establishing what soon became the standard street architecture of mid-century Huddersfield, the 'spacious' thoroughfares lined with 'elegant stone buildings', described by White.[92]

Castle Hill

The next group of projects had rather more chequered gestations. John Rumsby tells us that 'a tavern to cater for pleasure-seekers was first built on [Castle Hill, Almondbury] in about 1810–11,'[93] and through the nineteenth century the hill was a popular location for walkers, political rallies and for church and chapel outings. In 1848 Wallen wrote to the Ramsden Estate to request 'a site for a prospect tower on Castle Hill',[94] a project which he stated he had had in mind some years. He wrote again early the following year seeking the Estate's support: if approved, it 'may be finished this season',[95] Wallen claimed confidently. It seems there was much local support, 'a model was made, a committee formed and financed organised.'[96] The building was to have included 'a restaurant, museum and observation room',[97] and 'accommodation for private picnic parties [likely to be popular as] Huddersfield was without any place of attraction for visitors.' The tower was to be 'about 26 feet square

... and the total height [was to be] 95 feet so that the summit ... would be nearly 1,000 above the level of the sea' with extensive views. The cost was estimated at £1,200.[98] However, in 1849 Isabella Ramsden objected strongly, claiming that her son's 'antiquarian taste is quite shocked at the idea of the old fort ... on Castle Hill being disturbed for a new erection of any sort or kind.'[99] Nevertheless, in 1851, at the 'Huddersfield Brewster Sessions ... it was stated that the tower, talked of some time ago ... was now likely to be proceeded with and that Mr Wallen ... had his plans ready for that purpose.'[100] And in that year the Castle Hill Hotel opened, but, confusingly, this seems to have been an entirely separate project.

The narrative is further complicated by simultaneous discussions concerning a monument to Robert Peel. A letter signed 'Alpha' – could this have been Wallen using a pseudonym? – appeared in the *Huddersfield Chronicle* on 3 August 1850.

> A very pretty plan and model for a tower on Castle-hill ... were prepared by our talented architect, W. Wallen, with whom originated the idea of marking the spot where stood the old Roman fortress ... also to serve as an observatory for astronomical and other purposes for the whole county, which design would have been carried out but for some slight difference in respect of the ground. Now, it strikes me the same tower, if erected, might serve a twofold purpose, viz that for which it was originally intended, and a lofty base for a colossal figure of that statesmen.

It concluded, 'Should this meet the views of the committee formed for carrying out the proposed monument, it might also serve as an inducement to the trustees of the Ramsden Estate, to grant the necessary land for the purpose.' Clearly the Ramsdens were still not enthusiastic and nothing came of this proposal or the tower, although Wallen was to be involved in other schemes to honour Peel.

Was there any relationship between the Castle Hill Hotel and the Castle Hill Tower? Although sharing a similar location, their functions and intended clienteles were significantly different. It seems it was Ramsden opposition, as noted in Wallen's 1850 letter quoted above, that killed the tower project. But if the Ramsdens objected to a tower, why did they not also object to the hotel? Probably the hotel was a rebuilding of the existing inn in a style which reflected the vernacular traditions of the area and could almost have been mistaken for a seventeenth century yeoman's house.

38. Castle Hill hotel (1851), usually ascribed to William Wallen.
Huddersfield Local Studies Library

The Peel Monument

Following Robert Peel's death on 2 July 1850, the good citizens of Huddersfield lost no time in considering the erection of a fitting monument. A committee of forty-four was formed to consider proposals,[101] and early in 1851 a competition was organised which solicited as number of designs from architects. The *Chronicle* devoted much space to the project, beginning a long article with a discussion of possible sites, concluding the only sensible one was in the new square in front of the station, one the Ramsdens were reluctant to provide. It then proceeded to assess in detail eight anonymously submitted designs, concluding that design III 'was by far the most appropriate among the sketches we have seen.'[102] Later it transpired Wallen was the author of design III, which was a 57-feet high Classical column surmounted by 'a Funeral Urn'.[103] The committee was unable to agree on either a design or a location, and nothing further was done.[104] However, the project was revived in 1868 and eventually, in 1873, a statue of Peel was erected in front of the station [see Illustration 22, p. 59].[105]

Wallen's status in Huddersfield and final legacy

We have only scant details of Wallen's private life during his Huddersfield years. He appears to have lived the sort of life that could be expected of a successful professional gentleman. Initially he resided in Buxton Road/ Chapel Hill[106] but by 1842 he had moved to 41, West Parade.[107] In 1850 he was living a little further out from the centre in fashionable New North Road, at no 2.[108] His activities with the Yorkshire Architectural Society and lectures for the Geological and Polytechnic Society of the West Riding were regularly reported in the region's newspapers and must have brought him some academic eminence. Similarly, his earlier publications continued to be advertised, although his planned *Guide to Castle Hill, Almondbury, with Historical, Typographical and Antiquarian Notices*, advertised in 1852, remained unfinished.[109] And within his profession, he was sufficiently well-regarded to have been appointed as an arbitrator in the Leeds architect John Clark's dispute concerning the Leeds Industrial School competition in 1846.[110] Finally, in the early 1850s, he was one of around 50 'Directors' of the Agbrigg Savings Bank.[111] It all suggests middle-class respectability.

It had long been believed that Wallen died in 1853 or 1854, but Isaac Hordern, the Ramsden Estate's cashier, recorded that Wallen did not see the completion of the chapel at Aspley in 1854, 'as he had to go to a private doctor's home.'[112] It is now clear that he lived until 1888 and spent the last thirty-five years of his life as a patient at Bootham Park Hospital, York, the county's lunatic asylum. He was admitted on 8 September 1854 and died there on 1 May 1888.[113]

Wallen's legacy

After about 1850 Huddersfield's attitudes to where architects resided changed. No longer was employing a man with a local address the ultimate stamp of prestige; now a London address was pre-eminent. The town's two most significant churches from this decade – St John, Bay Hall (1851–3) [see Illustration 29, p. 136] and St Thomas, Manchester Road (1857–9) – were by eminent London designers; and while most of the impressive 1850s buildings surrounding St George's Square were by local men – Cocking, Pritchett and Wallen – in 1851 it was a London architect, William Tite, who was appointed to inspect designs and maintain standards.[114]

However, it is clear that Wallen had enjoyed a high reputation in Huddersfield. Aside from his architectural contribution to the town and beyond, he was a Fellow of the Society of Antiquaries and had been a committee member of the Yorkshire Architectural Society. He had published a number of significant archaeological books and pamphlets, and enjoyed some eminence as a lecturer. In one of the last newspaper notices of him – the opening of the chapel at Aspley in 1854 – the *Chronicle* referred to him as, 'the architect who has so well adorned the locality'.[115]

Wallen and the Ramsdens

What was Wallen's relationship with the Ramsdens and their agents? Pritchett was initially the family's favoured architect, a position seriously dented by the 1842 partial collapse, during reconstruction, of St Edward, Brotherton. In 1844, having read in the *Leeds Mercury* that Fitzwilliam had recently visited Huddersfield accompanied by Pritchett, Isabella Ramsden repeated a warning she had first issued to George Loch the preceding August:

> Now, he [Pritchett] must not be employed in his profession, on any work, for which the Ramsden family are expected to pay. – He has given us a lesson we shall not forget. – He must not be employed by the Trustees. – ... we [the Ramsdens] are resolved that we will not have any thing now to do with him.[116]

However, it seems Fitzwilliam was unmoved and Pritchett's most memorable addition to Huddersfield and one that was the result of Ramsden patronage – the railway station – was yet to be started.

Nevertheless, this spat can only have aided Wallen's position. Yet he too managed to fall out with Mrs Ramsden in 1849 over the Castle Hill Tower. More positively, in 1851 he prepared plans for 'covering the Market Place ... The idea seems to have originated with ... Isabella Ramsden who felt that the ladies of the area, who bought [items there] deserved some covered accommodation.' However, nothing came of the proposal.[117] In contrast, his 1848 commission to design the estate office at Longley Hall, the family's Huddersfield base, was successfully completed, [118] and probably in the same year Wallen began work on the new George Hotel. This was to be the Ramsdens' principal contribution to the 'New Town' of Huddersfield that came with the railway[119] and the choice of architect is unlikely to have been a matter of indifference. It was both Wallen's most significant project for the Ramsden Estate and his most memorable addition to Huddersfield.

More generally, the Ramsdens – or more usually their agent – seeking to maintain high standards of design, inspected all proposals for new buildings on land that formed part of the Estate and would thus have been familiar with other Wallen commissions. This was particularly the case from 1844 when George Loch was appointed Manager of the Estate – a responsibility he undertook much more diligently than his predecessor – and introduced strict supervision of new buildings. Thus in 1846 Wallen, seeking to have the Riding School 'covered before winter which is very desirable', complained of delays the inspection process generated.[120]

Any architect seeking success in the town after 1844 would have had to impress Loch; in this respect, Wallen probably had a distinct advantage.

Loch, father and son, had extensive metropolitan connections and would have known, or known of, Wallen's father, John, the 'principal quantity surveyor [in the 1830s] in the City'.[121] Estate managers might have had only limited interest in architectural niceties, but quantity surveying and the erection of functional buildings to increase mercantile efficiency – where John Wallen excelled – certainly came within their domain. It is thus very unlikely that the Lochs and the Wallens were unknown to each other. They would, in modern parlance, have 'spoken the same language'. However, when it came to ecclesiastical projects, in the 'new' world of Ecclesiological imperatives, any closeness between the families would have counted for little.

A Ramsden project that gives useful insights into both how the family saw itself as well as its relationship with Wallen and Pritchett is the new church of St John, Bay Hall, begun in the late1840s and closely associated with Isabella Ramsden. Following the debacle at Brotherton, employing Pritchett is unlikely to have been countenanced, but did they consider Wallen? He had, by this time, a succession of well-regarded, structurally sound churches to his credit. The answer is deeply embedded in the revolution of attitudes to the design of churches and to the liturgy that would take place within them, brought about by the Ecclesiologists whose influence from the early-1840s was enormous. It was a movement closely associated with elite groups at Cambridge University and, to a lesser extent, at Oxford. Concurrently, financing church building moved from being something the wealthy middle- and upper-classes often rather resented – as noted in Sir John Ramsden's grudging contribution to the rebuilding of Huddersfield parish church in 1834–6 – to something to be done with generosity and enthusiasm. The Ecclesiologists made 'medieval authenticity' in the style, layout and detail of new churches beyond question, while social reformers made the support of church building a Christian duty: 'Nothing can be so sacred, so public, so permanent, so really benevolent, so truly gracious an offering, as a building devoted to the Living God.'[122] The cynic might conclude that the support of church building became something of a fashionable past-time, although one undertaken with earnest.

Wallen made a name for himself building cheap, plain churches for 'Low' Anglican congregations of a type loathed by the Ecclesiologists – they are not churches at all, merely 'sermon houses', they thundered [see Illustration 36, p. 157].[123] These might have served Huddersfield's industrial worshippers perfectly well but, thanks to Ecclesiology, they would struggle to be accepted by polite society. Pritchett's completed churches were at least as unacceptable in the context of the new imperatives. His ecclesiastical solecisms included St Peter, Bafferton, North Yorkshire (1826–31) where he rebuilt the nave of the medieval church to create a 'preaching box' orientated north-south, sandwiched between the original tower and chancel, and, worse still, in 1816 he had built the new St Nicholas, Norton, East Yorkshire – in Fitzwilliam territory – in the Grecian style. Using 'pagan' idioms was, for the Ecclesiologists, the ultimate sin. If the Ramsdens were to capitalise on their generosity at St John's they needed to impress their equals at least as much as their tenants. Thus, while they were content to let Pritchett author the new railway station and Wallen design the estate office at Longley Hall or the George Hotel, neither could, in the new climate, be entrusted with a 'Ramsden' church; this was a job for a big-named metropolitan architect, one who carried the Ecclesiologists' stamp of approval. The initial choice was London-based Edward Blore who had recently completed Buckingham Palace and was currently engaged at Windsor Castle and Hampton Court; Loch would have known Blore through the latter's work on the Bridgewater estate at Worsley, Lancashire, where he was also the agent. It is a mark of Ecclesiological dogma that even an architect of Blore's eminence was pilloried for his churches: his Christ Church, Hoxton, London, was deemed a 'truly contemptible building' by an architect 'entirely unacquainted with the true spirit of Pointed architecture.'[124] His design was also too expensive and so the commission went to William Butterfield, widely seen as the Ecclesiologists' favoured son.[125] By 1851, when construction started, Butterfield was also busy with his designs for Adelaide Cathedral.

Thanks to the Ramsdens' careful oversight of Huddersfield, the mid-nineteenth century town was indeed 'one of the most handsome towns in the kingdom', and local architects played the major part in this. However, by the mid-1840s, church-building had become so over-laid with the demands of the High Church agenda that its funding needed to be approached with circumspection. If high profile donors like the Ramsdens were to capitalise on their largesse, they needed to build the 'right' sort of church.

Endnotes

1. Baines (1822), pp. 134–5; White (1853), p. 443.
2. Baines (1822), p 188; White (1853), p. 561.
3. Baines (1809), p. 44; Slade (1851), p. 467.
4. Baines (1822), p. 149; White (1853), pp. 142-3.
5. Although Pigot (1834), p. 261, does include Joseph Kaye in his Huddersfield Architects list.
6. Quoted in Wyles (1992), p. 303.
7. Attributed on the basis of its stylistic similarity to Pritchett's York County Savings Bank, York (1829–30).
8. Whitaker (1816), p. 65.
9. For a useful overview of Huddersfield in 1840, see Griffiths (2011a), pp. 176–8.

10 An 1848 commentator, quoted in Wyles (1992), p. 303.
11 White (1853), p. 596.
12 For Kaye's career, see Law (1989).
13 Among the books, Nicholson (1798) ran to many editions between 1798 and 1835. Examples of tradesmen turned 'architects' include, in Leeds, Lawrence Ingham and Benjamin Jackson, and in Wakefield, John Robson.
14 Pigot (1834), p. 261.
15 Soane (1788), p. 7.
16 For Pritchett, see *ODNB* (2004), 'Pritchett, James Pigott (1789–1868)' and Colvin (2008), pp. 834–7.
17 Jenkins (2017), p. 247.
18 *Sheffield Independent and Yorkshire and Derbyshire Independent*, 3 July 1830.
19 Wyles (1992), p. 308.
20 For details of his pupils, see Webster (2010), p. 10. This also provides more thorough coverage of Wallen's pre-Huddersfield activities.
21 Robson (1831), p. 173; Shepherd (1957), p. 167.
22 For a fuller account of Wallen's antiquarian pursuits, see Webster (2010).
23 Graves (1907), p. 291.
24 The committee meeting of 7 May 1835 received his application: Society of Antiquaries, Minute Book 36, pp. 488-9, 510.
25 Wallen (1836).
26 *Architectural Magazine*, 3, 1836, p. 227.
27 *Civil Engineer and Architect's Journal*, I, 1838, pp. 156-8.
28 Lambeth Palace Library, Incorporated Church Building Society archive, ICBS file 01422.
29 I am grateful to Christopher Marsden for information about Ward's places of residence.
30 ICBS file 01422, Lewis Jones to ICBS, 2 January 1838, asking the ICBS to tell Mr Chantrell what further changes it wanted.
31 ICBS file 01422, Jones to ICBS, 3 March 1838.
32 ICBS file 01422, Chantrell to Jones, 21 January 1839: 'on 18 March [1838] when you came over to Leeds with the Farnley Tyas Estimates [Chantrell was in the process of building this church in the Almondbury parish] and proposed to me to execute another person's design'.
33 ICBS file 01422, Wallen to ICBS, 17 March 1838.
34 *LI*, 2 June 1838; 1 August 1840.
35 WYAS, Wakefield, WDP12/178, Almondbury Parish Records, Minute Book, 1825–1885.
36 Foundation stone laying, *LI*, 30 March 1839.
37 Brook (1968), p. 199.
38 *LM*, 2 Feb 1839. Wallen was a shareholder, *LM*, 26 May 1838.
39 *LI*, 2 December 1838.
40 The precise date of opening seems not to have been recorded.
41 ICBS file 02999; WYAS, Leeds, BDP26, Farsley Parish Records.
42 *Bradford Observer*, 6 July 1843.
43 *LI*, 27 January 1844; WYAS, Bradford, BDP78, Oakworth Parish Records.
44 ICBS, file 03891.
45 *HC*, 11 March 1854 reported the opening stating the new chapel 'was not far from the old Lecture-room' which, presumably, was a temporary chapel. Clearly there were two

	discrete buildings but the new chapel was often referred to as 'the Lecture Room', e.g. *HC*, 25 January 1868.
46	ICBS, file 02498. The application was unsuccessful.
47	Tenders requested, *LI*, 14 October 1843.
48	*HC*, 26 June 1852.
49	Weatherhead (1913), p. 40. Weatherhead records that Wallen asked for only 'a donation of £10–0–0' for his professional services.
50	WYAS, Wakefield, WDP 24, Holmbridge Parish Records, nos 87 and 98.
51	Tenders requested, *LI*, 21 Sept 1844.
52	Tenders requested, *LI*, 28 December 1844.
53	WYAS, Wakefield, WDP 143, Marsden Parish Records, no 38.
54	Tenders requested, *LI*, 1 August 1846
55	Harman and Pevsner (2017), p. 353.
56	For the Cambridge Camden Society, see 'Introduction' in Webster (2003).
57	This appears in a hand-written statement in the YAS's first Minute Book (1842–6), p. 2: York Minster Library, YAS, 2001/178, box 10b.
58	The paper delivered in York is variously referred to as being on 'The Geometrical Principles of Gothic Architecture' and on 'The Geometric Principles of Gothic Tracery', whereas the Halifax one was on '… Gothic Architecture'. York Minster Library, YAS Minute Book, 1842–6.
59	Information about the society's meeting is to be found in Minute Book 1. Minute Book 2, covering 1847–50 is missing and Wallen is not mentioned as a committee member in the one covering 1851–7.
60	The society's membership records are patchy but from 1850 were published in *Associated Architectural Society Papers and Reports*. The first volume, for 1850, shows Wallen as a member.
61	Wallen (1842).
62	See Scholfield (1958), ch. 5; Morgan (1961), p. 17. For more on Wallen's contribution to the subject see Webster (2010), pp. 20–1.
63	Wallen (1842), pp. 5–7.
64	For instance, see the *c*.1842 plan for Farsley in WYAS, Leeds, BDP 26/31 and the plan of the finished building in ICBS, file 02999.
65	Ahier (1949), p. 229. The pre-Ecclesiological interior arrangement of Christ Church, Linthwaite (built 1827–8) still remained unmodernised at the end of the century. In a national context, it was a very rare survival.
66	In addition to the publications discussed already, Wallen subscribed to most of the parts of Poole and Hugall (1842–4), the best survey then of the county's medieval parish churches.
67	Wallen (1842), p. 7.
68	Wallen (1842), p. 20.
69	For more discussion of Wallen's views about church design, see Webster (2010), p. 23.
70	Wallen (1842), p. 4.
71	See Crook (2003), pp. 84–120.
72	*LI*, 5 October 1840.
73	*LI*, 11 October 1845. For more discussion of the reception of Wallen's churches, see Webster (2010), pp. 24–5.
74	*LI*, 11 October 1845.
75	I am grateful to Christopher Tyne for this information.

76   *LI*, 11 October 1845, although the [*London*] *Morning Post*, 18 November 1845, gives the number of seats as 602.
77   *HC*, 11 March 1854.
78   *LM*, 9 May 1840. I am grateful to Christopher Marsden for this reference. For a thorough discussion of the exhibition, see Griffiths (2011a), pp. 175–98.
79   DD/T/S/a/41, Thornhill Papers, Report on the Condition of Roofs at Fixby Hall, 26 September 1840.
80   *LI*, 27 January 1844.
81   Law (1986) p. 59. See chapter 1, pp.14-18
82   Tenders requested *LM*, 27 June 1846 (Riding School), 10 October 1846 (Druid Hotel).
83   Wyles (1992), p. 308.
84   White (1853), p. 596.
85   *HC*, 11 March 1854.
86   See chapter 2, pp. 61-2.
87   'Abstract of New George Hotel Building Account', quoted in Whomsley (1974), note 139. I am grateful to Brian Haigh for alerting me to this item.
88   Jenkins (2017), p. 248, even suggests Pritchett 'echoed' Fitzwilliam's mansion, Wentworth Woodhouse, built a century earlier.
89   White (1853), p. 596.
90   Wyles (1992), p. 312.
91   Tenders were advertised in *HC*, 26 June 1852.
92   White (1853), p. 596.
93   Rumsby (1992), p. 10.
94   DD/RE/C/50, Wallen to Loch, 10 July 1848, quoted in Law (1986), p. 58.
95   DD/RE/C/56, Wallen to Loch, 11 January 1849.
96   Law (1986), p. 58; *LM*, 3 March 1849.
97   Rumsby (1992), p. 11.
98   *HDC*, 3 July 1899. This 'Correspondence' from Isaac Hordern included a detailed account of Wallen's proposal and the names of those on the Management Committee: Hordern, 'Notes', 1851, p. 24; 1898, p. 197.
99   WYASK, DD/RE/c/59, Isabella Ramsden to Loch, 15 April 1849.
100 *LM*, 23 August 1851.
101 Minter (1996), vol. 2, p. 3.
102 *HC*, 15 March 1851.
103 The designs received much coverage in the *Chronicle* thanks to letters from 'Josephus J. Roebuck, Civil Engineer' criticising Wallen's designs and responses from Wallen. *HC*, 15 March 1851, 29 March 1851, 5 April 1851, 12 April 1851, 5 June 1852. Wallen had also submitted design V.
104 See chapter 2, pp. 73-4.
105 Minter (1996), vol. 1, p. 3.
106 Correspondence in ICBS, file 01422.
107 Williams (1845), p. 69.
108 *HC*, 5 June 1852. *HC*, 26 June 1852, confusingly still gave his address as West Parade.
109 *HC*, 9 October 1852.
110 *LM*, 4 April 1846. I am grateful to Christopher Marsden for this reference. See also C. Webster, 'John Clark (1798–1857)' in Webster (2011), pp. 132–3.
111 *HC*, 25 January 1851, 5 February 1853.
112 Hordern, 'Notes', 1853, p. 35.

113 University of York, Borthwick Institute, NHS/BOO/6/2/3/2, Registry of Admissions Book, 6 Nov 1850–10 Sept 1855. Many of the details that follow are based on information generously supplied by Gary Jones of Brisbane, Australia, a distant relative of Edward Jones, one of John Wallen's pupils. I am grateful to him for sharing this information.
114 Wyles (1992), pp. 308, 312.
115 *HC*, 11 March 1854.
116 WYASK, DD/RA/C/4/1, Isabella Ramsden to Fitzwilliam, 9 November 1844; see also DD/RE/C/3/26, Isabella Ramsden to Loch, 20 August 1844.
117 WYASK, DD/RE/C/90, Isabella Ramsden to Loch, 2 November 1851, quoted in Law (1986), p. 59; see chapter 2, p. 65.
118 See chapter 1, pp. 14-15.
119 Marsden (2018), un-paginated.
120 WYASK, DD/RE/C/25, Wallen to Hathorn, 1 June 1846.
121 *DNB* (1890), vol. 28, p. 408.
122 *British Critic and Quarterly Theological Review*, 26, 1839, p. 461.
123 Neale and Webb (1843), p. xxiii.
124 *Ecclesiologist*, 3, 1843, p. 99; *ODNB* (2004), 'Blore, Edward (1787–1879)'.
125 Brooks (2000), pp. 121–49. For Butterfield, see *ODNB* (2004), 'Butterfield, William (1814–1900)'.

CHAPTER SIX

Buying Huddersfield for the People

STEPHEN CAUNCE AND EDWARD ROYLE

'IT IS OFTEN TRICKY to decide when an agglomeration of huts and houses becomes a town with a sense of itself as a community, with a shared identity and aspirations.'[1] This process was particularly short and dramatic for many northern English textile towns, and Huddersfield's was one of the most truncated. When they received their first town charter as a municipal borough in 1868, many inhabitants celebrated this as a formal recognition of the threshold having been crossed, even though, as in every town, there were also significant numbers who resented anything which increased their outgoings and they perceived no personal gain from stronger administration. For ordinary people, it may all have seemed to be above their heads, but more and more of them did look forward to a time when real democracy would require the town's management to reflect the wishes and needs of the whole population.

Certainly, those who valued the charter also took it as a recognition from central government of the enormous amount they had achieved over the previous century in expanding their manufacturing and trade. The more practical gift of powers to manage their own affairs much more actively than in the past was, however, now clearly needed, especially in the central area which was until then classed as nothing more than a hamlet.[2] The wider township had also seen its population multiply rapidly, an increase which showed no sign of tailing off. Much had been achieved through determinedly adapting systems designed for running feudal villages, supplemented by the setting up of improvement commissions and other ad hoc bodies.[3] However, the age of muddling through in this way had to be superseded by forms of government more firmly embedded in the desires of the whole community. Even so, the powers and duties awarded were still limited compared to the present day, and this chapter recounts how Huddersfield was a pioneer in going further.

The Municipal Corporations Act of 1835 undoubtedly marked a sharp break with the previous history of towns in England, for charters awarded since Tudor times had mostly been about ceremony and prestige rather than the practicalities of running a community. In effect, the reforms of 1835 recognised that the manufacturing and mining towns had reset the whole urban agenda on their own terms, rather than their being absorbed into an existing system. Huddersfield was thus recognised as a thriving industrial settlement when it became a municipal borough in 1868, and would go on to be given county borough status as part of the formation of the new West Riding County Council in 1889.

This removed the town entirely from the county's administrative apparatus, but this chapter recounts how, after a delay, one further step which few other towns could ever have considered, and hardly any ventured upon, was undertaken. As the town's Liberal newspaper, the *Examiner*, commented at the time, when the Corporation decided to acquire the Huddersfield portion of the landed estates of the feudal overlord, the Ramsden family, that was but 'another step ... along the path of municipal progress which has been so consistently and successfully followed even before, and certainly since, the incorporation of the borough.'[4] The Ramsdens held extensive estates elsewhere, but the heart of their historic lordship lay, as the legal conveyance which ended their influence was to put it:

> in and around the Town of Huddersfield and in the townships of Huddersfield, Almondbury, Lockwood, Honley, and Dalton, or the Parishes of Huddersfield, Almondbury, Deighton, Kirkheaton and Fixby, comprising or including the Manor and Lordship of Almondbury, the Advowsons of the Rectories or Vicarages of St. Peter's, Huddersfield, All Saints, Almondbury, and St John's, Birkby, and the lands containing in the whole Four thousand three hundred acres or thereabouts delineated in the plans specially prepared.[5]

By acquiring this estate, the Borough Corporation at a stroke came to own nearly half the territory which it administered, including almost the whole of the commercial heart of the town, which was estimated to cover about three hundred acres.[6] It also acquired automatically what remained of the manorial system of administration from feudal times, and the right to appoint the clergy of three Anglican churches on the estate. In doing so it imposed a new unity across the chaotic mix of townships within huge ancient parishes which was typical of the industrial Pennines but very different from the arrangements taken for granted in the southern half of England. It effectively extended the practical powers of administration considerably further than even much larger urban areas enjoyed, or the framers of the reformed charters envisaged.

Clifford Stephenson, himself a councillor, looked back at the purchase some decades ago in a determinedly celebratory tone, setting out how it originated and how it was brought to fruition largely through the efforts of Councillor Wilfrid Dawson. A re-examination of the bound volume of documents known as the 'Dawson File', which Stephenson relied upon, certainly supports the factual aspect of his account as far as it goes.[7] However, he rather glosses over the manner in which negotiations both began and were carried through, almost to the point of completion, and leaves a number of important questions unanswered. In particular, according to Stephenson the process was nudged along by an astonishing series of coincidences which were apparently vital to its success. There are also some elements in the story which might suggest the possibility of sharp practice to modern minds used to suspicions of corruption and underhand dealing in such matters.

This chapter therefore goes over the process again, using an approach which would be associated today with the phrase 'due diligence' as applied to such enormous corporate financial dealings, in so far as such a thing is possible from such limited material. At the same time, it must be stressed that it was always clear that Dawson himself never stood to make any personal profit from the scheme. At his funeral the *Examiner* reported that

> a rumour [had been] rife at the completion of the bargain to the effect that Alderman Dawson had "made a profit, or drawn a commission" on the transfer – an insinuation that had hurt [him] very much. "Not by one penny piece", said Councillor Barlow, "did he or his firm benefit. Even on the completion, when he was offered a cigar he declined it so that for all time he could honestly say "Not a farthing in any shape or form came to me or mine through this transaction."[8]

The lengthy report from which this comes also reminded readers that Dawson never actually fought a council election. He was unopposed when he first stood as a candidate for Newsome ward, and the dramatic events of his first term led to his immediate selection as an alderman, a status which he maintained for the rest of his time on the council. Indeed, after a year he became mayor and served two years (1921–1923) in that office. Dawson was remembered as 'a great administrator, and a man whose shrewd and sound judgement, wonderful insight and wide experience have been of inestimable benefit to the town of Huddersfield'. The reported views of those who knew him suggest a man who was energetic and determined, a hard negotiator and one who could at some times be impatient yet at others show 'a generous disposition'.[9]

By profession Dawson was a stockbroker who developed a wide range of business interests. He was involved in the speculative buying of Lancashire cotton mills during the brief post-war boom (and lost money in the subsequent slump), and he was a director of several textile companies. These included the Amalgamated Cotton Mills Trust Limited, of which someone

39. Wilfrid Dawson (1871–1936), in 1921. Councillor (1917); Alderman (1920) and Mayor (1921–3); honorary Freeman (1934); Chairman of the Finance and Watch Committees (1921–36).
West Yorkshire Archive Service, Kirklees

40. Samuel William Copley (1859–1937), in 1933. Self-made banker and financier who funded the initial purchase of Huddersfield in 1919–20.
West Yorkshire Archive Service, Kirklees

else who was to play a significant part in the Huddersfield purchase, Samuel William Copley, was also a director. Another business associate and financier involved in cotton speculation was James White, who was also to enter the story of the Huddersfield deal.[10]

The existence of the Dawson File in itself leaves the researcher with a sense of confusion about motives and methods, which Stephenson largely ignores. Its creation shows that Dawson wanted to preserve a formal and comprehensive paper trail covering the course of his negotiations, which he knew were unorthodox, and yet it was effectively put away in a place where it was unlikely to be found, and where if found its significance would almost certainly be missed. It was thus far more likely to have disappeared for ever, than be utilised as it ultimately was – and presumably was intended – to be. Most of the 175 documents included seem unimpeachable individually, but the process they reflect, taken as a whole, is generally eccentric and at times bizarre. In that sense the File can sometimes seem almost designed to obscure the real significance of what was done. What is apparent is a fairly ruthless, driving urge by Dawson to achieve a personal goal which he knew his colleagues on the council did not actively share, much less the general public. A similar scheme had been proposed by Councillor E. A. Beaumont in 1894, apparently after talking about such matters to the financier Baron Rothschild, but it had then been firmly rejected as impractical.[11]

What may have motivated Dawson to ignore this is Huddersfield's unusual continuing dependence on a single manorial lord. The Ramsdens owned most of the land on which the town centre stood and, although they had previously been closely and positively involved in various aspects of the town's development, they now seemed increasingly detached.[12] When Dawson had first joined the council in 1917, he had stated that such a purchase was 'his great ambition', but in all his later comments on the actual purchase, he said that the initiative really came from the Ramsdens, not him.[13] The account given by Meriel Buxton in chapter 7 clarifies the issues by showing that Sir John Frecheville Ramsden had demonstrated a steadily diminishing emotional identification with his ancestral estate around the town, except perhaps for Longley Old Hall, which was not included in the sale.[14] Instead, there was a growing engagement with other sections of the family's lands, especially in Scotland. With a shift in the Ramsdens' economic attention to the Malayan plantations which they had fortuitously acquired and which proved highly lucrative, even the practical significance of Huddersfield as a source of income was reduced.[15] There is also some evidence in the Dawson File and elsewhere that the rise of socialistic politics in the town made it harder for paternalism to function in a way that satisfied the family. Finally, the rise of much larger, impersonal companies at the heart of the local economy must also have diminished any possibility of maintaining any real control of development by a feudal lord.

The work of Springett also suggests that the estate had been run for several decades in a rather unrealistic manner, and its long-term financial value therefore was far from clear, something which almost wrecked the search for agreement over what was a fair price to be paid.[16] In particular, when the Ramsden Estate had finally had to admit that tenancies-at-will were no longer acceptable to tenants in the commercial centre, their initial shift to 99 year leases in 1867 still did not actually go far enough to encourage developers and later owners to see them as long-term assets which would not depreciate discernibly over a short lifetime. Leases for 999 years were becoming the norm nationally, and were much preferred.[17]

Moreover, with regard to the development of housing, even though many contemporary commentators and historians have argued that developers should have built better houses than they did, it seems clear that when the Ramsdens set out to encourage this approach it had limited success. New North Road was developed in the 1850s and good villas were built around Greenhead Park from the 1860s and in Marsh from the 1880s, but most Huddersfield inhabitants could not afford such dwellings, and developers knew it. Consequently, whereas the adjacent Thornhill Estate became a scene of steady building, opportunities on the Ramsden Estate were neglected. Finally, the residual agricultural value of their undeveloped land was low, given the altitude and poor soils of the area. This remained true despite the relative success of the distinctive family dairying operations based on the direct retail of liquid milk to nearby consumers, which was the local norm. Whereas the Armytages of Clifton, for example, did feel a strong enough sense of history to resist the spread of Brighouse, and to accept the financial consequences, the Ramsdens no longer wished to maintain this approach.[18] Therefore, a sale of the whole estate would be the easiest way out of an economic impasse, especially as existing investments in high-quality town-centre buildings had proved an expensive way to try to get the town economy to catch up with the older centres of Yorkshire textile manufacturing. The alternative possibility, of breaking the estate up at auction, also existed but as far as we know this was never suggested.

The man who made Dawson's plan possible was Samuel William Copley (known as Sam), like Dawson a native of Berry Brow but whose subsequent career had taken him to Australia and back. Copley was born in Parkgate, Berry Brow in 1859, the son of a weaver who had turned his hand to hairdressing and then speculated in mineral waters and oatcakes. The son showed the same initiative. Leaving home at 17 with £1 in his pocket, Sam worked as a barber in Manchester, Blackpool and Wales, and in Pontypridd he branched out as a dealer in furniture, carpets and boots. In 1887, having saved about £400, he emigrated to Australia with his brother-in-law, where he joined his half-brother, Ben. He set up as a butcher and began cattle ranching and speculating in land, making and then losing money before starting out once more as a barber in Melbourne.

He continued his financial speculations and gradually became more successful, especially after moving to Freemantle in 1888 and Perth in 1890 where his business interests and speculative land purchases in the undeveloped suburbs were highly lucrative and he became a wealthy financier as well as owning the ferry across the River Swan. He returned to England for health reasons in 1914 and settled in London. He described himself as a banker in the conveyance which ultimately concluded the purchase of Huddersfield, having recently founded Copley's Bank in London, and in 1919 he was doing well in banking and insurance as chairman of both the Western Australia Insurance Company and the Atlantic Assurance Company as well as governing director of Copley's Bank. He died in 1937, having retired to Elstree in Hertfordshire where he farmed Red Poll cattle.[19] He cuts an exotic figure as a Huddersfield native from a poor background with an unbelievable record of making, losing and making again large amounts of money. As his long-term secretary, Florence Barrowclough, told Clifford Stephenson in 1973, 'S.W.C. was always willing to take a speculative chance'.[20]

If Ramsden's urge to sell the estate is credible, what is harder to accept is Dawson's assertion that the decision to sell to him in particular was a matter of pure chance. Since the paper trail in the Dawson File provides no evidence to support this, we are free to doubt in part or in whole Dawson's version that Charles Melville (referred to by Stephenson as 'The Mystery Man'[21]) was already 'acting in a confidential role for a vendor' by cautiously seeking out a credible purchaser for an un-named Yorkshire estate.[22] However, in an alternative account, to which Stephenson did not have access until 1974 (after publishing his booklet), Sam Copley gave his version of events which, although suspect in some parts, does provide a more credible introduction to the sale process.[23] In Copley's recollection, written in 1934, Melville may well have been acting opportunistically in his own interest on the basis of knowing of Ramsden's general dissatisfaction with his Huddersfield responsibilities but without having Ramsden's specific instruction to find a buyer.

Though Copley places himself at the centre of affairs in his account, the Dawson File states firmly that formal negotiations for the purchase of the Ramsden Huddersfield Estate were 'conducted by Councillor Wilfrid Dawson from his personal business office'. The File itself shows both men playing a leading role at various times, and it is clear that Dawson was always acting in a personal capacity, not as a representative of the council. Dawson later insisted that Sir John would never have approached the council directly, and it is probably true that if any other councillors had been the first to become aware of the possibility of the purchase then they would not have taken it up. Not only would the price have been completely unprecedented as an item of municipal expenditure, but also the council had no existing powers to proceed at all with such a large purchase. Only Parliament could enable such actions, and there was no precedent to suggest that it would. National government was at that time very wary of what could be seen as reckless spending by councillors sent giddy by the reformed local government system, even when identified as investment in their towns, for such things would have been quite unthinkable only a few decades earlier.

For Dawson to set the ball in motion as a private individual in this way, and then trust that the council would eventually endorse his action rather than condemn and disown it, was taking an enormous risk even though at the end of the process it was revealed that Dawson (who was deputy chairman of the Finance Committee) had had the support from the start of the mayor, Carmi Smith, and the chairman of the Finance Committee, Ernest Woodhead. Councillors Rowland Mitchell and Thomas Canby are also mentioned by Stephenson but their names do not occur in the Dawson File correspondence and they hardly constituted what Stephenson dignified as 'an unofficial very select committee'.[24] There is little to suggest that anyone on the council except Dawson was actively involved before the whole affair was made public in the local press. When significant difficulties over agreeing a specific price emerged, Sir John never implied that he knew of others who might be willing or eager to take over the purchase, which supports theory that it was Melville who had initiated the sale and was driving forward the deal with Dawson and Copley in order to get his commission.

Stephenson's story, whereby a chance first meeting at a social gathering led to Dawson spending a night in Melville's flat in 1919, and there almost by chance hearing that an estate somewhere in the largest county of England might be for sale, must feel contrived.[25] Given that Dawson was already on record as wanting to buy the Ramsdens out, we might suspect that there was more to it than that, especially as Dawson's private office was in the same building as the Ramsden Estate Office, which was on the floor above.[26] On the other hand it is true that Melville did ultimately get a substantial fee, presumably in return for doing something. If Copley's memory is correct, the story as he told it is more straightforward: Melville was paid his commission by Copley 'In consideration of your services in negotiating on my behalf terms for the purchase of certain estates in Huddersfield belonging to Sir John Ramsden'.[27] In practice this meant in the end that it was Melville who took Dawson's name to Sir John and then let his own solicitor, H. Acland Hood, act as the go-between.

So, it would appear that Copley was playing an important part in the initial proceedings before 15 March 1919 when he appears in the Dawson File as an associate who was willing to take on the role of actual purchaser, but with the declared intention of passing on the estate if and when the Corporation could get the legal powers to buy it.

When Copley came to record his version of events in 1934, his memory and some of the details may have strayed from what actually happened and he almost certainly compressed the time scale and exaggerated his own role, but there is some contemporary corroboration for his story and there are points at which his account helps fill some of the gaps in the Dawson File.[28] Copley, Dawson and White were all business associates at this time, and it was at White's office in London that Melville (whom Copley remembered as Melrose) first met the three men.[29] How or why this came about is not clear but it would seem from Copley's account that Melville may have known White and may well have 'happened' to come to his office on business. This seems far more credible than the story of the social gathering and the night at Melville's flat. Stephenson later noted 'That Melville's contact with Copley and Dawson was deliberately "set-up" is an interesting speculation'.[30]

The two accounts then diverge further, and here Copley may be exaggerating the extent to which he, and not Dawson, took the initiative. Nevertheless, Copley's dramatised account may contain a seed of truth when he recounted that Melville had said, on learning that Copley came from Huddersfield:

> My word! I went to school with Sir John Ramsden who owns Huddersfield. My God! he would be glad to sell it – he is sick of it. He is sick of all the battling with the Socialistic Council, as they are always at him about begging a bit of land here and a bit of land there for town improvements, and they are always quarrelling about raising rates and that sort of thing on the Estate, and he has told me many times how sick he was of owning Huddersfield.

At this point, Copley recalled offering to buy his 'native town'.[31] This gave Melville his opportunity, and he responded:

> I believe he [Ramsden] would sell it cheaper through me than anyone else, as he knows I am needing money badly and he would like to see me get a Commission.[32]

Copley offered a commission of £40,000 based on a purchase price of £1m and a net yield of 6 per cent. Both Copley and Dawson must have shared Melville's belief that if Ramsden would sell at all, it would be through him, hence their agreement to pay the commission for bringing the two parties together through his solicitor, Acland Hood. Dawson, whose desire to end Ramsden control of the town was as strong as Copley's, must have been dismayed to learn of Copley's independent ambition. However, after the two men had discussed the matter further, Dawson felt re-assured that Copley would sell the estate to the Corporation when they were in a position to buy it.[33] Here the two accounts come together again and, according to the documents in the Dawson File, on 1 April Melville's commission was halved when Ramsden's asking price proved to be higher than Copley had hoped. Perhaps Copley was beginning to feel he had overreached himself. This is certainly what his family feared might be the case.[34] It may be significant that it was Dawson (not Copley) who then gave his bank details to Acland Hood.[35]

A binding commission note was produced for Melville and signed by Copley eight days later, and the Ramsdens were then formally identified as the potential vendors.[36] Two days after that, the production of some figures on estate finances set actual negotiations in motion. A six-inch map of the estate was supplied, again to Dawson, not Copley, and a debate followed about the true levels of income being derived.[37] This opacity over who was really driving the deal runs through the entire transaction and there seems to have been no agreed procedure whereby one particular individual had the final say over the amount to be paid. Copley was clearly playing an active part in the negotiations to buy the estate, and was not merely a sleeping partner who would initially finance the deal, as Stephenson thought, which would support Copley's claim to have been involved from the start.

This is a part of the narrative where Stephenson exhibits the complacency of hindsight, for the consequences for Huddersfield could have been very serious indeed if it had all miscarried. If Parliament had refused to pass the Act enabling the Corporation to buy the estate, then Copley would have replaced Sir John in his crucial role as virtual monopoly landowner in the town centre, but without any commitments made as to what would follow. Copley took this possibility seriously and claimed to have benevolent plans to allow tenants to buy their freeholds, but he also had a record for swift action, not prolonged engagement, and the reverses he had suffered previously show he was a gambler rather than a far-sighted investor.[38] Dawson was later to admit publicly that Copley had made his money 'buying and cutting up estates' – what a later generation might term 'asset stripping' – and as he would have been so heavily committed financially, he might well have had to seek rapid sales for sections of the estate at the very least.[39] Because Dawson was acting in a personal capacity, the Corporation obviously had no power to intervene at any point, but would have been presented with a take-it or leave-it deal if Copley were indeed set to take over.

At this point, we should turn our attention to the solicitor, Acland Hood. His initial link was just to Melville, but he soon offered his services to Dawson for more general liaison with Sir John. The implication was that he would prove more effective than anyone else, which is what Melville had claimed for himself at the start, though why anyone should have been needed to act in this way is hard to understand unless it is true that Copley had agreed to pay Melville for liaising with Ramsden. Moreover, it was to become evident that Hood's role had never been clearly defined, not even how his fee would be calculated. That would be disputed even as negotiations reached a climax, adding an unwelcome distraction to an inherently unsettling process. Indeed, at one crucial point Hood effectively refused to do any more work, though this threat does not seem to have been carried through.[40] Admittedly, if any one person did liaise with both sides to keep the negotiations going, it was Hood, and a large number of the documents in the File originate with him. However, had this been an official Corporation negotiation, it would have been handled entirely without him. As Dawson presumably did not wish to involve his own staff, it was convenient to leave the negotiations to Hood.

An exchange of letters with more financial details during April 1919 showed that the serious work had now begun. On the 15th Copley commented that the estate revenues were 'way below what we were led to believe they were', though whether this was simply a negotiating ploy is not clear. Acting as buyer, he now stated that he wanted a personal profit of £40,000 from the deal if he did pass on the estate, a very substantial sum echoing Melville's original demand, and one not really subject to negotiation.[41] However, he did commit explicitly to giving 'sufficient time for the Corporation to obtain statutory authority for the purchase'.

While Copley was communicating his terms to Woodhead, Dawson also remained deeply involved, receiving detailed rental lists for inspection which he then passed on to Copley, and he took the initiative to suggest an opening bid of £1,000,000 for the estate, 'free of all encumbrances'. At this point he was assuming that net income would be about £55,000 a year, which at 20-years' purchase meant £1,100,000, so £1,000,000 was 'well worth it'.[42] This was the price he said he felt the council would accept. Informally, Ernest Woodhead, thought they could go up to £1,250,000, as 'we have to look not only at the present income but also at the future development of the town & at the advantages of control when building schemes and public improvement are desired'.[43] His recommendation carried weight even though Copley would have to find the extra money.

Melville was still hovering around the fringes of the bidding and now talked directly to Copley, with Dawson wanting what was discussed to be passed on. This may bear out Copley's later view of how the purchase had started but it was a very unlikely way to run a coherent negotiation, especially as so far Sir John himself had not yet come to the fore on the Ramsden side. Dawson feared the possibility of a secret deal getting out, and wanted to push on, but on 28 April Hood stated that they were bidding too low to hope to reach agreement. On their side, they queried whether sales of Woodhouse Mill and the Lion Arcade had been reflected in the price asked. Copley, however, was now satisfied over levels of outgoings.[44]

On 6 May it was agreed that a personal meeting might break the logjam, but nothing seems to have come of this before Sir John Ramsden's own solicitors, Capel, Curie and Bell, intervened on Sir John's behalf, explicitly demanding £1.4m.[45] Dawson insisted at this point that Copley was now in charge. He in turn pointed out that the return on the sum involved was less than would come from buying war bonds, hinting at that side of Copley which was simply looking for a good investment. James White was consulted and advised that sentiment due to the Ramsden connection might raise prices at an auction sale, should the sale fall through and the Ramsdens still wish to be rid of the estate.[46] It is not clear if this was mere speculation but, as already noted, such a course certainly never emerged as a real possibility. A summary of rentals less outgoings suggested an annual income of just short of £60,000 which at 20 years' purchase would amount to £1,200,000. Sir John now proved personally very determined not to reduce his price – 'If your side are really anxious to buy they ought to be able to come up to my price'[47] – so nothing was achieved over the summer. From early August to mid-September renewed attempts to meet also came to nothing as Sir John was spending most of the summer at Ardverikie. Finally, on 1 October, Hood commented that 'it is a shame' that the two sides were now stuck just £50,000 apart, with Sir John having brought his price down to £1.3m, and Dawson evidently having gone up.[48] There is a lack of documentation here. On the 16th Dawson was still adamant that he could not go any higher as his 'friends' would not sanction it. This is a possible reference to Woodhead and the wider Corporation, but it could just refer to Copley. In any case, the latter suddenly came round to Hood's view and gave in, which does seem to have been the only possible route to resolution.[49]

Though Dawson had undoubtedly seized the initiative in the matter of the purchase, he had to be confident from the start for the realisation of his (and Copley's) dream that he could deliver the Corporation as the eventual purchaser of the estate.[50] This is why Dawson informed the Mayor, Carmi Smith, of the plan immediately after his meeting with Melville in April, and then felt able to proceed secure in the knowledge that Smith and Ernest Woodhead had 'authorised him to ascertain the terms on which the estate might be purchased'. The responsibility of the three men was admitted when the minute of the General Purposes Committee came before the subsequent meeting of the Town Council and its adoption was moved by the Mayor, seconded by the Deputy-Mayor and carried unanimously:' I think', said Councillor Robson, 'that the Council should accord its thanks to the three gentlemen who have carried through these negotiations – to the Mayor, Councillor Dawson and Alderman Woodhead.'[51]

The speed with which the deal was concluded owed much to that fact that, on 23 October the *Yorkshire Observer* reported that the Ramsden estate had been purchased on behalf of the Corporation.[52] Ernest Woodhead, who was also co-proprietor and editor of the *Huddersfield Examiner*, had expected to break the news in his own paper when the time came, so he denied the accuracy of this.[53] This was, of course, correct in a literal sense, but it was clearly disingenuous, and as a consequence of the leak (though the *Observer* denied this) Ramsden's price was agreed next day. Copley then confirmed privately that a deal was being done at £1.3m, and that it would be finalised once a few small issues were sorted. On the 25th the news hit the national press and on the 26th Melville re-emerged to note that now things were completed, he hoped everyone was satisfied. This was presumably a hint to remember his commission.[54]

Two days later, Copley then not only confirmed to Dawson that, after completion, he would immediately offer the whole estate to the Corporation but also that he would forego his premium if they allowed him £20,000 to cover his personal expenses (the sum he had promised to Melville), plus his legal expenses, and if they agreed to send all future Huddersfield Corporation insurance business to his two insurance companies, as well as any other insurance business they could 'influence'.[55] Though generous in one respect – 'I decided I would be big for once in my life' is how he later put it – Copley the opportunistic businessman was never far away and, despite having a rider that such deals would be at 'a market rate', this would not have been regarded as acceptable practice today.[56] To say that Huddersfield Corporation would effectively become a sales representative for Copley's businesses is truly astonishing. However, no-one seems to have objected on the record at the time.[57]

Sir John now indicated his acceptance that he was actually selling to the Corporation when he agreed to delay completion till 24 June 1920 'to suit their convenience' to allow them time to obtain parliamentary approval. Clearly, he did not see Copley as his long-term successor as lord of the manor, though he must now have been aware that that might happen. On 30 October the *Yorkshire Evening Post* reported that

> this afternoon, the question of the municipality of Huddersfield becoming the owner of the freehold sites of the town, will be

discussed for the first time by the Town Council. It can be said at once that, in responsible quarters in Huddersfield, not the smallest doubt is entertained of the scheme going through. The self-appointed committee of three, which has been conducting secret negotiations with Mr. Copley for some months past, decline to make any statement on the point, one way or the other; but it can be taken for granted that the three gentlemen concerned would count their labours as wasted, and suffer keen disappointment if the Town Council refused to ratify what they have done.[58]

Though a few members of the Town Council were inclined at first to be incensed because, as they said, the negotiations had been carried on behind their backs by a committee which had no authority, they soon accepted that to buy the estate on behalf of the town the method pursued was the only practical one. The three members of the negotiating committee were all Liberals, and both they and the Conservatives were in favour of the purchase, as was the Labour group whose attitude was summed up by one of its members who was reported as saying that 'Surely, a proposal which means the land for the people is up our street.' There does seem to have been 'a small body of property owners in the business portion of the town who are not exactly enamoured of the prospect of their premises becoming municipalised and officialised' but there was no danger of letting slip what Dawson himself described as 'an unparalleled opportunity'.[59] Meanwhile, Copley would indeed keep the estate if they did not see their way clear to buy it themselves. Nothing suggests that he felt this was likely, but it was Copley who at this stage had to promise to provide the substantial down payment while Parliamentary sanction was gained.[60]

The whole deal was put to a meeting of ratepayers in the Town Hall on 12 January 1920,[61] but even then Sir John was still disputing what it was exactly that he had agreed to sell. At the start he had excluded Longley Old Hall and enough land to support it. He had also excluded a site he had promised to the Corporation for a war memorial in St Peter's Street and he thought he had excluded the advowsons of his three churches (the parish churches of Huddersfield and Almondbury and St John's, Bay Hall) which he intended to give to the Bishop.[62] There was also the matter of who should pay the pension to Lady Georgiana Legge out of the £30 a year rental income from the clergy house at Almondbury, topped up to £50 by Sir John himself. He was holding out on both these issues as late as February 1920, but had conceded both by 12 March.[63] It is interesting to note that during these final negotiations, Hood felt he should warn Dawson that 'Sir John Ramsden is not a particularly willing Vendor and is opposed to the idea of the Corporation acquiring the property.'⁶⁴ This is the only clear evidence to support Dawson's belief that he should conceal the identity of the eventual purchaser of the estate.

Once the news had broken, the newspapers could not resist telling the Sam Copley story. The weekly version of the *Yorkshire Observer* ran a 'Special Huddersfield Supplement' about Copley⁶⁵ and the *Examiner* published a review of his life, the general thrust of which can be summed up by its comment that

> few stories of the rise to eminence of great magnates of the last century possess such a romantic colour as the story of [his] career. The climax of his career, the purchase of the Huddersfield Ramsden Estate on behalf of his native town by one who little more than forty years ago was a barber's boy has a suggestion of a fairy tale about it. Not even Dick Whittington was more successful.'⁶⁶

This was the man who, in his own words, 'started to buy [Huddersfield] for myself, not for them … because it is my native town' but, as one of Dawson's circle of business associates, had then felt able to respond to the need for a wealthy benefactor to enable Dawson to accomplish the deal whereby Huddersfield bought itself.⁶⁷

On 12 January 1920 a draft contract was finally circulated but, with some things still to settle, Dawson, Hood and Sir John agreed that completion should be postponed to 29 September, Michaelmas Day, the traditional legal quarter day for land transactions. This would simplify the financial handover, since it was the first half-year rent day after an exchange of contracts could be expected, and would mark a clean break in that respect, easing the strain on both the estate office and tenants.⁶⁸ The one remaining hurdle was to secure for the Corporation the legal power to purchase the estate. On 4 February the Ramsden (Huddersfield) Estates Bill duly started its course in Parliament, and it was at this point that Hood effectively refused to act any further until the purchasers agreed to pay him at the rate he felt appropriate. However, the sale business as well as his complaints both continued and in the end Hood's reduced demand was paid. The final stages were now set in motion. On 29 April, a 'brief for the Huddersfield Corporation Lands Bill', ten pages long, went before Parliament's 'Unopposed Committee'. The Bill was opposed in the Lords by the Bishop of Wakefield on account of the advowsons being included in the sale, so an amendment was agreed requiring the Corporation to sell them to the diocese for £4,000, which Ramsden then refunded. In the brief, the estimated annual rental income was raised to £65,000, equating the actual price paid to the value at 20 years' purchase. The Lands Bill completed its passage through the Lords on 22 July and received the Royal Assent on 4 August 1920.⁶⁹

On 6 May the Borough Treasurer had confirmed to Dawson the implementation of Copley's requirement about the Corporation's insurance business, though no promises survive about influencing others.[70] On 16 July Dawson was negotiating over mortgaging the Estate with the Prudential to expedite payment, insisting that this was a very short term expedient, with repayment promised 'when the purchase by the Corporation takes place'. This seems odd given Copley's commitment to provide the interim funding, and suggests Dawson's awareness of their vulnerability at this crucial time. On 21 July Copley also caused some awkwardness when his secretary revealed that her employer had already promised one of the advowsons to a friend 'before he knew the Corporation was taking over the Estate' - a blatant mis-statement unless she had been kept in ignorance of Copley's intentions.[71] Was this to be a foretaste of potential asset stripping? On 30 July Copley was reported to be ill, which delayed things, for as the formal purchaser he needed to appoint a valuer to assess tenant right on un-let agricultural land, something then resolved by simply accepting the Ramsden figure. He also failed to deal with some mortgage issues, causing needless expenditure on interest. As late as 10 September such things were still arousing 'bitter complaint' from Sir John.[72]

Although the headline sum for the purchase had been agreed as £1,300,000, this included the clearance of existing Ramsden mortgages, at least some of which were associated with inheritance settlements within the family. The Corporation thus agreed to pay Sir John £1,258,500 directly, though it seems that only a deposit of £50,000 was actually paid by Copley at that time. The Corporation also accepted liability for the mortgage debts and the interest thereafter falling due on them. It is therefore not clear from the File whether or not Copley did pay over any further funds before the contract between him and the Corporation transferred his interest in the Ramsden Estate to the Corporation, now with appropriate Parliamentary authorisation. Everything was brought together on 29 September, and the historic deal was completed. The borough treasurer, Ernest Dyson, made his way with Dawson and others to London with over a million pounds in open drafts stitched inside his waistcoat.[73] The conveyance named Sir John Ramsden of Byram Hall, as the Vendor; Samuel William Copley as the Purchaser; and the Mayor, Aldermen and Burgesses of the County Borough of Huddersfield (the Corporation) as the third party.[74]

Was this a good deal for the town? The transaction was done at the peak of the short-lived post war economic boom, followed by a collapse leading into depression, so a higher price was probably paid than if the sale had been delayed a few years, even though wool textiles were less affected than cotton. Indeed, Dawson would soon have become aware of this personally through his own speculation in the boom and subsequent heavy losses. Moreover, the ongoing inter-war depression created an environment where it would have been hard to make the substantial gains from better management that were anticipated. However, the bulk of the purchase money was borrowed from Cardiff Corporation at a variable 6⅝ per cent and in fact interest rates had fallen to 4 per cent within two years – another gamble that turned out well. By 1970 almost all the loans had been paid off, a further £980,000 had been contributed to the rates and £435,000 to the capital fund. Two years later all debts had been cleared and almost £1,500,000 added to the town's revenue – enabling Stephenson to claim that literally 'the Town had bought itself'.[75]

However, with increasing inflation, ground rents fixed for 999 years were a growing liability. Stephenson himself, as Chairman of Estates, was instrumental in establishing new leases for the town centre redevelopment in the 1960s, which included ground rent review clauses allowing for periodic increases, albeit for shorter terms. In contrast in the 1990s most residential ground rents, by then costing more to collect than they brought in, were sold off.[76] By then, moreover, pressures on local government finance made the realisation of capital gains attractive even at the expense of future rents, and the freeholds of the central area redevelopment were sold to financial institutions.

Beyond these financial considerations, the fact that the Corporation had no need to seek the consent of any other landlord for developments in the town centre, or for small amenity schemes on open space, was over time seen as a positive result. This was clearly an advantage in the 1960s when the Central Area Shopping Precinct Redevelopment was undertaken.[77]

The vision set out in the brief for the Lands Bill had amounted to no less than a prescription for municipal socialism:

> The purchase will secure to the municipality which creates it any further increment in value. It will preclude the possibility of exploitation by private individuals for private gain. It will secure to the public complete control of the laying out of the undeveloped areas and the preservation of the amenities of life so often overlooked by private speculators. It will give the Corporation so far as the undeveloped land is concerned the fullest powers in the shape of Town Planning. It will allow Improvement Schemes being carried out without insuperable obstacles being raised. It will allow the Corporation to give facilities for the establishment and expansion of industries. In short it will facilitate almost every function of the Corporation acting through its Council in connection with Town Planning, Housing, the laying out of streets, the laying of sewers, drains, water and gas pipes, electric cables and in short enable the Corporation to exercise their powers as such to the best advantage of the community.[78]

In other words, it would resolve the tensions inherent in the position whereby a manorial landlord was able to inhibit the ambitions of an elected local authority in a rapidly developing town. Moreover, as the *Examiner* pointed out, this was a development in keeping with Huddersfield's proud history of pioneering municipal action, from the Model Lodging House opened by the Improvement Commissioners in 1854, to the first municipal tramways in 1882 and the production and distribution of municipal electricity in 1893.[79]

However, evidence from the Estates Committee minute book for the next five years suggests there was no readiness to take advantage of the purchase to strike out in new directions, for it was simply business as usual under a new name, with no change even of personnel for some time. Sections of the borough's existing estate were gradually transferred into the remit of the new Estate Committee and two extra staff were added, but the business was very humdrum for at least the first five years. Much of it was simple conversion of pre-1867 99-year leases to 999, rather than the implementation of any transformative master plan for the borough, such as happened in the 1960s. Dawson chaired the committee from 1920 until 1932.[80]

Taking all in all, the purchase does seem to have been decidedly in the long-term interests of the borough, despite Dawson's initial concern that they might be paying too much. However, we should still be careful of taking the contents of the Dawson File at face value. Dawson, with Copley's backing and support, in effect forced the hand of the Corporation by a purely personal initiative which he was known to favour. The mayor said that he and the chairman of the Finance Committee were informed at the start, but little in the File supports the idea that the informal committee of three was really in charge. So, it is important to consider what would have happened if this complex deal had not worked out as planned. As the *Yorkshire Evening Post* speculated on 25 October 1919, 'in the event of the Town Council not agreeing to the purchase, or anything else arising that would prevent the transfer, Mr. Copley would keep the estate. But no such contingency is anticipated.' [81] On the 30 October it expanded that:

> Mr. Copley, who is a far-seeing business man, is prepared for any contingency. This is only to be expected. If the estate is left on his hands, then, he says, he will give tenants of houses every opportunity to obtain final ownership of the premises they occupy, this by purchase in instalments. What his course would be in the case of the valuable business portion of the town he has not divulged, but there is no great apprehension on the point.[82]

This would fit with Copley's known attitudes, but he would not have intended to lose by his investment, and in any case working-class home ownership was unusual because people could rarely afford it. It was also noted at the time that

> there are a few who contend that the town has lost a good landlord, and that if the Corporation is able to proceed with the deal it may not perhaps be quite so considerate of the interests of individual lessees as was Sir John Ramsden. The larger number of people, however, hail this step with great satisfaction, even with exultation. They see in it an opportunity of becoming, by means of the Corporation, which they, through their elected representatives ought to control, virtually their own landlord.[83]

Whatever the risks of the unorthodox methods adopted by Dawson, the outcome of the decision to buy the Ramsden Estate was all that the optimists believed it would be and Alderman Stephenson's uncritical celebration of Dawson's deal, written in 1972, was able to echo the *Examiner*'s belief in 1919 that 'the ratepayers of Huddersfield have reason to congratulate themselves both on this wise decision and on the negotiations which have rendered it possible'.[84]

Note

References to the 'Dawson File' [DF] in this chapter are to the bound volume of numbered documents in the West Yorkshire Archive Service, Kirklees, at DD/RE/420b, entitled 'The Dawson File. Purchase of the Ramsden Estate'. This contains 175 contemporary documents plus some added later by Clifford Stephenson.

Endnotes

1 Beard (2015), p. 117.
2 See Griffiths (2008) and chapter 2, p. 45.
3 See chapter 2.
4 *HDE*, 29 October 1919.
5 Conveyance, 29 September 1920 – copy in DF 175.
6 See the map published in *HDE*, 8 November 1919.
7 Stephenson (1972). Apart from the Dawson File, Stephenson's main source appears to have been the 'Notes for Talks on The Ramsden Estate' made in 1946 by Harold Taylor, Huddersfield Estate Manager, 1934–1953 (copy in DF, Appendix XI). Stephenson's booklet is now available on the Huddersfield Local History Society, Huddersfield Civic Society and Huddersfield Exposed websites.
8 *HDE*, 12 August 1936.
9 *HDE*, 12 August 1936.

10   Stephenson (1972), p. 10. For Copley's Lancashire interests, see *HDE,* 28 October 1919, and for White, see *HDE,* 12 August 1936.
11   DF 66A, *Examiner* interviews, Alderman Beaumont, *HDE,* 27 October 1919; Stephenson (1972), p. 10.
12   See chapter 2, pp. 76-7.
13   Stephenson (1972), p. 10.
14   See chapter 7, pp. 208-10.
15   Buxton (2017), pp. 313–26.
16   Springett (1992), pp. 452–8 and 466–76; Springett (1986), pp. 40-52.
17   See chapter 3, p. 99.
18   Crump (1924), pp. 105–35.
19   *HDE,* 28 October 1919; *Yorkshire Observer Budget,* 'Special Huddersfield Supplement', 1 November 1919; obituary, *HDE,* 5 November 1937. He had been wrongly diagnosed with cancer in Australia but then recovered after a successful operation in London – see DF 179, 'Notes of Interview with the Family of Sam. Wm Copley by Clifford Stephenson', 19 August 1974.
20   KC 592/2/15, Clifford Stephenson Papers, notes of interview, 27 January 1973.
21   Stephenson (1972), p. 11.
22   DF 1, Hood to Dawson, 3 March 1919.
23   Sam. W. Copley, 'How I came to be interested in Huddersfield', 27 July 1934, copy at the back of the Dawson File (DD/RE/420b) and in KC/592/2/15, Stephenson Papers, Sam. W. Copley.
24   Stephenson (1972), p. 13. His source for these names appears to be Harold Taylor, 'Notes', DF, Appendix XI.
25   Stephenson (1972), pp. 10–11; his source for the meeting between Melville and Dawson appears to be Taylor, 'Notes', DF, Appendix XI.
26   DF, note on reverse of Contents page; Stephenson (1972), pp. 9–10.
27   DF 8, Commission Note, approx. 5 April 1919.
28   Copley, 'How I came to be interested in Huddersfield'. On seeing Copley's account for the first time, Stephenson commented that 'it agrees in essentials [with the Dawson File], though, not unsurprisingly, with more emphasis on the part played by Sam Copley personally' – note in DF (1975).
29   *HDE,* 12 August 1936.
30   DF, note in 1975.
31   Copley made this same statement to a reporter in 1919 – see *Yorkshire Observer Budget,* 'Special Huddersfield Supplement', 1 November 1919 (also in Huddersfield Local Studies Library, 942.74, Samuel Copley file).
32   For Melville's financial circumstances, see chapter 7, pp. 211-12.
33   Copley later claimed that this conversation did not take place until negotiations were almost completed, in October 1919 - Copley, 'How I came to be interested in Huddersfield', but the contemporary evidence in DF does not bear this out.
34   KC/592/2/15, Clifford Stephenson Papers, Sam W. Copley, 'Interview with the Copley family by Clifford Stephenson, 1974'. It was on this occasion that Stephenson was shown Copley's account of the purchase.
35   DF 7, Hood to Dawson, 1 April 1919.
36   DF 3, Dawson to Hood, 15 March 1919; DF 7, Hood to Dawson, 1 April 1919; DF 8, Commission Note, approx. 5 April 1919; DF 10, Copley to Dawson, 7 April, Copley to Melville, 8 April, and Copley to Hood, 8 April 1919.
37   DF 15, Hood to Dawson, 11 April 1919.

38   Yorkshire Observer Budget, 'Special Huddersfield Supplement', 1 November 1919.
39   DF 101, Speech at Town Hall, 12 January 1920.
40   DF 72, Hood to Copley, 30 October 1919); DF 125, Dawson to Hood, 20 February 1920; DF 145, Hood to Dawson, 19 March 1920; DF 149, Hood to Copley, 9 April 1920.
41   DF 19, Dawson to Ernest Woodhead, 16 April 1919. In 1934 Copley said Dawson had offered him £50,000 profit on sale to the Corporation.
42   DF 23, Dawson to Woodhead, 27 April 1919.
43   DF 21, Woodhead to Dawson, 18 April 1919.
44   DF 27, 28 and 29, 2, 5 and 6 May 1919, correspondence between Dawson and Hood; DF 30A, Ramsden Estate: Summary Rentals less Outgoings, May 1919.
45   DF 34, Capel-Cure & Ball to Hood, 22 May 1919.
46   DF 41, James White to Dawson, 19 June 1919.
47   DF 50, JFR to Dawson, 24 August 1919.
48   DF 54, Hood to Dawson, 11 October 1919.
49   DF 62, Copley to Dawson, 24 October 1919.
50   Copley spoke to the reporter in 1919 of 'the inspiring dream of his life': Yorkshire Observer Budget, 'Special Huddersfield Supplement', 1 November 1919.
51   DF 66, 28 October 1919, Examiner interviews, HDE, 27 October 1919, 'Local Opinions on Purchase of Ramsden Estate'.
52   Yorkshire Observer, 23 October 1919, repeated in Yorkshire Observer Budget, 25 October 1919.
53   DF 60, HDE, 23 October 1919.
54   HDE, 23 and 24 October 1919; DF 63, 25 October 1919; DF 65, Melville to Dawson, 26 October 1919.
55   DF 71, Copley to Dawson, 28 October 1919.
56   Copley, 'How I came to be interested in Huddersfield'.
57   DF 76, Huddersfield Corporation to Copley, 1 November 1919.
58   YEP, 30 October 1919; see also HDE, 28 October 1919.
59   YEP, 30 October 1919.
60   Copley's obituary wrongly stated that Copley had come forward for the first time to conclude the deal because of the leak on 23 October – HDE, 5 November 1937.
61   DF 101. Dawson's speech at Town Hall meeting.
62   DF 1, Hood to Dawson, 3 March 1919; DF 34, Capel-Cure & Ball to Hood, 22 May 1919; DF 106, Hood to Dawson, 24 January 1920.
63   DF 119, Hood to Copley, 13 February 1920; DF 129, Hood to Copley, 26 February 1920; DF 134, Hood to Copley, 12 March 1920.
64   DF 106, Hood to Dawson, 24 January 1920.
65   Yorkshire Observer Budget, 1 November 1919, supplement.
66   HDE, 28 October 1919.
67   HDE, 28 October 1919; interview with the reporter from the Yorkshire Observer,
68   DF 167, Hood to Dawson, 30 July 1920.
69   DF 156, J. Henry Field (town clerk) to Dawson, 28 April 1920; Parliamentary Debates, House of Commons 128, 3 May 1920; Hansard, House of Lords Debates, 9 June 1920 and Minutes, 22 July 1920; HWE, 24 July 1920; Taylor (2012), p. 52
70   DF 161, Ernest Dyson to Dawson, and Atlantic Assurance Co. to Ernest Dyson, borough treasurer, 6 May 1920.
71   DF 164, Florence Barrowclough for Copley to Dawson, 21 July 1920.

72 DF 167 and 169, Hood to Dawson, 30 July and 10 September 1920.
73 DF 169A, Ernest Dyson to Mr Johnson, 4 October 1941, and 'Delivery of Estate Purchase Money, 29 September 1920'.
74 DF 175, Conveyance – Ramsden Estates, Huddersfield, 29 September 1920. It then took several days for the loads of deeds to be physically handed over – *HDE*, 1 October 1920.
75 DF 176, Capital Account, August & September 1920; Stephenson (1972), p. 15.
76 Stephenson (1972), p. 19, and information from David Griffiths.
77 Stephenson (1972), p. 18.
78 DF 156A, Huddersfield Corporation Lands Bill – Brief, 29 April 1920.
79 *HDE,* 29 October 1919.
80 Stephenson (1972), p. 16.
81 *YEP,* 25 October 1919.
82 *YEP,* 30 October 1919.
83 *Sheffield Daily Telegraph*, 31 October 1919. One who contended that Ramsden was not a good landlord was G.W. Shaw of Botham Hall, Milnsbridge – see DF 84 and 162, Shaw to Dawson, 22 November 1919 and 3 July 1920.
84 *HDE*, 31 October 1919.

CHAPTER SEVEN

A Ramsden Family Perspective

MERIEL BUXTON

Mother and son: Isabella and John William

JOHN WILLIAM RAMSDEN HAD a lonely childhood. Before he was born his parents had already lost a son and daughter. One of his two surviving sisters died while he was still a baby, leaving only John William and his sister Charlotte, sixteen years his senior. He was too young to remember any of his other siblings. Worse still was to come when his father, John Charles, died suddenly in 1836, leaving his five-year-old son heir to the baronetcy and all the vast estates of the Ramsden family. Just before his eighth birthday, his grandfather also died. John William was now the fifth baronet.

He had been born on 14 September 1831 at Newby Park near Thirsk (now known as Baldersby Park) but this was only a rented house and his parents took the opportunity to buy Buckden House and its estate in Wharfedale not long before his father's death. John William's mother was the Hon. Isabella Dundas, daughter of the first Baron Dundas and, on her mother's side, a Fitzwilliam. Isabella had a profound influence on her son's life, both as a mother and in her capacity as one of his trustees. Throughout his minority the estate was administered by Trustees, the two longest serving and most influential of whom were Isabella herself and her first cousin and brother-in-law, Charles Wentworth-Fitzwilliam, 5th Earl Fitzwilliam. They proved a formidable team, with Isabella giving full support to Fitzwilliam in his determination to run the estate as efficiently as possible and to right the damage done in the last years of the fourth baronet's life when he had allowed his agent to let many matters drift, in particular with regard to the tenancies at will.[1] The fourth baronet's agent, John Bower, had with his employer's tacit agreement taken the line of least resistance on everything. Whenever John Charles had tried to alter things he had been met with mocking laughter.

The decision to appoint George Loch to sort out the most important issues was taken primarily by Isabella and Fitzwilliam. They were looking for a man with the right professional attributes and sufficient personality to drive through the necessary changes. Loch had been working with his father on the Bridgewater estate, where canals were the central feature. He had been called to the Bar and was able, in addition to his work in Huddersfield, to work in London on the legislation being put through Parliament relating to the Ramsden estate, which Earl Fitzwilliam was satisfied justified the high salary Loch demanded. He was initially asked to report on the condition of the estate and was highly critical of the appalling state in which he found it. He was then appointed auditor and manager.[2] While the tenancy issue was highlighted rather than resolved during John William's minority, Loch not only turned round many other management issues but also started to change the culture whereby people looked back to the fourth baronet's time as a golden age when the townspeople could do anything they liked. Loch succeeded in altering the public perception to an appreciation that in the long run good management of the Ramsden estates was of benefit to everyone in Huddersfield.

Loch sometimes went too far in refusing support for local projects, instinctively turning down all requests for new schools or support for the hospital. Fitzwilliam took issue with him here, concerned that John William, even before he came of age, could acquire a reputation for stinginess.[3] On such occasions, Loch would attempt, usually unsuccessfully, to play one trustee off against another. He knew that the two most senior trustees would usually support each other but also realised that Isabella in particular had immense confidence in his judgement and he saw her as a potential ally and means of influencing the other trustees.

The major issue of the time was the building of the railways. Traditionally the Ramsden position was to oppose the building of any railway close to Huddersfield because of the competition it would offer to their canal. A proposal from the Manchester and Leeds Railway Company to build a branch line to Huddersfield sparked strong reactions in the town. The townspeople were determined not to be excluded from the new age of steam. When an official publicly declared that 'Huddersfield is not worth stopping the engine for' the question also became a matter of pride.[4]

The Trustees then suggested that the proposal for a branch line should be rejected but that they should themselves build the line. Loch did not think that this was wise but instead entered into negotiations with a different railway company, having noted what generous terms the Huddersfield and Manchester Railway Company had been forced to offer in a comparable case. Once the decision had been taken, Loch faced a struggle to get the appropriate legislation through Parliament. He lost the first round but was determined not to give up and, against all the odds and with Fitzwilliam's help, he eventually emerged victorious. He had been aware throughout that this was only the first step. He must now strike a suitable deal with the railway company and knew that the Ramsden Trustees must own not just most but all of the land affected. Unfortunately, the fourth baronet's will stated that additional land could be purchased only when there was excess income to pay for it. There was none. The most important relevant block of land was the Bay Hall estate, outside the town centre but on the route of the proposed new railway.

Here is where Loch's good relationship with Isabella and her determination to do the best for her son came into play. The Trustees could do nothing to raise the necessary funds so Isabella personally borrowed from her brother-in-law, Charles Ramsden, the money to buy the land, putting Loch in a strong enough position to negotiate an excellent deal with the railway company. After Isabella had been repaid there were still sufficient funds for the rebuilding of the George Hotel, the opening up of what was now named John William Street and the purchase of the Greenhead/Gledholt estate.[5]

Isabella was equally successful in her relationship with John William himself. She remained throughout her life the one person who was always prepared to stand up to him whenever she felt that it was right to do so, usually with a sense of humour which seldom failed to win him round. She would happily tell him how uncomfortable his carriage was and that she would therefore avoid using his coach makers, or how dismal his servants looked in their new, all black livery. This continued throughout her life. Even aged 97, on noticing her son's receding hairline, she commented, 'Well, Sir John, and when are you going to buy a wig?'[6]

Highly intelligent, she would read a wide range of books, even ones in German when in her nineties, and she remained almost unbeatable at backgammon to the end: when her son played a move which did not impress her, she made her views extremely clear. Although she could be sharp with her son, she remained thoughtful and considerate to staff and to her companion, Bunny Dundas, an unmarried younger cousin who remained with her to the end of her life, an invaluable support and friend.

Not surprisingly, when she was seriously ill in 1879 and forced to endure the horrors of contemporary medicine (including treatment with a turpentine plaster and doses of brandy and ammonia), John William never left her side: temporary fluctuations in her condition created an emotional roller coaster for him. 'Oh if this can only last, but it is too much to hope that she is really getting better,' he exclaimed.[7] To his delight, she eventually confounded everyone, even the doctors, by surviving another nine years, weak but with her brain unimpaired, and dying only three years short of her century. A few months before her death she decided to celebrate the Queen's Jubilee in her own way. Letting only Bunny into the secret, she had her bedroom redecorated with

41. Sir John William Ramsden, 5th Bt (1831–1914), by Camille Silvy, albumen carte-de-visite, 26 June 1861.
Ramsden Family Collection

new wallpaper and a new carpet. She delighted in being surrounded by the family, counting the days till her ten-year-old grandson John Frecheville – her 'Monkey Boy' as she called him – came home from school.[8]

Yet even she made few demands on John William. In a fit of gloomy introspection at the age of 32, he confided to his diary that the only request she had ever made of him was that he should be up and ready for Prayers at 9 o'clock every morning and even this he rarely managed to achieve. He perceived himself at this time in his life as idle and lethargic – with neither quality was he associated in later life — and he gave the credit to his brother-in-law, Edward Horsman, husband of his sister Charlotte, for getting him more actively involved in the world around him.

After his marriage, Isabella's support took a practical form. She had an excellent relationship with his wife Guendolen, aware as she was of John William's many shortcomings as a husband, and indeed pointed them out to him bluntly if unavailingly: 'This being dear Guen's birthday and the day she comes of age … What a pity it is that you did not postpone the journey.'[9]

She offered practical support by stepping in when ill health restricted Guendolen's activities. Repeated pregnancies, too often ending in miscarriages, meant that she was unable to play a full part in John William's lifestyle of perpetual motion. His mother, and sometimes his sister Charlotte, would deputise as hostesses for him in London when the House was sitting. After the birth of Hermione Charlotte (known as Mymee), their first child, Isabella frequently had her, and later the other children, to stay at Buckden, or eventually Byram, for extended periods. Mymee and Isabella's companion, Bunny Dundas, remained close for the rest of Bunny's life. This gave Guendolen the opportunity to travel, which she loved, when her health and intervals between pregnancies permitted.

For many years, John William and his mother were united by their love for Buckden, where John William undertook a massive tree planting scheme, but eventually Buckden lost its appeal for him when he fell in love with Ardverikie, the Scottish estate which he first started to buy in 1870. He wrote his mother a marvellous letter at that time, setting out both the appeal of the place and his immensely complicated plans for acquiring all the land that he wanted there, plans which he later followed almost as a blueprint.[10] She gave him full backing, even supporting his sale of outlying parts of the Buckden estate to finance his plans elsewhere, while remarking that it was sad that he would never again care as deeply about Buckden as he had previously.[11]

John William was a man who loved places more than he ever loved people. Ardverikie became the abiding passion of his life. He also loved his other country estates, Buckden, Byram and Bulstrode, the Buckinghamshire estate Guendolen inherited from her father. His relationship with Huddersfield was quite different. If Ardverikie was his wife, his mistress, his favourite child, Huddersfield was his business. As such it remained of supreme importance to him. Despite his own misgivings about himself as a young man, John William was always a hard-working, capable businessman, enjoying to the full the many benefits life had conferred on him but, unlike his son, having no illusions about the responsibilities which accompanied those benefits. On the other hand, he was less of an idealist than his son. He had no burning ambition to improve the lot of the people of Huddersfield, merely to keep to

42. Sir John William Ramsden, 5th Bt (1831–1914).
Kirklees Image Archive

43. The Hon. Lady Helen Guendolen Ramsden (1846–1910), married to Sir John William Ramsden in 1865.
Muncaster Castle

Husband and wife: John William and Guendolen

Guendolen had a more powerful influence on her husband than was immediately apparent. The youngest of three daughters of the Duke and Duchess of Somerset, Guendolen was also descended through her mother Georgiana from the great playwright Richard Brinsley Sheridan, author of *The Rivals* and *School for Scandal*. They were a remarkably talented family: both Georgiana's sisters were writers and had many other accomplishments. Georgiana herself, whose wit and originality were legendary, was chosen to be the 'Queen of Beauty' at the Eglinton Tournament, which attracted 100,000 spectators in 1839. Guendolen's father was a politician, author of two books and served as Lord Lieutenant of Devon for a quarter of a century.[12]

Guen had a fey, almost unworldly side to her nature which was quite unlike her down-to-earth mother-in-law. This could cause her unhappiness and anxiety: a dream might leave her worrying and despondent, though when she had ether for an operation she came round feeling that much of the mystery of life had been made clear to her, leaving her blissfully contented. Sometimes John William was mocking but, especially as she got older, he became more considerate. Once a dream left her convinced that if he travelled to London for a meeting that day as planned, he would, against all probability, be drowned. Remarkably, he agreed to forgo attendance at the meeting.[13]

Guen had two brothers but the younger was killed by a bear in India. The older never married but had two children with a beautiful, fiery 17 year-old girl of gypsy extraction, Rosina Elizabeth Swan. While both children were still small, first their father and then their mother died. The Duke and Duchess never hesitated but brought up the two children, Ruth and Harold, as their own with Guendolen giving full support and remaining close to both for the rest of her life. While Harold devoted much of his life to a vain attempt to prove that his parents were married, making him a Duke and heir to all his grandfather's possessions, Ruth was later described in her obituary in *The Times* as 'One of the most vivid personalities [her friends] have known', a socialist, rebel and 'inveterate champion of the underdog.'[14] She married William George Frederick Cavendish-Bentinck. Two of their sons became successively 8th and 9th Duke of Portland.

When the Duke of Somerset died, the title passed to his brother but he ensured that his property was divided between his three daughters with his grandchildren too being provided for. This was how Bulstrode in Buckinghamshire passed into the ownership of the Ramsden family.

Guendolen, only 19 at the time of her marriage and immediately plunged into a seemingly never-ending cycle of child-bearing and ill health, did not succeed in producing the longed-for son and heir until she was over 30. But throughout those years she enjoyed the support of her mother-in-law and gradually grew in stature. Independent enough to pursue her own interests – travel, literature and the theatre – she eventually developed the confidence to impose views dictated by her own social conscience on her husband, as the following letter illustrates:

> I hear some more children have died of the scarlet fever Bunny heard and she hears Mr Haslam is sinking a well for the good of Brotherton at his own expense. Oh dear, what it is to have an UNenergetic husband. Have I not begged you to do something – a drain or a something as the water and everything stinks so. If my school children are ill I will whip you … Cotton has stopped his children from going to school I am glad to say. When are you COMING?
> Ever your loving wife.[15]

Whether Guendolen was as conscious of what was happening in Huddersfield in the early days as she was aware of events in Brotherton, the village close to Byram, is unlikely. She willingly and graciously played her part in any formal duties she was asked to undertake in Huddersfield but she was too far away at Byram to take the direct interest which she did, for example, in the school in Brotherton. But whilst neither she nor John William would have seen it as her place to devote the full day or more a week spent by John William on Huddersfield affairs, she was held in deep affection in the town and with increasing age shared more and more of her own interests with the people of Huddersfield.

She was a keen supporter of the Needlework Guild, entertaining the members annually, and when she wrote a play entitled *Beauty and the Beast* it was premiered for the Guild. Every Monday when in Yorkshire she would attend the meetings, referred to by John William as her Mothers' Meeting. Together with her two daughters, she came up especially from London to spend five days manning a stall at the Huddersfield Drill Hall Bazaar. When the people of Huddersfield put on an opera entirely composed and performed by local residents, she not only attended but was unreserved in her support and praise for the success of the venture. On opening the Art Gallery she made a speech so impressive that even John William dropped his usual ironic mockery and gave her unstinting praise. To celebrate the marriage of their son, John Frecheville Ramsden (known in childhood as 'Freshie' but later as 'Chops') to Joan Buxton, a special train was commissioned to bring 300

44. Opening of Somerset Bridge by Lady Guendolen Ramsden, 25 May 1874.
Kirklees Image Archive

people from Huddersfield to Byram to join the celebrations. No doubt here again the lead was taken by Guendolen rather than her husband.[16].

Family Matters: Yorkshire and beyond

With the passing of time John William and Guendolen took it for granted that their role would gradually be taken over by the younger generation. In 1898, soon after his 21st birthday, John Frecheville, rather than his father, gave the main speech and laid the cornerstone for the Victoria Tower on Castle Hill, at a ceremony attended by all the dignitaries of Huddersfield. In the main surviving photograph (see p. 204), which does not appear to include any women, John William Ramsden is in the centre of the front row with his son behind him and, standing close by, Isaac Hordern, treasurer of the Ramsden estate in Huddersfield who served the estate loyally for almost 64 years.

But the path of duty had little appeal for John Frecheville. His main struggles at Cambridge were to avoid being sent down from the university. His time and his dreams were focused on dancing, wine, horses, the internal combustion engine and the sister of an old school friend. Her name was Joan Buxton. Three years later he sought his father's approval, gladly given,

45. Portrait group at the Yorkshire Agricultural Show, 1888, taken outside Longley Hall entrance porch. From left to right: standing, Lord Harewood, Sir John William Ramsden, Lord Auckland; seated, F.W. Beadon, Col. Ramsden, Hon. G. Lascelles
Huddersfield Local Studies Library

46. Official party at the laying of the corner stone of the Victoria Tower, Castle Hill by John Frecheville Ramsden, Saturday 25 June 1898. Sir John William Ramsden is centre front; John Frecheville Ramsden is immediately behind him; Isaac Hordern is to his far right.
Ramsden Family Collection

before making her his wife. It was one of the best decisions of his life. But her Norfolk background was yet another factor in his drift southwards.

John Frecheville's older sister, Mymee, had long made her own life far from Yorkshire. An independent spirit, Mymee cared for none of the things which so attracted her brother, but her parents' way of life was not for her either. She travelled extensively, particularly in Norway, and resisted all attempts to find her a husband. A puzzle and something of a disappointment to her mother, she of all the family was the most willing to stand up to her father.

John William and Guendolen's middle child, a sweet and gentle girl named Rosamund, was close to her mother, in awe of her father and increasingly dependent financially and socially on her brother, John Frecheville. Later she made what the rest of the family viewed as an unwise marriage, had a son, then died while the child was still a toddler. Had she lived she would have been so proud of her son who went on to become the great art connoisseur Sir Brinsley Ford, an exceptionally charming and erudite man. She was probably more settled in Yorkshire than either her brother or sister, but she too eventually drifted south. After her marriage she bought a house in Sussex.

So gradually in a single generation the ties with Yorkshire were loosened. Guendolen herself really preferred to be at Bulstrode, her parents' old home, with easy access to London, to her sisters and to the doctors on whom she was increasingly dependent. Perhaps because of his nomadic lifestyle, constantly moving between Byram, London, Bulstrode and the place he loved more deeply than any other, Ardverikie, none of John William's family ever imbued his deep sense that, no matter where he might spend time, Byram was truly home.

In 1909, for the first time in his life, John William passed a whole year without spending a single night at Byram[17]. Guen's health was a major factor, but, even when he came up to Huddersfield to celebrate 70 years since he had inherited the estate, he stayed at Longley and returned south immediately afterwards without visiting Byram. However, of Huddersfield he wrote:

> My visit . . . was most satisfactory. Everybody was most cordial and the Town looks very prosperous. I am much impressed with the large amount of building going on in many different parts of the estate.[18]

His relationship with the town could be compared to that of an elderly married couple who have had many disagreements, some deep and bitter, but are indissolubly bound together by a lifetime of shared memories of every kind. In 1860 he had been amongst the officers who joined the 1st Yorkshire (West Riding) Artillery Volunteer Corps on its formation. More than 40 years later he was the sole survivor of that original intake. He alone had witnessed the work of Isaac Hordern in the estate office for more than sixty years.

47. Byram Hall (as remodelled from 1762 by John Carr); main house, demolished after 1945.
Matthew Beckett/Lost Heritage (www.lostheritage.org.uk)

When a Huddersfield church needed £1,000, he took for granted his duty to provide 10 per cent of this in response to the appeal.

After Guen's death in 1910, John William and Rosamund returned to Byram for a sad visit sorting out Guen's possessions. After Rosamund herself died the following year, her father only once returned to Byram before his own death in the spring of 1914. John Frecheville and Joan did their best to make his stay at Byram as happy and as close to the past as possible, bringing their children, arranging guests and shooting parties and even themselves returning briefly after the children went back to school. But soon John William was left alone for eight weeks, apart from the company of the old agent, Cole Hamilton, who worked with him as far as possible in the old way, interviewing tenants, going through accounts, clearing out the old Deed Room and even accompanying him on local expeditions. But Cole Hamilton himself was about to retire.[19]

John Frecheville and Joan did return to Yorkshire for a night once during this time, to entertain the Duke of Teck at Longley. John William sent grapes, flowers, cream and eggs from Byram but to his disappointment the party went straight back to their Northamptonshire home next day without visiting him at Byram.[20]

Father and son: John William and John Frecheville:

For such an intolerant and demanding man, John William was remarkably patient and tolerant with his son. Believing as he did that he himself had been idle and ineffective as a young man, without even the excuse, as he would have been the first to admit, of filling his time with all the social and sporting activities so dear to the heart of John Frecheville, he never doubted that the young man would eventually shoulder his responsibilities. There is no evidence that he in any way excluded John Frecheville from business matters: on the contrary, he did his best to involve him in everything, delighting in any sign of interest and grieving only when, as all too frequently occurred, John Frecheville found that important meetings clashed with his private amusements and he invariably prioritised the latter.[21]

The point has frequently been made that John William could have shackled his son's inheritance with trusts to ensure its survival for future generations. But the restrictions which his own grandfather had imposed had served only to make more difficult the position of his Trustees during his own minority, and he himself had always revelled in his freedom to take his own decisions, which he had done with spectacular success in financial terms throughout his life.

Remarkably Huddersfield was no longer the primary source of family income. Early in the 1870s, just when John William was so keen to put any spare cash available into Ardverikie, a family situation had arisen which was to have repercussions far beyond the lifetimes of any of those involved. John William's only sister, Charlotte, was married to a man named Edward Horsman, a reactionary politician chiefly remembered for his failed attempt to set up a third political party.[22] At first he provided a much needed father-figure for John William who gave him full credit for helping him to find his way in life at a difficult time.

As a young man Horsman had seen himself as an entrepreneur ahead of his time. He had invested in sugar plantations in Malaya and in 1851 set up the Penang Sugar Estates (PSE). Unfortunately, he lacked the determination, hard work, sound judgement and judicious investment necessary to make a success of such a project, particularly as he was attempting to run the enterprise from the other side of the world at a time when even a letter might take many weeks to come through. Almost inevitably he was soon begging his rich brother-in-law for financial assistance. John William was initially supportive, at least for his sister's sake. But matters showed no signs of improving and, as Horsman's debts continued to pile up, the position was not helped by his devious, ungrateful attitude.[23]

Finally, John William told him that matters could not go on in this way. He was prepared to pay off all the older man's debts, eventually revealed to be in excess of £300,000, but John William stipulated that the plantations must be made over to him and he refused to provide an income for his brother-in-law for the future. He saw this as the only way to save his sister from bankruptcy, but she and her husband erupted with fury. Relations between brother and sister never really recovered, despite, as is clear from the correspondence, John William's best attempts to heal the breach. This was sad: in earlier years they had had a good relationship. Charlotte gave children's parties for Mymee and teased her brother when, contrary to his own interests, he stubbornly refused to pay a groom's moving expenses from Byram to Bulstrode — 'I hate trouble and so do you'[24] — but now loyalty to her husband blinded her to her brother's point of view. She felt that he was being unreasonably harsh: presumably if it had been possible to sell the Malayan estates for a sum sufficient to cover his debts and leave something for himself as well, Horsman would have done so.

'Poor Siss!' John William later wrote to his mother, 'If she is still in the same frame of mind she was in last spring it can be no pleasure to her and certainly a great pain to me for us two to meet.'[25] But later, not long before her death, they were on good enough terms for her to write to him saying she longed to see mountains again, and for him immediately to invite her up to Ardverikie.[26] Almost equally indignant on the other side of the Horsman question were many of John William's friends and in particular his father-in-law. The Duke believed that if John William escaped without losing more than £80 −100,000 he would be 'well out of it.'

But John William had taken detailed professional advice throughout. He never set foot himself in Malaya but established a team out there whom he could trust, and a second team in London. He took a detailed interest himself, sometimes too detailed, but the business went from strength to strength. At precisely the right moment, they changed from growing sugar to growing rubber. From the mid-1880s through to the outbreak of the Second World War, the Malayan plantations, or the PRE (Penang Rubber Estates) as they became, were bringing in even more income than Huddersfield and were the primary source of family wealth.

The Malayan position no doubt had considerable bearing on John Frecheville's approach to Huddersfield. From his earliest memories, Huddersfield had ceased to be 'the family business'. Malaya was equally important and, to John Frecheville, who loved travelling, infinitely more attractive. Unlike his father, he did go out there on a number of occasions. At first this pleased his father, who listened eagerly to any suggestions he put forward, taking care, even if he disagreed, not to be discouraging.

Although John William's diary in the last years of his life gives occasional indications of his anxiety over the direction in which his son was moving, he continued to place total confidence in him. He had no alternative. Lloyd

George's controversial 1909 Budget increased death duties even in cases where property was passed on to the younger generation but the donor failed to live for a full three years after making the gift. So, without further consultation with John Frecheville, John William decided (in his own words) 'to abdicate'. This meant that provided he survived until the spring of 1913 no tax would be payable on the transition of the estate. In fact, John William died in April 1914. John Frecheville was astounded, suitably appreciative but did not even fully understand the basis on which the decision was taken. John William thereafter made no attempt to interfere, reserving for his diary his mistrust of the advice now being offered to John Frecheville by a young friend, who made 'a new proposal which I cannot say that I understand.'[27]

John William's death was immediately followed by the outbreak of the First World War. John Frecheville's letters home are full of plans for ways in which he might spend money once peace came, at his home in Northamptonshire, at Ardverikie and at Muncaster Castle in Cumberland. This had passed to him on the death of the last Lord Muncaster and his wife, both in 1917, following an agreement made by John William seven years before.[28] His letters contain few references to Byram or to Huddersfield. By 1918 the world had changed immeasurably from John William's time, which in itself would justify to John Frecheville a reversal of his father's policies. Further, the Huddersfield estate was no longer showing a profit. How much this was due to factors beyond John Frecheville's control and how much to bad management it is impossible to tell. Either way, this situation did little to increase his interest in or enthusiasm for the town.

Another factor too had come into his life, his fascination with Kenya. Even before the outbreak of war in 1914, both a sister and brother of John Frecheville's wife Joan had moved out to Kenya and settled there. Another brother and sister had joined them before the end of the war. John Frecheville and Joan themselves had visited the country first when coming home from Malaya. The wild outdoor life and the challenges of creating a new world attracted him, seemingly offering the best of British life free of the encumbrances he deplored in the modern world. Joan, on the other hand, much as she enjoyed spending time with her brothers and sisters, had reservations. The most sophisticated of the nine Buxton siblings, she had no desire to abandon the comfort and trappings of the modern civilised world. She did not want to spend long days in the saddle rounding up cattle, building a house miles from the nearest European neighbour or even welcoming a lion or cheetah cub into her home, as her siblings happily did. But she supported her husband when he started to buy land in Kenya.

A part of John Frecheville longed to emulate his father and create his own estate with a mansion designed and built by himself, just as John William had done at Ardverikie. Kenya offered the opportunity to do precisely that. Further, land in Kenya could be bought at subsidised rates by those who had fought in the War.

Early in 1919 John Frecheville started to buy land, initially at Marula. He also invested £900,000 in the Trust which he had set up for speculative investment in raw materials, mostly in Africa, and a further million pounds in Cox's Shipping Agency. Algernon Cox was the friend whose schemes had puzzled and concerned John William before the war. John Frecheville was spending capital which he did not have.[29]

The sale of Huddersfield

Little was known of the circumstances in which John Frecheville came to sell the Ramsden estate in Huddersfield to the Corporation until the Dawson File, detailing the course of events, came to light in 1970.[30] Even then, Stephenson knew little of the position, financial and psychological, of John Frecheville Ramsden; and nothing of the background of the 'Mystery Man' in his story.[31]

The precise sequence of dates is unclear but undoubtedly the financial pressure on Sir John Frecheville was rising within a few weeks of the end of the war, well summarised by the 'cryptically explicit' comment on the sale made to Clifford Stephenson by a member of the family: 'Because we owed eight hundred thousand pounds to the bank.'[32] But if Sir John had decided to sell, why did he not go on the open market, or approach the Council himself? Perhaps he could not believe that anyone would be prepared to buy the estate at anything approaching its full value, especially at a time when a number of estates were coming on the market.[33] Selling the estate piecemeal would have been quite a different proposition, and there is no evidence that this was entertained. Wilfrid Dawson may have seen an advantage in conducting negotiations in secrecy to prevent competitive bids. He also believed that Ramsden would not wish to sell to a corporate buyer and there is some evidence for this, but it is more likely that Ramsden was concerned about what others might think or say, and it is more likely still that he had not thought the matter through at all beyond his general desire to sell. He certainly would not have known what sort of reception the idea would be given by the Town Council. If he had thought about it he is likely to have considered it most improbable that the Council would either want or be in a position to buy the whole estate. The proposal put forward in 1894 by Councillor E. A. Beaumont for the Corporation to buy the Estate, had come to nothing.[34] There were strict limits on what councils could spend and they were not even allowed to buy land. There is no evidence that Sir John had even heard of Wilfrid Dawson or of his great ambition 'to see the Corporation own the Ramsden Estate'.[35] This was not widely known about even in Huddersfield at the time. Dawson was able to act as he did only because a man such as Sam Copley existed, both able and willing to finance the venture himself and happy, had things turned out differently, to keep the whole estate for himself.

If Sir John were minded to sell but without any clear idea about how or to whom, then this is where Stephenson's 'Mystery Man' comes in. It was he who brought the parties together and it was his solicitor who drove the negotiations forward, so who was he and why did he become involved?

It is clear from names included in the Dawson File that the 'Mystery Man' was Captain Charles Le Despencer Leslie Melville, seventh and youngest child of the fifth son of the Earl of Leven. Born and brought up at Branston Hall in Lincolnshire, he joined the Grenadiers, finishing the war as a captain. In 1911 he had married Rose Chesney at the fashionable church of St George's Hanover Square, but all was not as the family might have wished. Charles was the black sheep of the Leslie Melville family. He was declared bankrupt in 1912.

The family was well-known and respected in Branston. Charles' father was a banker, had been High Sheriff of Lincolnshire, and served as a magistrate and Deputy Lieutenant. There was no shortage of money at home and perhaps Charles began to pin his hopes on an inheritance. If so, he was to be disappointed. His parents in fact handled his bankruptcy with dignity, sensitivity and caution. His mother made a new will in 1912 in the light of the situation. Apart from a number of legacies for family, godchildren and staff, her main property was 338 acres of land in County Cork, known as her Irish estates. This land, or the capital representing it if it were sold, was put in trust with the income going to her husband during his lifetime and after his death to Charles as the main beneficiary.

Charles had an older brother, Alexander, also a captain in the army, but apparently a man more in the mould of his father. He and Arthur Tritton, probably a London banker, were the two trustees for what became known as Charles' Trust, with the extremely onerous duty of ensuring that the capital remained intact and deciding how the income was to be allocated. Everything was tied up as tightly as possible to ensure that neither Charles nor his creditors had access to the capital and it was for the trustees to decide whether the income went to Charles, his wife or any children.

His mother died in March 1918 and his father in the following January. His brother was an executor of both wills, together with other family members and, in their father's case, another local banker. Although their mother's estates, including the Irish land, were worth less than £17,000, their father left more than £120,000. Once again, everything was kept well away from Charles and his creditors. The family pearls might be worn by his wife or a daughter if he had one, but the likelihood of him attempting to sell them was foreseen and forestalled. His debts to his father were to be dealt with sympathetically but not totally written off: £5,000 and some further land was added to his Trust fund, and £1,000, partly in kind, was made available for furnishing a house, but everything else went primarily to his brother with a portion for his sisters.

His parents were determined that he should not have the opportunity to fritter away any more of the family money and the details of their settlements indicate how aware they were that they were dealing with a highly manipulative man, and one who would not hesitate to sacrifice not only his siblings but his wife and any future children for his own benefit.

From the time the contents of his father's will were known, early in 1919, Charles considered his position desperate. Precisely what happened next will probably never be known. In order to persuade Copley to pay him the huge commission of £20,000, having originally negotiated twice that amount, he must have been both convincing and determined. To prevent Copley and Dawson from thinking, as Clifford Stephenson later thought, that 'never was so much earned so easily'[36] he must have convinced both men that he, and he alone, could persuade John Frecheville to sell. This was Copley's recollection of events.[37] Though indubitably a rogue, Melville was evidently a plausible one. This was his opportunity in a lifetime: even the reduced figure of £20,000 was probably close to the capital value of his Trust fund and here there would be no meddling trustees or interfering lawyers to frustrate him.

There is nothing surprising about Melville's knowledge of John Frecheville's position. The two men were exact contemporaries. They had been at school together. Melville was a second cousin of John Frecheville's former sister-in-law Clare, originally married to Geoff Buxton, brother of Joan and a Kenyan resident. Another second cousin was David Leslie Melville, who, like John Frecheville, built himself a house in the Wanjohi Valley in Kenya, where Geoff Buxton was the first Briton to build. The two men could have met anywhere, in England, Scotland (where the Leslie Melville family owned an estate near Kingussie, not far from Ardverikie) or in Kenya. It is particularly easy to visualise the conversation taking place around the campfire in the African bush, John Frecheville's eyes lighting up with enthusiasm for all that he longed to do and commenting on how dearly he would love to exchange a future in Kenya for his fractious and unrewarding Huddersfield. It may be that Melville in exchange grumbled about his lack of money, with Ramsden even suggesting that Melville might secure for himself a healthy commission if he could arrange a sale. We shall never know, but Copley's recollection of what Melville told him at their first meeting suggests that all this is quite plausible – more plausible than Stephenson's string of coincidences.[38]

The story as told by Clifford Stephenson relies so heavily on coincidence that it almost beggars belief. That the group of Dawson's friends who met on the train, on the unusual occasion when Dawson himself was unable to go to his own flat in London, should happen to include a stranger, who by chance invited him to stay and only then discovered that he came from Huddersfield, so then casually asked if he knew anyone interested in buying a large estate there, stretches coincidence to breaking point. It also ignores the cunning displayed in other parts of the story by Charles Leslie Melville as well as his nature and circumstances. Copley's account seems much more probable: that the friends were Copley, Dawson and White and that he had met them in White's office where the initial Huddersfield conversation took place. It may have been a coincidence that Melville visited White's office when Copley and Dawson were there, or Melville may already have done his homework, found out about Copley's or Dawson's dreams for Huddersfield and made sure that he was himself in the right place at the right time so that the whole process could progress with a slickness engendered by careful planning.

The man who sold Huddersfield

John Frecheville was generous but not a good judge of character and he always kept his own counsel. His closest confidante was his wife, Joan. Their marriage was exceptionally close, despite the willingness of both to spend months apart when he was in Kenya and she was happier in the garden at home. In many ways they were very like each other but, in common with most men of his generation, he would not have discussed financial matters in depth with her. The one with whom arguably he should have discussed the whole issue of Huddersfield was his oldest son and heir, John St. Maur Ramsden, who was eighteen in 1920, a young man of high intelligence, sensitive, thoughtful, but also practical. There is no record of what he thought about the sale of Huddersfield but he spent much of the following year, 1921, with his father in Kenya, sometimes just the two of them and sometimes joined by John's uncle, Geoff Buxton. All the indications are that John became very close to his father at this time. He certainly fell in love with Kenya, where he was to spend much time later in his life, writing in his diary 'I speak of Africa and Golden Joys'.[39]

John was supposed to be going up to Cambridge in October 1921 but, at his father's instigation, a somewhat high-handed telegram was sent to the university informing them that he would not now be coming up until after Christmas. John, unlike his father, was a hard worker by nature and he eventually returned having prepared a presentation for the Pitt Rivers Museum in Oxford of an anthropological collection. Father, son and uncle all relaxed together, joking and enjoying the country.

48. Sir John Frecheville Ramsden (1877–1958).
Ramsden Family Collection

Yet John Frecheville's mind at this time was filled with the need to decide on the future of Byram, family home for the Ramsden family for hundreds of years and, now that Huddersfield was sold, their last real link with Yorkshire.[40] He discussed it with no-one, probably not even Geoff Buxton. When John eventually returned to England he picked up a copy of *Country Life*. As he wrote in his diary:

> I came on an advertisement for Byram to be sold. It is the first I have ever heard of it. I think it is a very good thing as it is expensive to keep up and we never live there. I really don't know the house at all and have no regrets about it but the garden with its beautiful terrace and statues by the lake and its wonderful yew fences, the highest I have ever seen, will be a loss. I am afraid Daddy who knows it well is very sad at parting with it. However it is such an expense to keep up and wants so much money spending on it before we could live there that it is hardly worth keeping it.[41]

John William, while making all the decisions himself, had allowed his son to make a playground of his empire, visiting Malaya in lordly style, in the hope that the young man would develop a sense of responsibility towards his inheritance. John Frecheville was a much more kindly and sensitive man than his father, yet he made no attempt to involve his children in any aspect until they were older, when John St. Maur in particular was sent out to undertake relatively menial duties in both Kenya and Malaya, where tragically he was eventually murdered.

On the other hand, even without knowing John's reaction to the sale of Byram, there can be no doubt that, had he been consulted on the sale of Huddersfield, he would have given his unconditional support: what seventeen-year-old would not choose the paradise on earth which Kenya then was for him to the responsibilities of Huddersfield? The people of Huddersfield benefited from the decision.

Conclusion

John William and John Frecheville were very different men. John William was never what in the modern world would be described as a 'people person.' He cared more deeply for places than for people. The lethargy of which he was so conscious in his youth perhaps sprang from a perception that his role in life demanded all the qualities which did not come naturally to him. He had no wish to socialise with his neighbours, take a kindly interest in the lives of his employees, show gracious charm when opening a new building in Huddersfield or, as an MP, win the hearts of his constituents. He was not what at the time would have been described as a 'clubbable man'. It was probably this aspect of his nature which led to the oft-quoted comment: 'From his childhood Sir John William Ramsden, the fifth baronet, lived with the reputation of being a dislikeable person.'[42]

John William's skills were rather those of the businessman or entrepreneur. Gradually he turned his life round so that he was doing the things at which he excelled. He gave up politics, in which he had little interest, and took on running his estates with total personal commitment. The acquisition of the Malayan plantations provided him with precisely the challenge he needed. Once he had a job which suited him, he worked as hard as anyone he employed. His interests too came to fit in well with his commitments. He derived enormous pleasure from planting trees on all his estates, initially in particular at Buckden and later at Ardverikie. Building and designing houses was another passion which accorded well with his position. Whilst never an easy man personally, as he found scope for the things at which he excelled he undoubtedly became a better husband, son, father and eventually grandfather.

On the other hand, he could be ruthless and vindictive. His treatment of the architect and his wife at Ardverikie is the classic example, with the couple dragged through the courts even after the unfortunate man's death in a lunatic asylum to which John William's behaviour had driven him for his misguided attempts to help his client, but there were many others. John William's habit of suing people whose performance had fallen short of what he expected at times resulted in him being unable to find anyone prepared to work for him.[43]

Yet his diaries in later life reveal a more sensitive, caring man than outsiders ever dreamed of. He undoubtedly mellowed with age. Many of his staff were extraordinarily loyal to him and stayed with him for most of their lives. Sometimes he struggled to see things from the point of view of others, in part because his personal life experience was so utterly different from that of the majority of people with whom he came in contact. If his system provided for paying bills on a six-monthly basis, it simply would not have occurred to him that this could create cash-flow problems for others. But, while he remained in charge, the jobs of his employees were secure. His empire was built on a sound foundation. In later years, his diary records numerous instances of his care and concern for members of his staff. He spent long hours sitting by the bedside of the much loved Ardverikie factor when the man was dying, talking to the doctors and undertaking various chores himself. Three years after Guen's death, and only a year before his own, he wrote in his diary:

> I walked to the Beaconsfield Lodge to enquire after old Mrs. Dancer, aged 85 [three years older than John William himself] the widow of old Dancer who died there some months ago. I am paying a nurse as her daughter seems incapable of tending her.[44]

This was not an isolated incident. Guendolen would have been proud of him.

With the family, his worst tendency was to bully where he could do so with impunity while respecting any demonstration of qualities matching his own unbending determination. Thus, while he often laughed at his independent daughter Mymee, she could speak her mind to him with absolute impunity while the gentle, loveable Rosamund, endlessly kind and considerate to her father, frequently dared not approach him. Yet it is apparent from his diary, as it was not apparent to Rosamund herself, that this was simply his habitual way of expressing himself. He adored his younger daughter, was immensely appreciative of all she did for him after the death of Guendolen, and found Rosamund's death at such a young age probably the most tragic and shattering event of his lifetime. Even in practical, financial terms, while offering little support to her husband, he ensured that her son was extremely well provided for.

John William's relations with Guendolen improved throughout his life as age, experience and the support of her mother-in-law built up her confidence. With John Frecheville, while the mockery was often to the fore, he never took off the kid gloves. Falling out with his only son was one disaster in life which he was determined to avoid at all costs. He often worried, sometimes despaired, strove to guide him in what John William believed to be the right direction, but ultimately he had no alternative. John Frecheville was his future. Had he had two sons, or even lived at a time when a daughter could be considered on an equal footing with her brother, he might perhaps have played one off against the other. It is impossible to tell. As it was, John Frecheville held the ace of trumps.

Considering the differences in their characters, it is remarkable that the two men got on as well as they did. But then it was so clearly in the interests of both that they should do so. Each ultimately wanted the relationship between them to work and neither ever risked seriously endangering it. The very skill which was John Frecheville's strength, and the absence of which was his father's weakness, helped the younger man immeasurably. He did have considerable charm, a natural way of getting on with people which stood him in good stead throughout his life and worked even with his own father.

His strengths and weaknesses were quite different from those of his father. John William only really flourished once he entered the commercial world. This was never an environment with much allure for John Frecheville, cultured, with wide interests, undoubtedly a 'people person'. John Frecheville was an urbane man with a large circle of friends, playing a prominent part in the social and sporting worlds of England, Scotland and Kenya, well-travelled, well-read, an immensely knowledgeable plantsman, interested in history and a number of scientific subjects where he was keen to attempt to turn such knowledge as he had into successful business ventures. He was also a practical man who earned his Swahili nickname Kimondo, referring to the bag of nails and basic tools he carried everywhere with him. He, almost alone amongst the European settlers, knew exactly how to build waterways on the land, something of vital importance when establishing new grazing areas. He and Arthur Cole, husband of his niece Tobina, had a shared enthusiasm for all such projects and delighted in working together to bring life-giving water to their arid estates.

Tobina (then Cartwright), as a young girl in Kenya, had lived in her uncle's house for extended periods, and described him some 70 years later as a giant among men. People of all ages and from different walks of life undoubtedly adored him. He would bring a young grandson into a group in a way which made the boy feel on equal terms with his grandfather's friends. With his own children as they grew up, however, he could sometimes lack imagination and if they were acting on his behalf he was frequently reluctant to accept their accounts of events, preferring the word of an unreliable employee: he did not always show good judgement when making appointments.

Whether John William would in fact have delegated authority had the young John Frecheville been willing to take responsibility was rarely tested.

John William certainly believed that he was keen to do so and only his son's total lack of interest prevented him from playing a prominent part in the family businesses. A generation later John Frecheville was not good at delegating to his children, all of whom in different capacities tried to undertake some of his burdens, only to have their efforts rebuffed. John St. Maur in both Kenya and Malaya, Bobbie at Muncaster and Joyce at Ardverikie all suffered from this.

More of an idealist than his father, John Frecheville was at one time keen to enter Parliament, fired with enthusiasm for the good he might achieve. John William had no such ideals: his principles were concerned rather with running a sound and successful business. John Frecheville's dreams were more uplifting and inspirational. Unfortunately, he rarely showed the determination necessary to put them into practice.

The fact that John William died in April 1914 (demonstrating, one is tempted to feel, his usual impeccable timing) meant that the transition of power from father to son (for, despite a few ominous rumblings, little of major importance changed in John William's lifetime after his so-called 'abdication') was simultaneous with one of the greatest watersheds in history. John William was not the only Victorian to build up an enormous business empire in an age of expansion. John Frecheville had to contend with two world wars and the Great Depression. Had their roles been reversed, it is interesting to speculate how the fortunes of all involved would have been altered.

John Frecheville would no doubt have settled into the role of a Victorian country gentleman as so many others did, enjoying a full social life, country pursuits, sport, books, developing and caring for some magnificent gardens and perhaps dabbling in some scientific experimentation, a relaxed, contented dilettante. He would happily have left the management of Huddersfield to an agent: the outcome would have depended upon the approach of the man in charge. The income it provided would have kept him in the style to which he was accustomed. He would not have taken on the challenge of Malaya.

John William, had he been dealt the same cards which life presented to John Frecheville, would have played his hand quite differently. Quick to spot opportunities and, with none of the temptations of Kenya which so attracted John Frecheville, he would have worked to retain a more dominant role in Malaya and to build up Huddersfield after the war. The sale of the complete estate – particularly at such a low price – to the Corporation would have been unthinkable to him. Nor would he have had dealings with a man such as Charles Leslie Melville: John William tolerated neither fools nor villains. So, Huddersfield owed its chance to become 'The Town That Bought Itself' to John Frecheville. His father would never have given the town that opportunity.

Note

Most of the information in this chapter is taken from private sources not accessible to the public. Enormous numbers of family letters, diaries and other papers are in the possession of the family but have never been catalogued. Thus any attempt to reference them would be meaningless. The author had access to some of this material for her book *Poverty is Relative* and this is the source for much of the material contained in this chapter.

Endnotes

1. See chapter 3, p. 89.
2. See chapter 2, pp. 56–7.
3. See above, chapter 4, p.120.
4. Whomsley (1974), pp. 191–2.
5. Whomsley (1974), pp. 198–200 and above, chapter 2, pp. 57–8.
6. JWR Diary, 1887.
7. JWR Diary, 1879.
8. Several references in diary of Sir John William Ramsden and in correspondence between JWR and his wife
9. Buxton (2017), pp. 71–4.
10. JWR to Isabella Ramsden, 4 September 1869.
11. Isabella Ramsden to JWR, 1869.
12. Buxton (2017), pp. 69–71.
13. JWR Diary.
14. *The Times*, 3 February 1953; see also *ODNB* (2004), 'Bentinck, Ruth Mary Cavendish- [née Ruth Mary St Maur] (1867–1953).
15. Guendolen Ramsden to JWR, 1874.
16. Various letters from JWR to Guendolen Ramsden.
17. JWR Diary, 1909.
18. JWR Diary, 1909.
19. JWR Diaries, 1910–14.
20. JWR Diary.
21. JWR Diaries.
22. *ODNB* (2004), 'Horsman, Edward (1807–1876)'.
23. Cumbria Record Office, Whitehaven, Pennington-Ramsden Papers, DPEN 383/10, Correspondence regarding Edward Horsman's accounts, including a detailed list of £17,000 of Horsman's general debts on 30 Jun 1876; and 386/4, Correspondence mainly between Sir John Ramsden and Edward Horsman concerning their efforts to raise money to ameliorate Horsman's financial situation, 1874–6; Buxton (2017), pp. 114–17.
24. Charlotte Horsman to JWR.
25. JWR to Isabella Ramsden.
26. JWR Diary.
27. JWR Diary.
28. Correspondence between JWR and 5th Baron Muncaster.
29. Buxton (2017), pp. 247–78.

30 Stephenson (1972), pp. 9–16. See chapter 6 for details, pp. 175-7.
31 Stephenson (1972), p. 11.
32 Stephenson (1972), p. 16.
33 Beard (1989), pp. 38–54.
34 *HDE*, 28 October 1919; see chapter 6, p.177.
35 DF 77, W. P. Raynor to Dawson, 1 November 1919.
36 Stephenson (1972), p. 11.
37 KC/592/2/15, 'How I came to be interested in Huddersfield' – see chapter 6, p. 181.
38 KC/592/2/15, 'How I came to be interested in Huddersfield' – see chapter 6, pp. 181-2.
39 John St Maur Ramsden Diary, 1921.
40 See Wickham and Lynch (2019).
41 John St Maur Ramsden Diary, 1921.
42 Although a number of authors quote this, I have been unable to trace its original source.
43 Buxton (2017), pp. 102–9.
44 JWR Diary, 1913.

Bibliography

Manuscript sources

Cumbria Record Office, Whitehaven
  DPEN Pennington-Ramsden Papers
  DPEN/311 Ramsden Letters

Leeds University Library, Special Collections
  MS 491, Isaac Hordern, 'Notes Relating to the Ramsden Estate and Huddersfield' (also in WYASK, DD/RE/419).

The National Archives, Kew
  HO 107/2294/15/23: 1851 Census, Longley Hall.
  RG 10/4356/94/20: 1871 Census, Longley Hall.
  RG 11/4375/14/21: 1881 Census, Longley Hall.

Swindon, Historic England Archive
  MD60/00034 – MD60/00038, Longley Hall Agent's House, Plans of Cellars, Ground Floor, Bedroom Floor, Roofs and East Elevation and Sections.

University of York, Borthwick Institute
  NHS/BOO/6/2/3/2, York Asylum, Registry of Admissions Book, 6 November 1850–10 September 1855.

West Yorkshire Archive Service, Bradford
  BDP78, Oakworth Christ Church Parish Records

West Yorkshire Archive Service, Kirklees
  CBH/A/321, Huddersfield County Borough architects.
  DD/AH/92, Philip Ahier Papers
  DD/R, Ramsden Papers
  DD/RA, Ramsden Family Papers
  DD/RE, Ramsden Estate Papers
  KC592, Clifford Stephenson Papers
  KMT18, Huddersfield County Borough records
  KX486/2 Dennis Whomsley, 'Unpublished typescripts for an intended history of the Ramsden family', including 'The Ramsden family, 1670-

1776'; 'The Ramsden family, 1769-1839'; 'Sir John William Ramsden, Part I, 1831-1857'; and 'Sir John William Ramsden and the West Riding, 1859-1867'.
  WYK1628/33, Edward Law Papers,
West Yorkshire Archive Service, Leeds
  BDP26, Farsley St John the Evangelist Parish Records
West Yorkshire Archive Service, Wakefield
  QE13/2/9 and QE13/2/15, Land Tax Returns, 1780–1832
  The John Goodchild Collection
  WDP12, Almondbury All Hallows Parish Records
  WDP24, Holmbridge St David Parish Records
  WDP143, Marsden St Bartholomew Parish Records
York Minster Archives
  2001/78, box 10b, Yorkshire Architectural Society, Minute Book 1842–6.

Newspapers

Bradford Observer
Huddersfield Chronicle
Huddersfield and Holmfirth Examiner
Huddersfield Daily Examiner
Huddersfield (Weekly) Examiner
Leeds Intelligencer
Leeds Mercury
Leeds Times
Yorkshire Observer
Yorkshire Observer Budget

Secondary Sources

Ahier, Philip (1950), *The Story of the three Parish Churches of St Peter the Apostle, Huddersfield*, part 3. Huddersfield: Advertiser Press.

Aikin, J. (1795), *A description of the country from Thirty to Forty miles around Manchester.* London: John Stockdale.

Baines, Edward (1809), *The Leeds Directory.* Leeds: Edward Baines.

Baines, Edward (1822), *History, Directory and Gazetteer of the County of York*, vol. 1. Leeds: Edward Baines

Beard, Madeleine (1989), *English Landed Society in the Twentieth Century*. London: Routledge.

Beard, Mary (2015), *SPQR: A History of Ancient Rome*. London: Profile Books.

Beardmore, Carol, Steven King and Geoff Monks (2016), *The Land Agent in Britain*. Newcastle: Cambridge Scholars Publishing.

Broadbent, G. H. (1956), 'The Life and Work of Pritchett of York', in W. A. Singleton, *Studies in Architectural History* II, pp. 102–24.

Brook, Roy (1968), *The story of Huddersfield*. London: Macgibbon & Kee.

Brooks, Chris (2000), '"the stuff of Heresiarch": William Butterfield, Beresford Hope and the Ecclesiological Vanguard', pp. 121–49 in C. Webster and J. Elliott (eds), *'A Church as it should be'*. Donnington: Shaun Tyas.

Brown, Roger Lee (2001), *"Welsh patriotism" and "Justice to Wales": the Association of Welsh Clergy in the West Riding of Yorkshire*. Welshpool: Tair Eglwys Press.

Buxton, Meriel (2017), *Poverty is relative*. Leicester: Woodperry Books.

Cannadine, David (1980), *Lords and Landlords; the Aristocracy and the Towns, 1774–1967*. Leicester: University Press.

Cannadine, David (ed.) (1982), *Patricians, power and politics in nineteenth-century towns*. Leicester: University Press.

Cant, David (2001), 'Longley Old Hall', *Yorkshire Buildings*, 29, pp 58-67.

Chadwick, Stanley (1976), *'A Bold and Faithful Journalist'; Joshua Hobson 1810–1876, Centenary Memorial*. Huddersfield: Kirklees Libraries and Museums Service.

Clarkson, D. L. (1989), 'St George's Square and the new town of Huddersfield', *Old West Riding*, 9, pp. 7–12.

Colvin, Howard (2008), *A Biographical Dictionary of British Architects*. New Haven and London: Yale University Press.

Cooksey, P. (1999), *Public Lives: The Family of Joseph Woodhead*. Huddersfield: Local History Society.

Coomber, R. (2017), 'Parliamentary enclosure in Shipley: process and effect', pp. 343–67 in N. Smith (ed.), *History in the South Pennines: The Legacy of Alan Petford*. Hebden Bridge: Local History Society.

Crook, J. M. (2003), *The Architect's Secret*. London: John Murray

Crump, W. B. (1924), 'Clifton and its Common Fields: A Survey in 1788', *Papers, Reports, etc.'*, Halifax Antiquarian Society, pp. 105-35.

Crump, W. G. & G. Ghorbal. (1935), *History of the Huddersfield Woollen Industry*. Huddersfield: Tolson Memorial Museum.

Dawson, W. N. (1973), *History on your doorstep*. Driffield: Ridings Publishing Co.

Dyson, Taylor (1932), *The History of Huddersfield and District: From the Earliest Times Down to 1932*. Huddersfield: The Advertiser Press.

Elliott, John (1996*), 'Palaces, Patronage & Pills – Thomas Holloway - His Sanatorium, College & Picture Gallery'*. Egham: Royal Holloway University of London.

Engels, F. (1845), *The Condition of the Working Class in England*. London: Penguin edition, 2005.

Evans, B. (2018), 'A Liberal town? The politics of Huddersfield borough, 1868 to 1918', pp. 85–101 in Griffiths (2018).

Fletcher, J. S. (1900), *A Picturesque History of Yorkshire*, vol II. London: Dent.

Foster Joseph (1874), *Pedigrees of the County Families of Yorkshire*, vols 1, 2. London: Joseph Foster.

Gash, Norman (1953), *Politics in the Age of Peel*. London: Longmans, Green & Co.

Gibson Keith, and Albert Booth (2005), *The Buildings of Huddersfield*. Stroud: Tempus.

Giles, Colum (ed.) (1986), *Rural Houses of West Yorkshire, 1400-1830*. London: HMSO.

Girouard, M. (1990), *The English Town*. New Haven: Yale University Press.

Griffiths, David (2008), *Pioneers or Partisans? Governing Huddersfield, 1820-48*. Huddersfield: Local History Society.

Griffiths, David (2009), 'Building an alliance for urban improvement: Huddersfield, 1844-1848', *The Local Historian*, 39:3, pp. 192–206.

Griffiths, David (2011a), '"Blending Instruction with Amusement": the Huddersfield Philosophical Society Exhibition of 1840', *Yorkshire Archaeological Journal*, 83, pp. 175–98.

Griffiths, David (2011b), *Secured for the Town: The story of Huddersfield's Greenhead Park*. Huddersfield: Friends of Greenhead Park.

Griffiths, David (2011c), 'Springwood, Huddersfield's lost park', *Huddersfield Local History Society Journal,* 22, pp. 16−25.

Griffiths, David (2012), 'Before the Corporation: Huddersfield's early civic buildings', *Huddersfield Local History Society Journal*, 23, pp. 14−20.

Griffiths, David (2015), 'Huddersfield in turbulent times, 1815−1850: Who Ruled and How?', *Northern History*, 52:1, pp. 101−24.

Griffiths, David (ed.) (2018), *Making up for Lost Time: The Pioneering Years of Huddersfield Corporation.* Huddersfield: Local History Society.

Haigh, E. A. Hilary (ed.) (1992), *Huddersfield, A Most Handsome Town.* Huddersfield: Kirklees Cultural Services.

Haigh, E. A. Hilary (2001), *Huddersfield Town Hall; An ornament to the town.* Huddersfield: Kirklees Council.

Halstead, John (1991), 'The *Voice of the West Riding*: Promoters and Supporters of an Unstamped Newspaper, 1833-34', pp. 22−57 in *On the Move: Essays in Labour and Transport History Presented to Philip Bagwell*, ed Chris Wrigley and John Shepherd. London: Hambledon Press.

Halstead, John (2012), 'The Huddersfield Short Time Committee and its radical associations, c.1820−1876', pp. 91-144 in *Slavery in Yorkshire: Richard Oastler and the campaign against child labour in the Industrial Revolution*, ed John A. Hargreaves and E. A. Hilary Haigh. Huddersfield: University Press.

Halstead, John (2018), 'The Charter and Something More! The Politics of Joshua Hobson, 1810-1876', pp. 83−122 in Hargreaves (2018).

Hargreaves, John A. (1992), '"A Metropolis of Discontent": Popular Protest in Huddersfield, c.1780−c.1850', pp. 189−220 in Haigh (1992).

Hargreaves, John A. (ed.) (2018), *The Charter our Right! Huddersfield Chartism re-considered.* Huddersfield: Local History Society.

Harman, Ruth and Nikolaus Pevsner (2017), *Buildings of England, Yorkshire West Riding: Sheffield and the South*. New Haven and London: Yale University Press.

Hemingway, Vivienne (1992), 'Parliamentary politics in Huddersfield, c.1832−53', pp. 481−500 in Haigh (1992).

Hewitt, John (1862-4), *The History and Topography of the Parish of Wakefield.* Wakefield: John Hewitt.

Hey, David, Colum Giles, Margaret Spufford and Andrew Wareham (eds) (2007), *Yorkshire West Riding Hearth Tax Assessment, Lady Day 1672.* London: British Records Society.

Hilton, K, (1989), 'Huddersfield 1837–1854: The influence of the landlord and land steward on the development of the town.' Unpublished dissertation, Huddersfield Polytechnic.

Hinchcliffe, Gerald (1963), *A History of King James's Grammar School in Almondbury*. Huddersfield: Advertiser Press.

Hulbert, Charles Augustus (1882), *Annals of the Church and Parish of Almondbury.* London: Longmans.

Hulbert, Charles Augustus (1885), *Supplementary Annals of the Church and Parish of Almondbury*. Huddersfield and London: Longmans.

Jenkins, Simon (2017), *Britain's 100 Best Railway Stations*. London, Penguin Books.

Jenkinson, Brian (1963), *Moldgreen Parish Church, 1863–1963*. privately printed.

Jenkinson, Brian (1988), *St Mary's, Longley, 1888–1988*. privately printed.

Law, Edward J. (1985), *18th Century Huddersfield: the day-books of John Turner, 1732–1783*. Huddersfield: Edward J. Law.

Law, Edward J. (1986), 'Architects of Huddersfield and District to 1860', no. 7 in *Essays in Local History*. Huddersfield: unpublished typescript. (also at http://homepage.eircom.net/~lawedd/ARCHITECTS.htm).

Law, Edward (1989), *Joseph Kaye, Builder of Huddersfield c.1779-1858*. Huddersfield: Local History Society.

Law, Edward (1992), 'Markets, Fairs and Tolls in Huddersfield', pp. 65–84 in Haigh (1992).

Law, Edward (2001a), 'Huddersfield maps: a caution', at http://homepage.eircom.net/~lawedd/CAUTION.htm

Law, Edward (2001b), 'William Henry Crossland, Architect, 1835-1908, Part 1', at homepage.eircom.net/~lawedd/WHC1.htm

Lawton, George (1842), *Collections Relative to Churches and Chapels within the Diocese of* York, new edn. London: Rivington.

Linstrum, Derek (1978), *West Yorkshire Architects and Architecture*. London: Lund Humphries.

Lobban, Michael (2004), 'Preparing for Fusion: Reforming the Nineteenth-Century Court of Chancery, *Law and History Review*, 22:2, pp. 389–427 and 22:3, pp. 565–99.

Marsden, Christopher (2018), 'Huddersfield Architects ... an A–Z Listing'. Huddersfield: privately printed.

Mills, D. R. (1980), *Lord and Peasant in Nineteenth Century Britain.* London: Croom Helm.

Minter, Gordon and Enid (1996), *Discovering Old Huddersfield*, 4 vols. Huddersfield: Barden and Co.

Moore, D. C. (1976), *The Politics of Deference.* Hassocks: Harvester Press.

Morgan, B. G. (1961), *Canonic Design in English Medieval Architecture.* Liverpool: University Press.

Morris, R. (1990), *Class, sect and party: The making of the English middle class – Leeds, 1820-50.* Manchester: University Press.

Navickas, K. (2016), *Protest and the politics of place and space, 1789-1848.* Manchester: University Press.

Neale, J. M. and Webb, B. (1843), *The Symbolism of Churches and Church Ornaments.* London: Rivington.

Nicholson, P. (1798), *The Student's Instructor in Drawing and Working the Five Orders of Architecture.* London: J. Taylor.

Ormrod, W. Mark (ed.) (2000), *The Lord Lieutenants and High Sheriffs of Yorkshire, 1066-2000.* Barnsley: Wharncliffe Books.

Oxford Dictionary of National Biography (2004): Oxford: University Press.

Pearce, Cyril (2018), 'A pioneer in municipal enterprise: Huddersfield, 1868-1920', pp. 37–60 in Griffiths (2018).

Phillips, George Searle (1848), *Walks Round Huddersfield.* Huddersfield: Bond & Hardy (first published in *Bradford & Wakefield Observer*, 27 September 1847).

Pigot, James (1834), *Pigot and Co.'s National Commercial Directory &c.* London: Pigot and Co.

Poole G. A. and J. W. Hugall (1842-4), *The Churches of Yorkshire,* 2 vols. Leeds: T. W. Green.

Redmonds, George (1982), *The Heirs of Woodsome*, Huddersfield: G. R. Books.

Redmonds, George (2003), *The Making of Huddersfield.* Barnsley: Wharncliffe.

Richardson, Harry W. (1971), *Urban Economics*. London: Penguin Education.

Richardson, M. (1903), *St John's Church, Bay Hall, 1853-1903.* privately printed.

Roberts, Matthew (2018), '"God Save the Paddock Flag": Anti-Poor Law and Chartist Banners, 1837-1844', pp. 39–61 in Hargreaves (2018).

Robson, T. (1831), *Robson's London Dictionary*. London: Robson & Co.

Royle, Edward (1996), 'Owenism and the Secularist Tradition: the Huddersfield Secular Society and Sunday School', pp. 199–217 in *Living and Learning*, ed M. Chase and I. Dyck. Aldershot: Scolar Press.

Rumsby, John H. (1992), '"A Castle Well Guarded": the Archaeology and History of Castle Hill, Huddersfield', pp. 1–15 in Haigh (1992).

Rushworth, John (1721), 'Proceedings in Parliament: November 1st–December 1st 1648,' in *Historical Collections of Private Passages of State: Volume 7, 1647-48.* London: D. Browne, pp. 1315-48. British History Online, accessed October 7, 2019, http://www.british-history.ac.uk/rushworth-papers/vol7/pp1315-1348.

Schofield, D. (1883), 'Huddersfield Sixty Years Ago', *Huddersfield Examiner*, 15 September.

Schofield, Isobel (1999), 'Bruce of Huddersfield', pp. 89–101 in I. Schofield (ed.), *Aspects of Huddersfield*. Barnsley: Wharncliffe Publishing.

Scholfield, P. H. (1958), *The Theory of Proportions in Architecture*. Cambridge: University Press.

Scott, W. Herbert (1902), *The West Riding of Yorkshire at the Opening of the Twentieth Century.* Brighton: W. T. Pike.

'Senex' [Josiah Bateman] (1880), *Clerical Reminiscences*. London: Seeley, Jackson and Halliday.

Shepherd, F. H. W. (ed.) (1957), *Survey of London, Spitalfields*, vol. 27. London: Athlone University Press.

Slade, William (1851), *Slade and Roebuck's Directory of the Borough and Neighbourhood of Leeds, &c.* Leeds: Slade and Co.

Smail, John (1994), *The origins of middle-class culture: Halifax, Yorkshire, 1660–1780*. Ithaca: Cornell University Press.

Soane, John (1788), *Plans, Elevations and Sections of Buildings*. London: Messrs Taylor.

Spring, David (1963), *The English Landed Estate in the Nineteenth Century: Its Administration*. Baltimore: The Johns Hopkins Press.

Springett, Jane (1979), 'The mechanics of urban land development in Huddersfield, 1770-1911'. Unpublished Ph.D. thesis, University of Leeds.

Springett, Jane (1982), 'Landowners and urban development: the Ramsden estate and nineteenth century Huddersfield', *Journal of Historical Geography*, 8:2, pp. 129–44.

Springett, Jane (1986), 'Land development and house-building in Huddersfield, 1770-1911', pp. 23–56 in M. Doughty (ed.), *Building the industrial city*. Leicester: University Press.

Springett, Jane (1992), pp. 449–80 in Haigh (1992).

Stephenson, Clifford (1972), *The Ramsdens and their Estate in Huddersfield. "The Town that bought itself"*. Huddersfield: The County Borough of Huddersfield.

Sykes, D. F. E. (1898), *The History of Huddersfield and its Vicinity*. Huddersfield: Advertiser Press

Taylor, Kate (2012), *Wakefield Diocese: celebrating 125 years*. Norwich: Canterbury Press.

The Church at Longroyd Bridge, 1859–1899 (1899). Huddersfield: privately printed.

Thrush, Andrew and John P. Ferris (eds) (2010), *The House of Commons 1604–1629*. Cambridge: University Press.

Tolson, Legh (1929), *The History of the Church of St John the Baptist, Kirkheaton*. Kendal: privately published.

Trainor, Richard (1993), *Black Country Elites: The Exercise of Authority in an Industrialized Area, 1830-1900*. Oxford: University Press.

Turvey, Ralph (1957), *The Economics of Real Property: An Analysis of Property Values and Patterns of Use*. London: Allen & Unwin.

Venn, Henry (1836), *The Life and a Selection from the Letters of Henry* Venn, 4th edn. London: J. Hatchard.

Venn, John and J.A Venn (1924), *Alumni Cantabrigienses*, part 1 volume 3. Cambridge: University Press.

Venn, John and J.A Venn (1953), *Alumni Cantabrigienses*, part 2 volume 4. Cambridge: University Press.

Walker, David M. (1976), 'William Burn: the country house in transition', in J. Fawcett, (ed.), *Seven Victorian Architects*. London: Thames & Hudson.

Wallen, William (1836), *The History and Antiquities of the Round Church at Little Maplestead, Essex*. London: John Weale.

Wallen, William (1842), *Two Essays Elucidating the Geometrical Principles of Gothic Architecture*. Leeds: Edward Baines.

Weatherhead, Arthur S. (1913), *Holy Trinity, Huddersfield. Three lectures on the history of the church and parish, 1819 – 1904*. Huddersfield: privately printed.

Webster Christopher (ed.) (2003), *'temples ... worthy of His presence': the early publications of the Cambridge Camden Society*. Reading: Spire Books.

Webster, Christopher (2010), 'An Alternative to Ecclesiology: William Wallen', *Ecclesiology Today*, 42 (June), pp. 9–28, published as G. Brandwood (ed.), *Seven Church Architects 1830–1930*. London: Ecclesiological Society.

Webster, Christopher (2011), 'John Clark (1798-1857)' in C. Webster, (ed.), *Building a Great Victorian City*. Huddersfield: Northern Heritage Publications.

Whitaker, T. D. (1816), *Loidis and Elmete*. Leeds: Robinson, Son and Holdsworth.

White, William (1853), *Directory and Gazetteer of Leeds, &c*. Sheffield: W. White.

White, William (1894), *Directory of the Borough of Huddersfield*, 15th edition (pp. 391–546 from *The Clothing District Directory*). Sheffield: W. White.

Whittaker, L. J. (1984), 'W. H. Crossland'. M.A. Dissertation, University of Manchester.

Whomsley, Dennis (1967), 'William Ramsden of Longley, Gentleman, 1514–1580, Agent in Monastic Property', *Yorkshire Archaeological Journal* 42, pp. 143–50.

Whomsley, Dennis (1974), 'A Landed Estate and the Railway: Huddersfield 1844–54', *Journal of Transport History*, new series II, no. 4, pp. 189–213.

Whomsley, Dennis (1984), 'Market forces and urban growth: the influence of the Ramsden family on the growth of Huddersfield, 1716–1853', *Journal of Regional and Local Studies*, 4:2, pp. 27-56.

Whomsley, Dennis (1987), 'Radical Politics in the 1850s and 1860s: Joshua Hobson and the Tenant Right Dispute in Huddersfield', *Journal of Regional and Local Studies*, 7:1, pp. 14–33.

Whomsley, Dennis (1992), 'The Ramsdens of Longley 1530–1690', pp. 37–63 in Haigh (1992).

Wickham, Louise and Karen Lynch (2019), *Yorkshire Gardens Trust. Selby District Historic Designed Landscapes Project. Byram Park,* published at https://www.yorkshiregardenstrust.org.uk/byram-park.

Williams, J. (1845), *Williams' Directory of the borough of Leeds, &c.* London: J. Williams.

Woodhead, T. W. (1939), *History of the Huddersfield water supplies.* Huddersfield: Tolson Memorial Museum.

Wyles, David J. (1992), 'Architectural Design in Nineteenth Century Huddersfield', pp. 303–40 in Haigh (1992).

Index

Acland Hood, *see* Hood
advowsons 46, 115, 127-30, 174, 176
Almondbury 2, 3, 5, 8, 115-17, 123, 130, 138, 151, 174
    parish church (All Hallows) 8, 117, 123, 127, 130, 135-7, 138, 152, 186,
    school, 153;
    Grammar School, 118, 152
Andrews, George Townsend (1804-55), architect 151
Architectural Society 150
Ardverikie estate 24, 119, 177, 184, 199, 205, 207-10, 212, 215-16, 218
Armitage Bridge, St Paul 131, 142n50
Armitage, George 95
Aspley Mission 138, 153, 159, 165, 169n45

Baptists 122, 125;
    New North Road chapel, 122
Bardsley, Rev. James 126, 128, 130
Barrowclough, Florence 179, 188
Bateman, Rev. Josiah 62, 63, 123, 132
Bay Hall Estate 45, 58, 63, 67, 83n58, 118, 134, 135, 143n76, 197
Bay Hall, St John 19, 63, 67, 80, 118-19, 121, 123, 127, 128, 131, 134-6, 138, 139, 140, 167, 168, 174, 186,
    vicarage 135
Beadon, Frederick William (1853-1933), agent 34, 36, 40n104, 78, 79, 80, 119, 123, 126, 128, 129, 204
Beasley, John (1801-74), land agent 27, 40n83
Beaumont, E.A., councillor 177, 210
Bensted, Rev. Thomas 121, 128
Bentinck, Ruth Mary Cavendish- (née Seymour) (1867–1953) 201
Berry Brow 106, 178;
    New Connexion chapel 125

Blore, Edward (1787-1879), architect 10, 12, 22, 134, 168
Booth, James, agent 53
Booth, John 95
Bower, John, agent 10, 52, 53, 55, 56, 63, 83n28 89, 195
Bradford 47, 145, 161
Brick Buildings 7, 43, 49, 51
Bright, Mary (Countess Rockingham) 117-18
Britannia Building 99, 162
Broadbent, Thomas H. 101
Brook family of Meltham Mills:
    Charles 135
    Joseph 60, 63-5, 85n97, 159
    William Leigh 159-60
Brook, Jabez 101
Brook, James 91
Brook, Joseph, agent 89, 94, 105
Brook, Thomas, agent 12, 82n6
Brooke family of Armitage Bridge 131
    Edward 125
    John 98, 113n44
    Thomas 119, 135
Brooke, John of Fenay Hall 129
Brotherton 5, 89, 118, 202
    St Edward 134, 148, 166, 167
    school 202
Broughton, John 101
Brunswick Street Free Wesleyan chapel 95, 123
Buckden 95, 96, 98, 103, 109, 195, 199, 215
Bulstrode 34, 119, 128, 199, 201, 205, 208
Burn, William (1789-1870), architect 18, 24-9
Butterfield, William (1814-1900), architect 134, 136, 168
Buxton, Geoffrey (1879-1958) ('Bobby') 212-14

Byram 4, 5, 7, 8, 19, 26, 33-5, 46, 52, 54, 72, 103, 108, 119, 188, 199, 203, 205, 206, 208, 209, 214, 215
Byram Arcade 77
Byram Buildings 33, 40n97
Byram Street 43, 77

Calvert, Rev. W.B. 128
Camden Society/Ecclesiologists 155, 157, 158, 167, 168
canals 43, 47, 48, 53, 55-7, 75, 78, 81, 82n21, 83n49, 196
Canal Act (1774) 43, 48
Castle Hill 162-3, 165, 166
  hotel 62, 164
  Victoria Tower 203, 204
Catholics 125, 136, 144n88
  St Patrick, New North Road 122, 146,
  schools 121, 122
Chantrell, Robert Dennis (1793-1872), architect 146, 151-3, 156, 169n32
Child, John (c.1790-1868), architect 146
church rates 125, 134
Clay, Bradley, agent 53
Cloth Hall 7, 10, 14, 43, 47, 48, 50, 51, 58, 65, 75, 81
Coates, Rev. John 117
Cocking, William (1817-74), architect 162, 165
Cole, Prudence Tobina, née Cartwright (1928-2016) 217
Colling, William Bunn (1813-86), architect 27
Congregationalists, *see* Independents
Copley, Samuel William (1859-1937) 176-88, 190, 192n19, 211-13
Cowcliffe schools 121, 135
Crook, Rev. Harcar 117
Crosland, George 95
Crosland, Joseph 121, 131
Crosland, Thomas Pearson 110, 112n19
Crossland, William Henry (1835-1908), architect 14, 15, 28-33, 40n90, 70-1, 77, 79, 85n117
Crossley, Rev. Owen Thomas Lloyd 129, 130
Crowder, John, agent 10, 52, 82n21, 89

Dalton 45, 76, 77, 80, 138
Dartmouth, Earls (Legge family) 116, 139
  William (1731-1801), 2nd Earl 117, 131, 140
  William (1784-1853), 4th Earl 118
  William Walter (1823-91), 5th Earl 135
Dawson, Wilfrid (1871-1936) 175-88, 190, 191, 210, 211, 212, 213
Dawson File 175, 177, 179, 180-3, 188, 190, 191, 210, 211
death duties 209
Deighton 47, 76, 174
Dinsley, Thomas, surveyor 51, 89
donations 64, 73, 76, 119, 120-4, 127, 130, 131-2, 134, 135
Drawbridge, Rev. Charles 121-2
Dundas, Bunny 197, 199, 202
Dyson, Ernest, borough treasurer 188
Dyson, Lee 89, 105, 110, 111n3

elections 44, 53-4, 71, 82n6, 112n6, 112n18
Engels, Friedrich 52, 55, 83n31, 146
Estate Office, Longley Hall 10, 12-15, 25, 27, 70, 89, 160, 166, 168
Estate Office, Westgate 27-8, 70, 111, 180
Evangelicalism 24, 117, 127-30, 131, 140, 155, 157

Farnley Tyas, St Lucius 153, 169n32
Fartown Grammar School 152
Fenton, James Crosland 56, 64, 131
Fenton, Lewis 53
First World War 79, 80, 209, 210, 211, 218
Firth, Thomas 45, 65, 77, 82n10, 86n139
Fitzwilliams of Wentworth Woodhouse 46, 53, 54, 117, 134, 140, 168, 195
  Charles William Wentworth-Fitzwilliam, 5th Earl Fitzwilliam (1786-1857) 10, 16, 19, 23, 56, 63, 118-22, 125, 134, 147, 148, 159, 161, 166, 195, 196
Fixby 116, 159, 174
Fowler, Charles Hodgson (c.1823-1903), architect 138
Freeman, John, lawyer 95-8, 100

George Hotel 10, 57, 59, 62, 63, 65, 71, 75, 160-2, 166, 168, 197
George Inn 10, 50, 57

INDEX

Gledhill, Wright 106-7
Golcar 116
　St John 143n64
Gothic architecture 14, 21, 70, 85n117, 134, 138, 151, 155-6, 158, 159
Graham, Richard Hewley (1834-85), agent 24-6, 28, 29, 32-4, 68-71, 72-4, 78, 119, 122, 126
Greenhead 45, 58, 66, 67, 73, 124, 131, 155, 197
Greenhead Park 66, 72, 73, 80, 121, 124, 132, 178

Halifax 29, 47, 54, 61, 66, 145, 146, 148, 156
Halstead, Benjamin 100, 101
Hathorn, Alexander (1816-92), agent 11-17, 19-21, 23, 24, 39n69, 56, 57, 60-2, 668, 90-3, 100, 105, 109, 119, 149, 161
highways 46, 68
　Highways Act (1835) 53
　Board of Highways Surveyors 53
Hillhouse 63, 100, 126, 134
　Free Wesleyan chapel 125, schools 135
Hobson, Joshua (1810-76), editor 16, 52, 57-8, 62, 65, 66, 84n75, 87-8, 90-102, 104, 107, 111, 112n19
Holliday, Read 94
Holmbridge, St David, 151-2, 153, 158, parsonage 153, schools 153
Holt family 8, 13, 17, 20, 38n22
Honley 116, 174
　St Mary 116, 122, 142n50, parsonage 122
Hood, H. Acland, solicitor 180, 182-4, 186-7
Hordern, Isaac (1829-1912), estate cashier 11, 12, 21-4, 28, 29, 34, 122, 123, 165, 203, 204, 205
Horsman, Charlotte Louisa, née Ramsden (1815-95) 91, 102, 195, 199, 207, 208
Horsman, Edward (1807-76) 91, 199, 207, 208
Hoste, Rev. Charles Dixon 129-30
housing 49, 52, 58, 75, 78, 79, 80, 87, 153, 155, 178, 189, 190

Huddersfield 5, 27, 45, 68, 115, 130, 145, 146, 174, 202, 205, 207, 209, 212, 215
　Georgian 43, 50, 51, 57, 67, 81
　New Town 57, 58, 64, 67, 74, 75, 76, 78, 81, 166
　Huddersfield Corporation/Town Council 68-74, 76-80, 174, 175, 177, 179-91, 210, 211, 218
　incorporation 43, 44, 58, 68, 69, 70, 78, 174
　Corporation Act (1897) 44, 76
　purchase 34, 35, 36, 79, 177-80, 183-8, 210-15, 218
Huddersfield Art Gallery 77, 79, 86n139, 202
　Cemetery 62-4, 66, 73, 80, 124
　Commission for Lighting, Watching and Cleansing (1820) 53, 54, 58, 60
　court leet 46, 53, 68, 69
　Improvement Commission 57, 58, 60-68, 70, 71, 72, 81, 90, 190
　Infirmary 8, 55, 76, 86n139, 124, 134, 146, 147, 148, 160
　Mechanics Institute 23, 124
　Technical School 125
　YMCA 125-6
Huddersfield churches: parish church (St Peter) 10, 50, 51, 75, 77, 79, 118, 123, 130, 132-4, 135, 146, 148, 167, vicarage 130, 155, parish (Seed Hill) schools 46-7, 118
　Holy Trinity, Trinity Street 122, 131, 146, schools 153
　St Andrew, Leeds Road 127, 131
　St Mark, Lowerhead Row 127
　St Paul, Ramsden Street 51, 74, 118, 120, 123, 124, 131, 134, 146, 147, 148, schools 124
Huddersfield College 146, 153, 154
Huddersfield Collegiate School 121, 152-3, 154
Huddersfield Chronicle 16, 17, 28, 61, 66, 88, 90, 92, 96, 97, 103, 107-10, 112n22, 161, 163, 164
Huddersfield Examiner 92, 96, 97, 103, 106, 107, 108, 112n22, 174, 175, 185, 187, 190, 191
Hulbert, Rev. Charles Augustus (1804-88) 2-3, 5, 6, 36, 127, 128, 135, 136
Hurndell, Rev. W.A. 153

Improvement Acts: (1848) 44, 68
  (1871) 72
  (1876) 74
Incorporated Church Building Society 151-2
Independents/Congregationalists 104, 117, 125, 134, 148
  Highfield 117, 124, 126
  Milton 125, schools 125
  Paddock 124
  Ramsden Street 10, 51, 75, 122, 123, 134, 146, 148 149, 153, schools 122
Irish 141n29

Jebson, John 100
John William Street 43, 57, 75, 99, 162, 197
Jones, Charles Henry (1800-84), mayor 69, 71, 72
Jones, Frederick Robert, jnr, lawyer 88, 99-101, 103, 106, 107, 109-11, 114n52
Jones, Rev. Lewis (1824-66) 117, 127, 138, 142n50, 151, 152

Kaye, Jere 95, 97
Kaye, Joseph (c.1779-1858), builder 135, 147
Kayes of Woodsome 3, 116, 135
Kenya 209-10, 212, 213, 215, 217-18
Kilner, Thomas 93, 105
Kirkheaton 138, 153, 174
  schools 153

Leeds 16, 29, 47, 55, 57, 145-6, 151, 153, 156, 158, 159, 161, 165, 196
Leeds Intelligencer 152, 158
Leeds Mercury 108, 166
Leeds Times 101
Legge, Augusta Georgiana (1854-1931) 186
Leslie-Melville, Charles le Despencer (1877-1929) 179-85, 210, 211-13, 218
libraries 55, 66, 77, 79, 86n139
Lindley 45, 100
  St Stephen 143n64, 148, 153
Lingards 116, 142n53
Linthwaite 95, 116
Lion Building 162, 184
Lister-Kaye, John Lister (1801-71), 2nd Bt 45, 77, 101, 138

Loch, George (1811-77), agent 9, 10, 12-16, 19-23, 56-7, 58, 60-4, 87-9, 90-1, 92, 101, 112n4, 119, 122, 123, 125, 149, 161, 166-7, 168, 195-7
Lockwood 45, 65, 95, 116, 131, 146, 174
  Emmanuel 121, 128, 131, 142n50, 143n64, 146
Longley, St Mary's 138
  Primitive Methodist schoolroom 138
Longley (Old) Hall 1-3, 36, 37, 135, 177, 186
Longley (New) Hall 2-8, 10, 12-36, 70, 96, 98, 101, 105, 107, 111, 118, 119, 131, 138, 204-6
Longley Hall (Girls) Central School 36
Longroyd Bridge, St Thomas 127, 131, 138, 165
Longwood 55, 116
  Grammar School 152
Lowe, Rev. John 117, 118

Malaya 177, 207-9, 214-15, 218
Mallinson, Thomas 95, 98, 99, 100, 103, 106, 123
markets 5, 22, 47, 65, 70, 72, 76, 81
  Market Hall 70-2, 75
  Market Place 7, 43, 47, 50, 51, 53, 57, 65, 74, 75, 86n133, 166
  market rights 43, 44, 46, 51, 65, 68, 69, 72, 73, 81
Marsden 116
  St Bartholomew 153, schools 153
Mellor, Wright (1817-93), mayor 72, 85n124, 98, 103, 104, 106, 108, 126, 128
Meltham 116, 135
  St Bartholomew 160
Meltham Mills 155, 159
  St James 155, schools   155
Melville, Charles *see* Leslie-Melville
Methodists 122, 125
  Free Wesleyan: Brunswick Street 95, 123; Hillhouse 125; Sheepbridge 122
  New Connexion: Berry Brow 125; High Street 51
  Wesleyan: Paddock 121, 125; Queen Street 10, 51, 122, schools 122
  Primitive: Longley 138
Micklethwaite, Robert (1819-88) 90, 112n6
Milbanke, John 118

Miller, T. McGregor 126
Milnsbridge, St Luke 142n50, 153, 157-9, parsonage 153
Moldgreen 77, 101, 138
    Christ Church 132, 138, schools 122
    St Michael 131, 138-9
Moore, John White 99
Muncaster Castle 2, 35, 41n110, 209, 218
Municipal Corporations Act (1835) 58, 173, 174

Nelson, Thomas Wright (1802-83), agent 23, 62, 64, 66, 67, 70, 88, 92-4, 96-7, 106, 111, 112n18, 122, 123
New North Road 75, 95, 99, 122, 153, 165, 178
Newsome 175
    St John 119, 131, 138, 142n50
Noble, John, agent 24, 106-7
Nonconformists 63, 95, 122-6, 140, 148, 153
    see also under individual denominations
Norris, Rev. W. Foxley 138, 139

Oastler, Richard 55, 83n49, 112n6
Oates, John (1793-1831), architect 146, 148, 153, 160

Paddock 98, 100, 105, 120
    All Saints 120, 125, 131, 143n64, 148, schools 121
    Congregational chapel 124, schools 95
    Wesleyan chapel 121, 125
Paddock Brow, Johnny Moor Hill Mission 121
parks 65, 66, 72, 73, 74, 76
    see also Greenhead Park
Parliament 4, 27, 53, 72, 74, 76, 89, 95, 100, 101, 111, 180, 182, 185-8, 196, 218
    parliamentary 4, 5, 43, 44, 45, 53, 54, 77, 119, 131, 143n64
parsonages/vicarages 122, 131, 130, 131, 135, 148, 151, 153
patronage (church) 115, 116, 117, 123, 127-30, 135, 142n50
    see also advowsons
Peel, Robert (1788-1850) 59, 71, 73, 74, 163, 164

Philosophical Hall 55, 74, 100, 146
politics 5, 53, 54, 61, 81, 82n6, 90, 95, 112n6, 125, 140, 215
poor, poverty 109, 118, 120
    poor law 46, 53, 55, 62
Pope, Richard Shackleton (c.1793-1884), architect 151
population 44, 52, 87, 108, 115, 173
Primrose Hill, St Matthew 131
Pritchett, Charles Pigott (1818-91), architect 62, 147
Pritchett, James Pigott (1789-1868), architect 57, 59, 62, 132-4, 146-8, 149, 150, 152, 153, 154, 160-2, 165, 166, 167, 168
Public Health Act (1858) 68

railways 16, 55-6, 57, 58, 61, 64, 81, 140, 161, 166, 196-7, 202
    Huddersfield Railway Station 10, 19, 43, 52, 57, 59, 74, 75, 134, 146, 148, 166, 168
Ramsden Charity 118
Ramsden Estate 10, 16, 21, 23, 27, 34, 35-7, 43, 44-5, 46-51, 54-6, 57-8, 62, 63-4, 70, 76-7, 80-1, 89, 115, 120-1, 143n62, 149, 174, 178, 187-8, 196, 211
    Ramsden Estate Act (1844) 58, 65, 92, 93, 102, 106, 109
    Ramsden Estate Act (1848) 58, 60, 63, 65, 68
    Ramsden Estate (Leasing) Act (1859) 65, 88, 92, 97, 98, 100, 101, 102, 107, 109, 111
    Ramsden Estate Act (1867) 28, 33, 65, 70, 78, 89, 106, 111, 178
    Ramsden (Huddersfield) Estates Bill/Lands Act (1920) 182, 187, 189
Ramsden Tenure Dispute, *see* Tenure Dispute
Ramsden Trustees (4th Bt) 10, 134
    (5th Bt) 16, 54-6, 58, 60-2, 64, 89-91, 119, 120, 124, 134, 147, 159, 161, 163, 195-7, 207
Ramsden, Charles (1801-91) 197
Ramsden, Elizabeth (Mrs Weddell) (1749-1831) 118
Ramsden, Geoffey William Pennington (1904-87), 7th Bt ('Bobby') 37, 218

Ramsden, Helen Guendolen, née Seymour (1846-1910) 33, 34, 36, 119, 144n86, 199-203, 205-6, 216
Ramsden, Hermione Charlotte ('Mymee') (1867-1951) 199, 205, 208, 216
Ramsden, Isabella, née Dundas (1790-1887) 8, 9, 10, 12, 13, 19, 56, 58, 63, 65, 83n58, 87, 112n4, 118, 119, 131, 134, 135, 139, 140, 148, 149, 161, 163, 166, 167, 195-7, 199, 216
Ramsden, Joan, née Buxton (1881-1974) 139, 202, 203, 206, 209, 212, 213
Ramsden, John (1594-1646), Kt 4, 5
Ramsden, John (1648-90), 1st Bt 5, 35, 41n109, 115, 118
Ramsden, John (1698/9-1769), 3rd Bt 5, 8, 47, 49, 117, 140
Ramsden, John (1755-1839), 4th Bt 5, 7, 8, 43, 45, 48, 49, 52-4, 56, 63, 87, 116, 117, 118-19, 134, 147-8, 167, 195, 196, 197
Ramsden, John (d.1591) 1, 4, 6, 115
Ramsden, John Charles (1788-1836) 8, 9, 10, 53, 87, 118, 134, 135, 140, 148, 195
Ramsden, John Frecheville (1877-1958), 6th Bt 34, 35, 37, 79, 139, 177, 180-8, 191, 198, 202, 203-5, 206, 207-18
Ramsden, John St Maur (1902-48) 213-15, 218
Ramsden, John William (1831-1914), 5th Bt: life and family 9, 10, 19, 21, 22, 64, 79, 116, 119, 195, 198, 200, 205-6, 207, 209, 215, 216-17
  character 23, 54, 62, 63-4, 67, 69, 120, 130, 131-2, 135-6, 138, 139, 196, 198-9, 201, 202, 215-18
  Longley 24-29, 33-4, 204
  Huddersfield 16, 17, 46, 61, 64, 66, 69, 71-4, 87-9, 120, 199-201, 204, 205-6
  tenancy issues 91-3, 95-8, 99-106, 106-111
  businessman 78, 80, 124, 177, 199, 207-8, 215, 218
  religion and philanthropy 118, 120-5, 125-7, 127-30, 136, 140, 198, 216
Ramsden, Margaret (Bright), née Norton (d.1775) 5, 117-18
Ramsden, Margaret (Lady Ducie) (d.1786) 118

Ramsden, Rev. John (c.1762-1807) 116
Ramsden, Rev. Robert (c.1543-98) 116
Ramsden, Rosamund (1872-1911) 205, 206, 216
Ramsden, Thomas (1709-91) 47, 49, 52, 57
Ramsden, William (c.1513-80) 1, 115
Ramsden, William (1558-1622/3) 4, 115, 118
Ramsden, William (1625-79) 5, 118
Ramsden, William (1672-1736), 2nd Bt 5
Rashcliffe, St Stephen 131, 142n50
Redfearn, John 93-4, 96, 105, 109
Reform Act (1832) 43, 53
rent dinners 23, 67, 98
Riding School 160, 162, 166
Riland, Rev. John 117, 118
Riley, Jeremiah (1801-65) 60, 61
Ripon, Bishop of: Thomas Longley (1794-1868) 153, 159
  Robert Bickersteth (181684) 128
  William Boyd Carpenter (1841-1918) 126, 130
ritualism 124, 127, 128, 129, 140
Robinson, Thomas (1799-1861+) 91, 100, 101, 114n56
Roebuck, Josephus Jagger 99
Rolt, Rev. Cecil Henry 129
Rushforth, John 95

Sale, Rev. Thomas Rawlinson 129
Sandford, Rev. Folliott G. 128, 130
Scammonden 116
schools 115, 120, 122, 130, 131, 139, 140, 148, 151, 153, 196, 202
Schwann, Frederick 107
Secularists 126-7
Seymour, Edward Adolphus (1804-85), 12th Duke of Somerset 34, 144n86, 201, 208
Shaw, Bentley 95, 98, 100, 131
Shepley, St Paul 153, 157
Skyrme, J. J. (1825-58) 90, 112n6, 112n19
Slaithwaite 116, 117, 130, 142n53
  St James 116, 117, 128, 130, 131
Smith, Carmi, mayor 180, 184, 185
Smith, William 100, 101
Snowden, Rev. Edmund 127-8
Socialism 79, 177, 179, 181, 189, 201
Somerset Bridge 138, 144n86, 203
Somerset Road 131, 138, 139

South Crosland 116, 142n50, 143n64
Springwood 45, 65-7, 73
St George's Square 57, 61, 70, 71, 73-4, 75, 77, 160-1, 164, 165
Stephenson, Clifford (1903-92) 174-5, 179-82, 189, 191, 191n7, 210-13
Stewart, John 100, 104
Story, Rev. Charles Edward 128
streets 43, 49, 50, 51, 57, 60, 71, 74, 75, 76, 123, 161
Swallow Street Mission 121
Swan, Rosina Elizabeth 201
Swift, Frederick 92, 93, 94, 105, 108, 109

Taylor, James 104
Taylor, Thomas (c.1778-1826), architect 146
Tenure Dispute 16-17, 27, 66, 87-9, 92-8, 99-106, 106-111, 120, 122-3
 leases 23, 58, 65, 67, 70, 88-9, 90, 92-3, 95-8, 99-100, 102-4, 107, 109-11, 120, 122, 178, 189, 190
 tenancies-at-will 52, 65, 89-93, 97, 105-6, 108-11, 111n3, 178, 195
 Ramsden v. Dyson 89, 111n3
 Thornton v. Ramsden 88-9, 98, 105
Tenant-Right Defence Association 88, 100, 101-5, 106, 107, 111
Thornhill, Thomas (1780-1844) 159
 Thornhill Estate 45, 65, 67, 88, 93, 99, 100, 101 116, 178
 Thornhill Act (1853) 93
Thornton, Joseph 100, 101, 105, 106, 108, 109, 110
Tite, William (1798-1873), architect 12, 22, 57, 62, 161, 162, 165
Town and Country Planning Act (1909) 79-80
Town Hall 61, 62, 64, 72, 74-6, 79, 126, 186
Trotter, Rev. Joseph 117
turnpikes, roads 47, 48, 49

Unitarians Fitzwilliam Street chapel 122-3

Varley, John 126
Venn, Rev. Henry 117, 128, 140

Wakefield, Bishop of: William Walsham How (1823-97) 131, 138
 George Rodney Eden (1853-1940) 128, 129, 187
Wallen, William (1807-88), architect 14-16, 18, 57, 59, 65, 145-6, 147-62, 162-8
Ward, Henry, architect 151, 152
waterworks 47, 55
Waterworks Commissioners 51, 53, 55, 62, 69
Waterworks Acts (1827) 53, 55, 68
 (1845) 68
Wentworth, Charlotte (1746-1833) 118
White, James, financier 177, 181, 184, 213
White, Oswald, architect 139
Willans, James Edward (1842-1926) 125
Wilson, Rev. G.S. 128
Woodhead, Ernest (1857-1944) 180, 183, 184-5
Woodhead, Joseph (1824-1913) 75-6, 103, 106, 108
Woodhouse, Christ Church 131

Yorkshire Archaeological Association 136
Yorkshire Architectural Society 155-6, 159, 165
Yorkshire Observer 185, 187

Zetland, Dundas, Thomas (1795-1873), 2nd Earl 112n4, 119, 159
Zetland Hotel 160

INDEX

INDEX

INDEX